The Political Economy of Greek Growth up to 2030

Series Editor
Panagiotis E. Petrakis, Department of Economics, National and Kapodistrian University of Athens, Athens, Greece

This book series analyzes the medium to long-term prospects of Greece's political economy by studying concepts such as sustainability, sustainable governance and political functioning, economic inclusivity, cultural behaviors, and economic dynamic growth through an evolutionary approach. This series also publishes policy-oriented books outlining steps for increased economic growth and a sustainable future for the Greek economy. This series stands out in that the books depict the conditions that must prevail for the Greek economy to escape the economic stagnation that has lingered from persistent economic recession.

Using Greece as a lens to discuss pressing questions, this series will be of interest to economists interested in Eurozone policies, economic growth, evolutionary economics, and more.

Panagiotis E. Petrakis
Editor

Interconnections in the Greek Economy

Between Macro- and Microeconomics

palgrave
macmillan

Editor
Panagiotis E. Petrakis
Department of Economics
National and Kapodistrian University
of Athens
Athens, Greece

ISSN 2662-7248 ISSN 2662-7256 (electronic)
The Political Economy of Greek Growth up to 2030
ISBN 978-3-031-31334-9 ISBN 978-3-031-31335-6 (eBook)
https://doi.org/10.1007/978-3-031-31335-6

This Palgrave Macmillan imprint is published by the registered company Springer Nature Switzerland AG
The registered company address is: Gewerbestrasse 11, 6330 Cham, Switzerland

Preface

The series of books with the general title of "The Political Economy of Greek Growth up to 2030" analyze the medium- to long-term prospects of the Greek reality—including the COVID-19 pandemic—in view of the political economy. They combine the notions of sustainability, sustainable governance and political operation, the inclusivity of the economic system, and cultural behavior, with the requirements of economic dynamic growth. The concurrent influence from those five areas, through suitable structural reforms, is a necessary prerequisite to change the production prototype of the Greek economy, which will ensure a medium- and long-term economic development and growth. This viewpoint has an evolutionary foundation. The view supported is that conditions can be created for the Greek economy, after the 2008 depression, to avoid losing another decade due to COVID-19 and to create the necessary conditions for a great growth transformation up to 2030.

The target of this book series, presented in successive volumes, is to assess the current situation of the Greek economy and detect future potential for development and growth, particularly on a medium- to long-term horizon. It represents the next step in a series of books: The Greek Economy and the Crisis, Challenges and Responses, P. E. Petrakis (2011), New York and Heidelberg, Springer; and A New Growth Model for the Greek Economy, Requirements for the Long-Term Sustainability, P. E. Petrakis (2016), New York, Palgrave Macmillan. These books marked the conditions in which the Greek economy entered Great Depression (2008–2018) and put forth initial thoughts on exiting the crisis. In this current book series, conditions for the exit of the economy from the crisis are analyzed, along with its entry into a new period of development and growth.

Athens, Greece Panagiotis E. Petrakis

Acknowledgments

I would like to thank the main collaborator Mrs. E. Giouli, as well as the other collaborators in my office, who offered me the opportunity to deal with the completion of our research. National and Kapodistrian University of Athens offered its support. Our families offered us their patience.

Panagiotis E. Petrakis

Praise for *Interconnections in the Greek Economy*

"This book is an excellent addition to the literature in this field of economic interconnections and networks as it provides a framework for understanding and explaining economic, institutional, national, and social interactions and relationships. Moreover, the book offers policy implications on how to mitigate vulnerabilities resulted by incoherent interconnections, focusing on the Greek economy, which is service-oriented and characterized by low dynamism. Overall, it will be of great value to researchers, students, and practitioners alike."

—Dimitrios Kenourgios, *Professor of Department of Economics, National and Kapodistrian University of Athens*

"This book provides a rich and innovative portrayal of the Greek economy and its challenges. By focusing on sectoral interconnections, relations among industries and corporate networks it links macroeconomic evaluation with microeconomic detail necessary for more refined industrial policy design. The varied and transdisciplinary approaches of the contributing authors illuminate both our understanding of the Greek government debt crisis and the ways to achieve sustainable development. Students, researchers, and policymakers will have much to gain from reading this book."

—Andreas Papandreou, *Professor of Department of Economics, National and Kapodistrian University of Athens*

Introduction

Economic interconnections and networks are at the center of economic analysis since they provide a way to understand and explain economic, institutional, national, and social interactions and relationships. Traditionally, network economics and interconnections have been studied at a microeconomic level through game theory. Taking a step forward, the objective of the present book is to optimally pair the fields of microeconomics and macroeconomics in relation to interconnections and networks. Such an analysis is mostly concentrated in Greece in order to trace the quality of interconnections in the economy. The Greek economy is service-oriented and characterized by low dynamism. Hence, at a micro level, we study the interconnections of various Greek companies, property relations, and overlaps in management boards. At a macro level, we emphasize the economic relations between the various sectors of the Greek economy.

In the present book, the Greek economy is perceived as a complex institutional process that relies on the quality of interconnections between different sectors and industries. The quality of interconnections is a determining factor of dynamism, which is crucial for economic resilience and shock responsiveness. The higher the intensity and level of interconnection, the better for the labor market's dynamism because communication, competitiveness, and job transitioning are facilitated. Nonetheless, incoherent interconnections result in economic vulnerabilities due to contagion effects during a severe shock. A way to mitigate this adverse effect is to improve the quality of interconnections through diversification and institutional resilience by expanding economic activities across different sectors and industries. This strategy reduces the economy's vulnerability by spreading the risk across different sectors, leading to new value chains and economic growth opportunities.

Essentially, we unfold the structure of the Greek economy and address the internal relations that drive productivity trends, efficiency, and welfare. Methodologically, we rely on an interdisciplinary perspective that accounts for both traditional methods such as input-output analysis and network analysis based on the "influence and information flow" approach.

The book is divided into three parts: Part I comprises an analysis and evaluation of the Sectoral Interconnections in the Greek Economy; Part II concerns the Relations Among the Several Greek Industries; and Part III emphasizes the structure of interconnections and networks and its impact on addressing economic shocks, megatrends, and envisioning the future. Each part of this book consists of three chapters. We shall present each part and its corresponding chapters, starting with Part I.

In Chapter 1, Maria Markaki and Stelios Papadakis emphasize the importance of an industrial policy that improves the production-export structure in the short term and long term. Short-term benefits regard promoting productivity, which results in higher growth rates, while long-term benefits arise from technological advancements, improved capabilities in critical economic sectors, and increased international appeal. They propose a methodology for optimizing the economy's structural transformation using input-output analysis (IOA). IOA offers a structural perspective on industrial relationships and is frequently used to analyze the economic consequences of structural economic changes.

In Chapter 2, Maria Markaki and Stelios Papadakis review the unfavorable structural characteristics of the Greek economy and the policies followed, which led to the severe consequences of the Great Recession of 2008. The accumulated knowledge is used to provide useful policy-making insights for transforming the Greek production structure. They present an optimal economic structure to boost the GDP growth rate and reduce the deficit in the balance of goods and services to solve an optimization problem. This optimal structure serves as a basis for policy-makers to design a mix of sectoral and macroeconomic interventions to promote development and growth.

In Chapter 3, Pagiavla Georgia and Pisinas Yorgos utilize input-output tables as an empirical dataset and theoretical tool for examining an economy's internal structure and interconnections. Recent interest is focused on the regional level due to recognizing that the economy is not a non-spatial entity with interregional trade playing a significant role in the relationship between the periphery and the center. Thus, the authors present a method of producing input-output tables for Greece's regions to provide a fundamental framework for the sectoral/regional interconnections that occur in the country.

Part II focuses in the analysis of microeconomic interconnections, between individuals and companies, a much more thorough presentation of the economic interconnections of Greek companies in various vital sectors of the Greek economy.

In Chapter 4, Giorgos Vasilis examines graph theory at an introductory level and describes various forms of graphs used in economics and social sciences. He distinguishes two main types of relationships, namely interlocking directorates and interlocking ownership, and offers an analysis of their significance along with a critical literature review. Consequently, the chapter offers a general overview of the various forms of international corporate interlocks, followed by a focus on Greek business networks, which have lower levels of interconnections than the rest of Europe. The author concludes by discussing the possibilities and future directions for research in social network analysis for businesses.

In Chapter 5, Michalis Vafopoulos, Charalampos Agiropoulos, Artemis Gourgioti, and Michalis Klonaras focus on analyzing corporate interconnections to understand better the complexity and composition of corporate networks in Greece. By examining board-level interlock networks, the authors address questions related to power concentration, anti-trust investigations, corporate knowledge transfer, macroeconomic implications, and business strategy. The last section of this chapter applies the analysis of board interlock networks to a particular economic sector in Greece, providing compelling evidence of interconnectivity.

In Chapter 6, Charalampos Agiropoulos, Michalis Vafopoulos, Artemis Gourgioti, and George Galanos refer to the potential for anti-competitive risks associated with shared ownership. They assess the current methods that are used to measure market concentration and propose a new approach incorporating the connected corporate network method to measure competition more accurately. The proposed index is being tested across multiple sectors of the Greek economy. The authors evaluate its effectiveness compared to traditional measures like the Herfindahl-Hirschman index and the m-firm concentration ratio.

Part III elaborates on how the Greek economy has to transform its production prototype under structural constraints, opportunities for economic diversification and inclusive growth, and the pressure of economic shocks. As this section and book come to a close, the focus shifts to evaluating network externalities to assess the impact of powerful forces.

In Chapter 7, Kyriaki I. Kafka reviews the consequences of the economic crises in Greece and their effects on economic development, growth, and decision-making processes. More specifically, the author investigates how different economic sectors have been affected by these shocks between the first quarter of 1998 and the third quarter of 2022 to identify which sectors are more vulnerable or resilient. The findings of this study offer policymakers insights for transforming the Greek economy. The originality of this chapter concerns the analysis of various sectors of the Greek economy in terms of economic policy uncertainty (EPU).

In Chapter 8, Pantelis C. Kostis states that a country's production structure sets a country's economic path, including diversification, growth, and sustainability. The author examines Greece's structural impediments and possibilities for economic diversification, sustainable development, and growth. The author examines the Greek production structure and identifies its vulnerabilities, highlighting the need for a more diversified, sustainable, and inclusive economic model. Thus, the author presents policymaking directions based on a quintuple Helix model. Such a model emphasizes the importance of cooperation and collaboration among the government, industry, civil society, the environment, and knowledge and innovation systems.

Lastly, in Chapter 9, which closes the present book, Anna-Maria Kanzola discusses how networks and interconnections operate in an era of trending divergence with regard to several global trends. That is, this chapter presents a theoretical discussion of utilizing network theory—with countries as agents—as a means to access the future of global cooperation based on some compelling and time-resilient characteristics of human societies. Evidently, this chapter goes beyond the geographical boundaries of Greece as a country of reference and points out the relevancy of network analysis for assessing complex socio-economic phenomena, which is at the core of this book.

Having said that, the present book offers the opportunity to understand network analysis beyond its traditional setting and apply it to evaluate country profiles and their structural characteristics. It aspires to achieve a fresh glance at network analysis and emphasize its interdisciplinary nature.

Prof. Em. Panagiotis E. Petrakis (Editor)

Contents

Editor and Contributors

About the Editor

Panagiotis E. Petrakis is Emeritus Professor in the Department of Economics of the National and Kapodistrian University of Athens in Greece. He serves as Scientific Coordinator of Distance Education Training Programs at the same University. He has served as Chairman of the Department as well as Director of the Sector of International Economics and Development. He is the author of numerous scientific articles and monographs and has extensive publications in recognized academic journals on economic development and growth, entrepreneurship, and cultural background.

Contributors

Charalampos Agiropoulos is a senior Lecturer at the Department of Economics of the University of Piraeus. In 2015, he was appointed as the Academic Director of Postgraduate Programs at the University of Bolton and in 2018 he became GM of the New York College. Since 2018, he has been serving as the head of several Committees for the TMEDE Fund and he is currently the CEO of TMEDE Microfinance Solutions. He holds a Ph.D. in Economics, M.Sc. in Applied Statistics, and B.Sc. from the Department of Mathematics, University of Athens. His research interests focus on Applied Econometrics using ML techniques.

George Galanos is Assistant Professor in the field of Economic Policy and Competitiveness in the University of Piraeus, Department of International and European Studies He holds a Ph.D. in International Economics and Tourism Competitiveness from the University of Piraeus, an M.B.A. and a B.Sc. degree in Economics.. He was member of Academic Council of Wilfried Martens Centre for European Studies. He has published in academic journals and books, such as the World Economy, Intereconomics, International Research Journal of Finance and Economics, Research Journal of International Studies, International Bulletin of Business Administration etc and has also participated in international conferences.

Pagiavla Georgia completed an undergraduate degree at Panteion University in the Department of Economic and Regional Development (DERD) and a postgraduate degree at the University of Glasgow in Economic Development. She attended a postgraduate degree at the Athens University of Economics and Business in Economic Theory and completed a second postgraduate degree at Harokopio University in the Department of Geography. Now she is in the 4th year of her Ph.D. program at Panteion University in DERD researching the European Regional Policy of the EU.

Artemis Gourgioti is a senior data analyst. She is an honors graduate of the M.Sc. Business Analytics and Data Science of the University of Macedonia. Since 2019 she is a leading member of the Analytics Department of the award-winning startup Linked Business that provides market intelligence solutions based on open data and AI.

Kyriaki I. Kafka is Adjunct Lecturer of Economics in the Department of Economics at National and Kapodistrian University of Athens in Greece. She has published articles in distinguished academic journals including Journal of Comparative Economics, Journal of Business Research and Journal of Innovation and Knowledge. She is also the author of several books regarding economic development and growth and economic policy. Her research interests include economic development and growth, economic policy, cultural economics, institutional economics, behavioral economics, innovation and macroeconomics.

Anna-Maria Kanzola has a Bachelor of Science in Economics from the National and Kapodistrian University of Athens and a Master of Science in Applied Economics and Finance, both with the highest distinction from the same institution. Since 2019, she has been a member of the research team under Professor Panagiotis E. Petrakis at the National and Kapodistrian University of Athens. She has published in high-profile international scientific journals and participated in international conferences. Microeconomics, scenario planning, human behavior, and economic growth are among her scholarly interests. She is a Ph.D. candidate in behavioral and labor economics at the National and Kapodistrian University of Athens, Greece.

Michalis Klonaras is a highly skilled Electrical & Computer Engineer specialized in Telecommunications (M.Sc.) with over 20 years of working experience. Since 2012 and after acquiring his M.Sc. In Web Science, he participated in several projects in Linked Open Data ecosystem. He is specialized in Graph analysis and data visualization techniques. He is currently working in Hellenic Telecom Organizationas a Section manager in Imathia.

Pantelis C. Kostis is Assistant Professor of Economic Development in the Department of Economics of the National and Kapodistrian University of Athens. He is also a Member of the Collaborating Teaching Staff of the Hellenic Open University and has also served as Visiting Professor in other Universities. His research has been published in distinguished international academic journals including the Journal of Comparative Economics, Journal of Business Research, Economic Modeling and the Journal of Socio-Economics. He is also the author of several books regarding economic development and growth. He serves as Associate Editor and Guest Editor in several scientific journals.

Maria Markaki is an Assistant Professor of Applied Economics in the Department of Management Science and Technology at the Hellenic Mediterranean University. She holds a 5-year M.Eng. Degree in Mechanical Engineering and a Ph.D. in Applied Economics from the National Technical University of Athens. She has many published scientific papers in international refereed journals and collective volumes and has made numerous contributions to international conferences. In addition, she participated in 20 research projects funded by National or European sources. Maria's research interests include Input-Output Analysis, Development Economics, International Economics, Industrial Structure and Structural Change, and Economic Policy.

Stelios Papadakis is a Professor at the Department of Management Science and Technology of the Hellenic Mediterranean University, located in Crete, Greece. He received the diploma of Electrical and Computer Engineer in 1994 from the Department of Electrical and Computer Engineering of Aristotle University of Thessaloniki, Greece, and his Ph.D. in computational intelligence, from the same Department. He has published many articles in scientific research journals, performed many announces in international scientific conferences and participated in many research projects. His recent scientific interests include Computational intelligence and Machine Learning, as well as bigdata analytics with applications to Management Science and Economics.

Michalis Vafopoulos is a leading expert in data science. In 2013 he wrote the book «Living with the Web», about the sociotechnical aspects of the Web. In 2019 he was appointed as a member of the Board of Directors of the Hellenic Land Registry in charge of digital transformation. In 2020 he was invited to participate as a member of the Sectoral Scientific Council for Data Policy and Artificial Intelligence of the National Council for Research, Technology, and Innovation. He is currently the CEO of the award-winning startup Linked Business that provides market intelligence solutions based on open data and AI.

Giorgos Vasilis is a researcher in the Center for Training and Lifelong Learning (E-Learning) at the National and Kapodistrian University of Athens (NKUA), Greece. He holds a B.Sc., degree with honours (8.8/10), in Economics and an M.Phil. in Economic Science from the NKUA. Since 2019, he has been working as a graduate research assistant at NKUA under the supervision of Professor Panagiotis E. Petrakis. His main research interests are in the fields of political economy, the history of economic thought, economic history, and microeconomics.

Pisinas Yorgos studied (B.Sc. Hons) Economics at the Athens University of Economics and Business (AUEB) and completed (in 2021) his M.Phil. in Economics at the University of Athens (UoA). Currently, he is a Ph.D. candidate at the University of Patras, expanding on his interest in Ecological Economics and Political Economy. He has worked as a Research Assistant for e-learning programmes in the Department of Economics of UoA under Prof. Petrakis working on issues of Development and Human Capital Theory.

Abbreviations

CILQ	Cross-Industry Location Quotient
CME	Coordinated Market Economies
CR	Concentration Ratio
DVX	Domestic Value Added in Exports
ECI	Economic Complexity Index
EL.STAT.	Hellenic Statistical Authority
EPU	Economic Policy Uncertainty
EU	European Union
FDI	Foreign Direct Investment
GA	Genetic Algorithms
GDP	Gross Domestic Product
GECR	General Electronic Commercial Registry
GVA	Gross Value Added
HH	Herfindahl-Hirschman index
HT & MHT	High and Medium-high tech
IOA	Input-Output Analysis
IOT	Input-Output Table
LME	Liberal Market Economies
LQ	Location Quotients
NIOT	National Tables of Inputs-Outputs
PD	Power of Dispersion Index
PSO	Particle Swarm Optimization
R&D	Research and Development
RIOT	Regional Tables of Inputs-Outputs
SD	Sensitivity of Dispersion Index

US	United States
VAR	Vector Autoregressive Model
WMR	Region Western Macedonia

List of Figures

List of Tables

PART I

Sectoral Interconnections in the Greek Economy

CHAPTER 1

Industrial Policy and Productive Transformation: An Optimization Approach Based on Input–Output Analysis

Maria Markaki and Stelios Papadakis

1.1 Introduction

The economic crisis of 2008, followed by a long period of recession, revealed the structural failings of many economies, creating the resurgence of interest in industrial policy. Much of the interest in industrial policy derives from its potential implications for solving dramatic socioeconomic problems, such as high unemployment rates, expanding trade imbalances, and poverty. Additionally, changes in the production systems

M. Markaki (✉) · S. Papadakis
Department of Management Science and Technology, Laboratory of Data Science, Multimedia and Modelling, Hellenic Mediterranean University, Heraklion, Greece
e-mail: mmarkaki@hmu.gr

S. Papadakis
e-mail: spap@hmu.gr

P. E. Petrakis (ed.), *Interconnections in the Greek Economy*, The Political Economy of Greek Growth up to 2030, https://doi.org/10.1007/978-3-031-31335-6_1

due to the expansion of global value chains force countries to confront challenges arising from their level of integration within the new pattern of international trade (Di Tommaso et al., 2017). The rejuvenation (Stiglitz et al., 2013) or renaissance (Mazzucato et al., 2015; Savona, 2018) of industrial policy attracts several schools of thought in economics to a debate on the nature, the significance, the efficiency, and the instruments of industrial policy. The structural, the evolutionary, and, surprisingly, the neoclassical schools of thought all contribute to the debate, highlighting different perspectives and objectives as well as different directions for industrial policy.

The debate on industrial policy is not new. It can be traced back to the foundation of capitalism, with the controversy between two major theoretical streams of thought, mercantilism and liberalism (Maneschi, 1998). The neoclassical school of thought dominated the intense debate of academic and policy circles from the mid-1970s to the early 1980s. At that specific conjuncture, the majority of countries and world organizations adopted the position that the outcomes of industrial policy are limited, or even negative for the economies. Based on the neoclassical tradition, protectionism and infant-industry strategies only have adverse results and will probably lead to government failure. Thus, market-based strategies (liberalization, privatization, deregulation) and macroeconomic measures to ensure fiscal and financial stability were considered the only effective government policies (Chang & Andreoni, 2016; Rodrik, 2008). The neoclassical theoretical framework was strongly challenged by Chang (2002), who examined the economic history of developed economies and found no example of a country that developed following free-trade and market-based policies. On the contrary, all advanced countries developed on the basis of protectionism and infant-industry policies, the same policies which are rejected as ineffective and obsolete nowadays.

Based on the neoclassical agenda, industrial policy should only attempt to improve the business environment. Such interventions are commonly referred to as horizontal (also called functional) measures and include, among others, educational and training programs, R&D investments, FDI attraction, and infrastructures. In addition to horizontal measures, government interventions for overcoming market failures are accepted into the neoclassical school of thought. On the contrary, mainstream economists considered vertical industrial policies (also called selective) for the promotion of specific sectors or groups of sectors, or even for improving the supplementarity of the whole economic system, to be ineffective (Chang & Andreoni, 2019; Warwick, 2013). Salazar-Xirinachs et al. (2014, p. 20) identify a contradiction in the distinction between horizontal and vertical policy measures. They note that "the distinction between 'horizontal' measures (presumed to be neutral across sectors) and 'vertical' measures (supporting specific industries) is something of a false choice, as even the most 'general' policy measures favor some sectors over others". Even more, according to Stiglitz et al. (2013, p. 8), horizontal policy measures end up supporting "certain industries more than others and therefore shape the sector allocation of the economy". In reality, the only policies that can strictly be called horizontal are those concerning basic education and public health care. Nevertheless, referring to policy concerning these as industrial is "stretching the concept beyond reason" (Chang et al., 2016, p. 29).

The inability to develop a neutral, horizontal industrial policy does not mean that there is no difference between horizontal and vertical measures. Horizontal and vertical industrial policies have different objectives, and neutrality is only a part of the picture. Horizontal policies are consistent with improving the workings of markets and institutes, whereas vertical policies are consistent with the notion of structural change and the productive (or structural) transformation of the whole economy.

The term structural transformation refers to the "interrelated processes of structural change that accompany economic development" (Syrquin, 1988, p. 206). Advanced economies progressively shift their structure of production and exports to activities of higher value-added and more sophisticated products (Fortunato & Razo, 2014; Ocampo et al., 2009). The impact of the productive structure and its effects on economic development is frequently neglected by mainstream economics, despite its high relevance for development, international theory, and economic policy. As discussed by Rodrik (2009, p. 5), economic development "is fundamentally about structural change: it involves producing new goods with new technologies and transferring resources from the traditional activities to these new ones". The radical economic tradition offers significant contributions highlighting the fundamental role of changes in the composition of aggregate production and employment, and how they affect economic growth and development (Andreoni & Scazzieri, 2014; Hirschman, 1958; Kaldor, 1967; Prebisch, 1962; Robinson, 2016).

As analytically discussed in Scazzieri (2018), the structural dynamics of an economic system can be used as the basis for determining different paths of structural changes. In this framework, the role emerges of industrial policy as a mechanism for detecting and selecting the path (or trajectory) toward specific macroeconomic targets (such as the attainment of a specific level of development, improvement of the exporting profile, unemployment reduction, trade deficits shrinkage, etc.) For the purposes of this research, industrial policy is defined as sector-specific interventions in an economic system toward productive transformation and the achievement of economic development. Thus, industrial policy has a mainly vertical character and systemic impact inasmuch it stimulates specific economic activities and promotes structural change (Rodrik, 2008).

Policy measures referred to in the literature as horizontal-type industrial policies, should not be neglected in the process of structural transformation. On the contrary, their implementation is complementary to an industrial policy strategy. Research and development (R&D) investment, environmental regulation, support for small and medium-sized enterprises, educational and training programs, infrastructure and measure ensuring financial stability are important aspects of the policy agenda worldwide. However, given their macroeconomic character, their inclusion in industrial policy is rather disorienting in terms of the industrial policy debate.

The design of an industrial policy plan requires an in-depth knowledge of the examined economy and the theoretical and empirical background to approach the complexity and complementarity of the different features of the economic system in question. Furthermore, determining the optimal industrial policy for an economic system should also consider the different challenges arising from the international economic environment and the evolution of technology.

The structure of the chapter is the following: Sect. 1.2 presents the link between production transformation and Input–Output analysis. Then Sect. 1.3 focuses on different aspects and prospects of productive transformation. The next Sect. 1.4 presents the methodological approach. In Sect. 1.5, the formulation of the mathematical model for the Greek economy is elaborated. Finally, Sect. 1.6 discusses the future directions of the research.

1.2 Productive Transformation and Input–Output Analysis

A productive transformation strategy requires a methodology that reflects the complexity and complementarity of the economy in question and can be used to formulate an optimization model for determining the optimal productive structure. To this end, Input–Output Analysis (Leontief, 1986) is employed in the literature. The reason for the extensive use of IOA in this type of problem is that it is essentially a methodology that provides a structural view of sectoral interlinkages. Therefore, understanding the underlying mechanisms and the drivers of structural transformation is a critical issue for industrial policy, and IOA is recognized as a suitable approach in this regard.

In IOA, the production of an economic system is disaggregated into *n*sectors of economic activity and the transactions of goods and services among them are determined. Each sector produces a single type of product (or service), and it is assumed that all producers within a sector employ the same production technology. Moreover, each sector absorbs inputs from the other sectors and provides its production as input to other sectors and to the final demand of the economic system. Thus, the production process of the whole system is articulated in a tabular form, i.e., the Input–Output table (IOT) of monetary values. The IOT describes the transactions between the different sectors (intersectoral flows) and the sectoral distribution of value-added and final demand. IOA focuses on the intersectoral flows of the IOT, a square table with dimensions nxn, depicting how intermediate products and services are combined in analogies defined by the production technology of each sector, to generate the sector's output. Analytically, a typical row of the square matrix represents the distribution of the output within the other sectors and a typical column of the square matrix reflects the composition of inputs demanded from other sectors for the specific sector's production. Thus, the typical element z_{ij} of IOT represents the ith sector's output required by the jth sector for the production of jth sector's gross output. Furthermore, a typical technological coefficient a_{ij} represents the ith sector's output required for a unit production of the jth sector and a typical allocation coefficient b_{ij} represents the share of a unit production of the ith sector used as intermediate input from the jth sector (Miller & Blair, 2009). The matrices of the technological coefficients A_d (known as the Leontief approach) and allocation coefficients B_d (known as the Ghosh approach) provide a full view of the economic structure and are widely used for studying the economic effects of structural changes within an economy, both in sectoral and aggregate level. Particularly, the impact of structural shifts in final demand, in the Leontief model and value-added, in the Ghosh model, for the economic system can be simulated with the use of the A_d and B_d matrices, respectively (Ghosh, 1958; Miller & Blair, 2009; Belegri et al., 2011).

Nevertheless, a productive restructuring strategy requires the reverse process, i.e., the identification of the required shifts in production (expressed by final demand or value-added structure) for achieving macroeconomic targets under certain constraints. Thus, for addressing the productive transformation strategy, the macroeconomic objectives and constraints should be formulated into a constrained optimization model, the resolution of which will provide the optimal productive structure of the economic system.

Up to date, several studies have identified an economy's optimal productive structure. Most of these investigate the optimal structure of economic systems for addressing environmental pressures (such as greenhouse gas emissions and energy usage) and achieving macroeconomic objectives. Cho (1999) determined the optimal productive structure of the Chungbuk Province of Korea for addressing unemployment and resource scarcity. Oliveira and Antunes (2004) optimized the production structure of Portugal with a view to environmental (minimization of the acidification potential and the energy imports) and socioeconomic (maximization of employment and GDP) objectives. San Cristóbal (2010) defined the optimal structure of the Spanish economy when GDP is maximized and greenhouse gas emissions are minimized. Hristu-Varsakelis et al. (2010) used scenario analysis of GDP maximization and energy conservation to optimize the structure of Greece. Likewise, De Carvalho et al. (2015) approached the optimal productive structure of Brazil for different scenarios involving the maximization of GDP and employment and the minimization of greenhouse gas emissions and energy consumption. Chang (2015) investigated China and determined the optimal structure of the country when GDP is maximized and carbon dioxide emissions are minimized. Mi et al. (2015), in a regional study for Beijing, determined the productive structure of the city for maximum production and environmental objectives. In more recent studies, Tian et al. (2017) and Lin et al. (2019) investigated the optimal structure of China when GDP is maximized and energy consumption is minimized. Sánchez et al. (2019) found the optimal structure of Australia for the maximum GDP and employment and the minimum greenhouse gas emissions. Furthermore, in Papadakis and Markaki (2019), the optimal structure for the minimization of greenhouse gas emissions intensity is determined. Finally, Markaki and Papadakis (2021) identified the optimal structure of the Czech economy, ensuring that a decrease in global demand for vehicles will not affect the country's international competitiveness. In all cases, the optimal productive structure varies considerably from the current structure, highlighting the importance of productive transformation. Furthermore, the significant impact of a potential structural transformation on macroeconomic and/or environmental objectives in all the examined countries, constitutes a mutually reinforcing argument in favor of industrial policy strategies.

Although all the aforementioned studies successfully determine the optimal productive structure of the examined economic systems, they do not provide a robust methodological framework to explore different aspects of productive transformation. Moreover, the diversity of the set targets and the different types of constraints makes it difficult, in certain cases, even to recognize the common denominator in all the different approaches, i.e., the application of Input–Output Analysis. Consequently, there is a necessity for a robust methodological approach to productive transformation based on IOA, as support for different empirical applications. Such an approach will provide the tools to classify, compare, and evaluate different productive transformation plans.

1.3 Productive Transformation: Different Aspects and Prospects

A productive transformation that shifts production within different sectors through the reallocation of production factors, can address the structural weakness of the economy. Furthermore, such progress can increase aggregated production and exports, achieving significant improvements in the economy's level of development (Chang & Andreoni, 2016). Although the specific objectives and the restrictions of a productive transformation are country-specific, the broad outlines of an industrial policy toward a productive transformation can be drawn to derive factors that account for the main determinants. In this research, four structural economic factors are considered as a means of ensuring the effectiveness of productive transformation in an economic system. The share of manufacturing in production, the share of technologically advanced sectors, the strengths of intersectoral linkages, and the complexity of the economic system. The literature on industrial policy identifies these factors as crucial for the structural change of an economy from the supply side (Bresser-Pereira, 2016; Chang et al., 2013, 2016; Reinert, 2019). In this section, the role of each factor is discussed in terms of its contribution to growth and development.

1.3.1 Promoting Industrialization

Industrial policy is mainly associated with targeted interventions in specific industrial sectors (i.e., manufacturing, mining, utilities, and construction sectors), promoting industrialization in favor of an improved productive structure. However, the literature approaches the special role of industry in the process of structural transformation through several complementary aspects.

Firstly, industrial products, especially those sourcing from the core of industrial activities, i.e., manufacturing, have high tradability compared to the non-tradable character of most services activities (Rodrik, 2007; Stöllinger et al., 2013). Thus, industry products contribute to a favorable external balance of goods and services in the economy.

Secondly, as observed by Kaldor (1967, p. 8), there is a positive relationship between labor productivity growth rates and "the excess of the rate of growth of manufacturing production over the rate of growth of the economy as a whole". Thus, industry exhibits higher productivity gains than the rest of the economic system and promotes the aggregated labor productivity growth of the economy.

Contrary to the traditional view that productivity gains cause economic growth, Ocampo (2005) revised the arrow of causality. He pointed out that the link between increased productivity and growth is two-way. The productivity gains increase economic growth and vice versa. The crucial point in his approach is that the quality of economic growth, as expressed in the country's macroeconomic performance, determines the level of productivity gains. Compared with a strong macroeconomic performance, poor performance is characterized by a substantial decline in the rate of productivity growth (see also Ocampo, 2014). As a result, an economy with poor macroeconomic performance is characterized by structural weakness, usually reflected in negative terms of trade and trade deficits

(Economakis et al., 2015). Thus, the role is emphasized of industrial policy in ensuring a strong macroeconomic performance.

Thirdly, in addition to the "great importance to the role of the manufacturing sector in overall economic activity, is its role as a driver of innovation and technological change... [as long as] the manufacturing sector still accounts for the bulk of business expenditure on R&D" (Pilat et al., 2006). The industrial sectors are a major source of technological progress for an economy, indicating that a country with a strong industrial base has the potential for technological upgrading. Even though industrial sectors are not homogenous in their technological level, industry significantly contributes to the diffusion of technology and, thus, operates as the "learning centre" of the economy (Baumol, 1967; Cardinale & Scazzieri, 2019; Chang et al., 2013). The constant renewal of manufacturing production (creation of new products or the improvement of the existing) is facilitated with innovations and modern technologies. In addition, industrial sectors' high capital accumulation level and higher capital intensity allow industrial products to embody state-of-art technologies (Szirmai, 2012).

Fourth, both backward and forward intersectoral linkages in the industry are much stronger than in services and agriculture. Stronger backward linkages indicate that the sector demonstrates high inputs from other sectors. Stronger forward linkages indicate that the sector is essential as a supplier of inputs required by other sectors (Dietzenbacher, 2002; Hirschman, 1958; Markaki & Papadakis, 2021). Strong linkages create a powerful spillover of knowledge and technology from industrial sectors to the rest of the economy. Sectors with strong interdependencies have a central role in economic activity, and their promotion provides extended effects to the economic system.

Fifth, from the demand side of the economy, the relative income elasticity of the demand for industrial (mainly manufacturing) products is higher than those from the primary and service sectors. This is because an increase in a country's income creates a higher demand for products of high-income elasticity of demand than those of low-income elasticity of demand, as a result of Engel's law. Thus, the inability of a non-industrialized economy to satisfy the increased demand for manufacturing products occurring as a result of economic growth will lead in the long run to the increase of imports and possible balance of payment problems (Economakis et al., 2018; Krugman, 1988).

The aspects of industry sectors discussed above stress the unique role that industry could play in the productive transformation of an economy. In the words of Cimoli et al. (2006), "an increase in the share of manufacturing in the overall economy would be required for activities with low productivity to converge upon high-productivity ones. The industry was seen as the main driver of productivity growth. [] ...industrial development would generate the forward and backward linkages, spillover effects, capital accumulation and technological externalities needed to sustain increasing returns".

1.3.2 Promoting Product Sophistication and Diversification

Despite the undeniable contribution of industrial sectors to the process of productive transformation, the industry is not a homogenous group of sectors. Industrial sectors differ considerably in terms of, among others, capital and labor intensity, technological level, skills required, and productivity level. Industrial policy should provide the ground for developing a diversified economic base and, simultaneously, for upgrading production from simple to more sophisticated. On the one hand, productive diversification reduces the economy's vulnerability to external and internal shocks. On the other, technological progress is in line with the promotion of relatively sophisticated sectors (Lin, 2011). Empirical studies show that mature industrialized countries typically produce a wide range of goods, and the process of development is connected with a less concentrated (more diversified) productive structure (Economakis & Markaki, 2023; Imbs & Wacziarg, 2003; Markaki & Economakis, 2022).

Furthermore, Petralia et al. (2017) found that more developed countries tend to specialize in producing more diverse and valuable products by using more complex and less concentrated technologies compared to less developed countries. This finding supports the position of Lall (2000), who highlighted the importance of the technological structure of manufactured exports as an indicator of "quality" and the position of Rodrik (2009, p. 9) that "productive diversification is a key correlate of economic development".

The term economic complexity is introduced in the literature to express both diversification and sophistication of production. Economic complexity is assessed "based on the diversity of exports a country produces and their ubiquity, or the number of the countries able to produce them, and those countries' complexity. Countries that can sustain a diverse range of productive know-how, including sophisticated, unique know-how, can produce a wide diversity of goods, including complex products that few other countries can make" (Simoes & Hidalgo, 2011). Even though manufacturing sectors provide the ability to increase product diversification to a higher degree, by comparison to the primary and service sectors (Hausmann & Klinger, 2007), some service sectors could also promote diversification due to their knowledge intensity (Evans, 2008). By the term service sector, the relevant literature mainly refers to business services (such as transport, logistics, management, consulting, design, communications, warehousing) providing activities outsourced by manufacturing firms to the service sector. Business services are closely linked to manufacturing production, followed by wholesale and retail trade, financial intermediation, and transport (UNIDO, 2013). Thus, the procurements of business services depend on the manufacturing sectors; hence business services cannot operate optimally in an economy with a weak industrial base (Chang et al., 2016). Consequently, the expansion of service sectors which are strongly linked to manufacturing increases the diversification of the economy.

Thus, the process of productive transformation cannot only be expressed by the reallocation of production within the different sectors, but also as a process of diversification and technological updating of economic activities throughout the economy.

1.3.3 Promoting Interconnectedness

The structural weaknesses of an economic system resulting from a non-articulated economic structure act as an obstacle to structural change, even in diversifying and technologically advanced systems. Gains related to spillover effects "in terms of technology transfer and absorption" O'Donovan and Rios-Morales (2006, p. 55) reinforce productive activities, providing technologically advanced sectors are strongly linked to the rest of the economy. Otherwise, in the case of weak intersectoral linkages, diversification and sophistication of production will increase the demand for imported intermediate inputs, extending trade imbalances and slowing down industrialization and development.

Thus, the interconnectedness of the whole economic system is a crucial factor for the effectiveness of productive transformation. IOA describes the economy as a complex network of relationships between different activities, quantifying their interconnectedness by backward and forward linkages (Miller & Blair, 2009). For example, a developed industry is connected to a more complete and articulated economic structure (Leontief, 1986, pp. 169–170) with important productive linkages, spillover effects, capital accumulation, and technological externalities (see Cimoli et al., 2006; Hirschman, 1958). On the contrary, service sectors are more independent from other sectors by comparison to the manufacturing sector (Pilat et al., 2006).

Strengthening an economy's backward and forward linkages requires policy interventions focused on the increased portion of intermediate demand satisfied by domestic production. This intervention will empower economic activities both as a producer and a consumer of intermediate products and services. Import substitution policies targeting the intermediate productive structure, as it is expressed by the matrices of technological and allocation coefficients, is a one-way road toward addressing structural weaknesses sourcing from weak linkages.

1.3.4 Toward a Methodology for Productive Transformation

The approach to productive transformation adopted in this research builds on the position that to transform their production structure successfully, countries must undertake policies of diversification, interdependencies, and technological change simultaneously. Furthermore, this methodological approach stresses that productive transformation relies on both diversification and sophistication of production and that improving productive linkages is essential to sustain macroeconomic gains.

From the policy point of view, policies for diversification and technological upgrading, as well as import substitution policies focusing on both the final and the intermediate demand, could lead to an improvement of the country's external balance of goods and services and a reduction of the risk of adverse effect on production due to macroeconomic imbalances (Milberg et al., 2014). The combination of these types of policy interventions will enhance the potential for growth and development.

1.4 Productive Transformation and Industrial Policy: A Methodological Approach

In this research, a primary question is addressed: which sectors should a productive transformation strategy target to optimize the productive structure, satisfying specific macroeconomic targets in parallel? The term "productive transformation" is more accurate from the term "structural transformation", as the proposed methodology is quantified, focusing on the optimal distribution of production among the sectors, and not on all the interrelated aspects of the socioeconomic environment which the term structural transformation implicates. Section 1.5 provides the mathematical formulation of the proposed methodology for the Greek economy (Fig. 1.1).

The proposed methodology is structured in three stages:

In the first stage, the productive structure of the examined economy is expressed by the selected sectoral classification. The applied classification should be in line with the corresponding classification of the available input–output tables.

The second stage involves the determination of industrial policy target(s) and their mathematical modelling is built based on input–output analysis. Given that the proposed methodology has a strictly country-specific nature, the target(s) of different countries could be highly diverse, from macroeconomic to social, environmental, or any combination thereof. In this stage, taking in the advantage of the IOA to provide a mathematical model for the real-world economic system (Leontief, 1982), the target(s) of the industrial policy is expressed in connection with the productive structure of the examined economy at an analytical sectoral level.

In the third stage, potential constraints are considered. Potential constraints could guide the transformation process in order not to inhibit the effectiveness of industrial policy measures. They are determined based

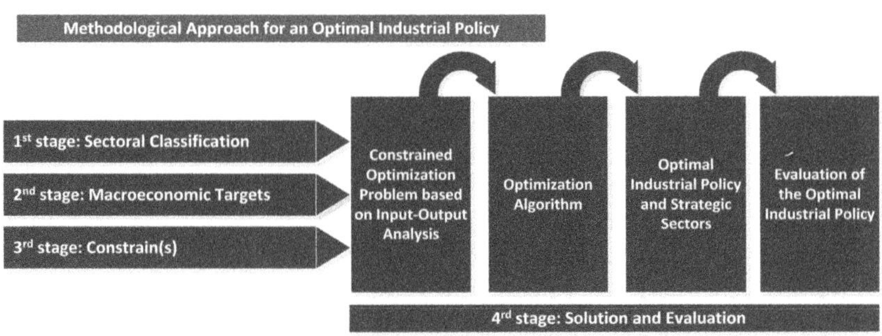

Fig. 1.1 The methodological approach of productive transformation (*Source* Authors' creation)

on economic and social features (such as technology, resources, skill level) of the economy examined.

Finally, the fourth stage includes the solution of the constrained optimization problem and evaluating the optimal economic structure. During the evaluation stage of the methodology, it is critical to investigate the optimal productive structure against socioeconomic aspects not included in the constraints in order to identify possible adverse effects. A revision of the 2nd and the 3rd stage is possible. New constraints could be included in order to prevent or counteract adverse effects.

1.5 The Formulation of the Mathematical Model for Greece

This section provides the background required for the formulation of productive transformation as a constraint optimization problem for the case of Greece. The productive transformation aims to reduce the trade balance deficits once macroeconomic targets (GDP growth rate and economic complexity) are achieved. The GDP growth rate is determined based on the projections of Oxford Economics (2020), while this growth rate should be linked to the increased complexity of the economy. GDP growth rate and economic complexity are constraints in the optimization process. The optimal productive structure should be determined for minimizing the trade balance deficits when GDP growth rates and economic activity reach specific values. The process of productive transformation concerns two aspects of the economic system: the decision variables.

The first aspect is the sectoral allocation of the value-added. The GDP share of each sector, expressed in the form of a vector, is the first decision variable of the model. The literature provides two alternatives for the determination of the decision variable. The first alternative is the use of value-added allocation (Mi et al., 2015; Oliveira & Antunes, 2004; Tian et al., 2017; Yu et al., 2016) and the second one is the use of the sectoral distribution of final demand (De Carvalho et al., 2015; Sanchez et al., 2019). The selection of the sectoral allocation of the value-added as a decision variable is due to the importance of the GDP growth rate constraint. GDP is the summation of value-added across the sector; thus, the first decision variable is directly connected with a constraint.

The second aspect is the distribution coefficients. Following an approach proposed by Papadakis and Markaki (2019), the network of sectoral interlinkages is optimized using the import substitution processes of imported intermediate inputs. The matrix of the distribution coefficient is used as the second decision variable, as an expression of the sectoral linkages. The use of the distribution coefficient instead of the technological coefficients is due to the origin of the first in the Ghosh approach, as discussed later in this section. In the Ghosh approach, value-added is considered exogenous; thus, both decision variables coexist in the Ghosh model and their impact on the objective function can be directly assessed.

The novelty of this approach is that it captures the full economic potential of productive transformation. The assumption that the economic system linkages will remain stable after a productive transformation cannot be valid. The promotion of a sector is connected with its ability to produce to satisfy both intermediate and final demand. Without capturing the improved position of a sector as a potential intermediate producer, a crucial segment of the economy is omitted. Thus, an in-depth productive transformation should simultaneously consider the reallocation of production among the sectors and the substitution of imported intermediate inputs with domestic production (Fig. 1.2).

This section provides the background required for formulating productive transformation as a constraint optimization problem. The approach of this research requires the expression of the objective function (trade balance deficit) and the restrictions (GDP and economic complexity) as a function of the decision variables (the structure of the value-added and the distribution coefficients of the sectors). To this end, firstly, the basic input–output model is described in matrix formation and, secondly,

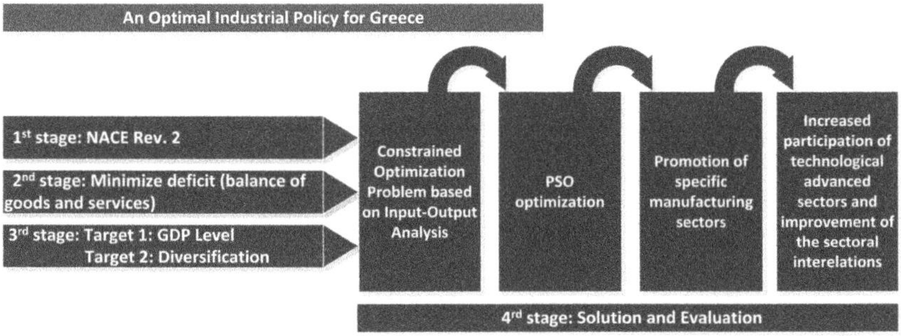

Fig. 1.2 An optimal industrial policy for Greece (*Source* Authors' creation)

the domestic content of exports and the GDP are defined in connection with the decision variables. An analytical description of the structural weaknesses of the Greek economy and the requirements of a productive transformation process is included in Chapter 2 of this volume.

1.5.1 The Leontief Model

In an economy with *n*sectors of economic activity, the total output of each sector i, x_i expresses the total level of production by an economic sector, which covers both intermediate and final demand. Given a vector $\boldsymbol{x} \in \mathbb{R}^{n\times 1}$ denoting the total output by sector of economic activity, the distribution of output is expressed by Eq. 1.1.

$$\boldsymbol{x} = \boldsymbol{Z}_d \cdot 1_n + \boldsymbol{f}_d \tag{1.1}$$

where,

$\boldsymbol{Z}_d \in \mathbb{R}^{n\times n}$ represents the matrix of domestically produced intermediate demand. The typical element z_{ij} of $\boldsymbol{Z}_d$ represents the production of sector i, which is used as an intermediate input by sector j.

$\boldsymbol{f}_d \in \mathbb{R}^{n\times 1}$ is the vector of the final demand components (analytically exports, public and private consumption, gross capital formation, and change in inventories), which are domestically produced.

$1_n \in \mathbb{R}^{n\times 1}$ is an n-dimensional vector, each element of which equals one.

As discussed in Leontief (1991), $\boldsymbol{Z}_d$ is a share of the economy's total output $\boldsymbol{x}$. Dividing the typical element of $\boldsymbol{Z}_d$, z_{dij} by the total output of sector j, the technological coefficient $a_{ij} = z_{ij}/x_j$ is defined. The technological coefficient a_{ij} represents the direct requirement of sector i's output, needed to produce one unit of sector j's output. The matrix of technological coefficients $\boldsymbol{A}_d \in \mathbb{R}^{n\times n}$ (or the matrix of direct requirements) is defined as:

$$\boldsymbol{A}_d = \boldsymbol{Z}_d \cdot \hat{\boldsymbol{X}}^{-1} \Rightarrow \boldsymbol{Z}_d = \boldsymbol{A}_d \cdot \hat{\boldsymbol{X}} \tag{1.2}$$

where and $\hat{\boldsymbol{X}} \in \mathbb{R}^{n\times n}$, a diagonal matrix whose diagonal elements are the elements of vector $\boldsymbol{x}$.

Taking into account Eq. 1.2, Eq. 1.1 is transformed to:

$$\boldsymbol{x} = \boldsymbol{A}_d \cdot \boldsymbol{x} + \boldsymbol{f}_d \Rightarrow \boldsymbol{x} = (\boldsymbol{I}_n - \boldsymbol{A}_d)^{-1} \cdot \boldsymbol{f}_d \tag{1.3}$$

The matrix $(\boldsymbol{I}_n - \boldsymbol{A}_d)^{-1}$ is the well-known Leontief inverse matrix (Miller & Blair, 2009). A typical element $i, j \in [1, n]$ of the Leontief inverse matrix shows the sector's-i product, which is required, directly and indirectly, for the production of one unit of the final demand of the sector's-j output.

Consider a vector $\boldsymbol{v_a} \in \mathbb{R}^{n \times 1}$. A specific element of $\boldsymbol{v_a}$ represents the value-added of a particular sector. Given a vector $\boldsymbol{v} \in \mathbb{R}^{n \times 1}$ representing the intensity of employment by sector of economic activity, then $\boldsymbol{v}$, can be computed by Eq. 1.4:

$$\boldsymbol{v} = \hat{X}^{-1} \cdot \boldsymbol{v_a} \tag{1.4}$$

A typical diagonal element of $\boldsymbol{v}$ represents the value-added by unit of a sector's output.

1.5.2 The Ghosh Model

Ghosh (1958) suggested an alternative interpretation of the Leontief model where gross output equals the primary inputs entering the economic system, expressed by Eq. 1.5.

$$\boldsymbol{x} = 1_{\boldsymbol{n}} \cdot \boldsymbol{Z_d} + 1_{\boldsymbol{n}}' \cdot \boldsymbol{Z}_m + \boldsymbol{v_a} = 1_{\boldsymbol{n}}' \cdot \boldsymbol{Z} + \boldsymbol{v_a} \tag{1.5}$$

where, $\boldsymbol{Z_m} \in \mathbb{R}^{n \times n}$ represents the matrix of imported intermediate demand and $\boldsymbol{Z} \in \mathbb{R}^{n \times n}$ represents the matrix of the total intermediate demand, both domestic and foreign. The typical element z_{ij} of $\boldsymbol{Z} = \boldsymbol{Z_d} + \boldsymbol{Z_m}$ represents the total production of sector i (domestic and foreign) needed for the production of the sector j.

Following the Ghosh approach, the matrix $\boldsymbol{B_d} \in \mathbb{R}^{n \times n}$ of the distribution coefficients of domestic intermediate inputs is defined as:

$$\boldsymbol{B_d} = \hat{X}^{-1} \cdot \boldsymbol{Z_d} \Rightarrow \boldsymbol{Z_d} = \hat{X} \cdot \boldsymbol{B_d} \tag{1.6}$$

The matrix $\boldsymbol{B_m} \in \mathbb{R}^{n \times n}$ of the distribution coefficients of imported intermediate inputs is defined as:

$$\boldsymbol{B_m} = \hat{X}^{-1} \cdot \boldsymbol{Z_m} \Rightarrow \boldsymbol{Z_m} = \hat{X} \cdot \boldsymbol{B_m} \tag{1.7}$$

And from Eq. 1.6 and Eq. 1.7:

$$\boldsymbol{Z} = \boldsymbol{Z_d} + \boldsymbol{Z_m} = \hat{X} \cdot (\boldsymbol{B_d} + \boldsymbol{B_m}) = \hat{X} \cdot \boldsymbol{B} \tag{1.8}$$

where, $\boldsymbol{B} \in \mathbb{R}^{n\times n}$ and $\boldsymbol{B} = \boldsymbol{B_d} + \boldsymbol{B_m} => \boldsymbol{B_m} = \boldsymbol{B} - \boldsymbol{B_d}$.

Based on Eq. 1.8, Eq. 1.5 is transformed to:

$$\boldsymbol{x} = \boldsymbol{x} \cdot \boldsymbol{B} + \boldsymbol{v_a} \Leftrightarrow \boldsymbol{x}^{\boldsymbol{T}} = \boldsymbol{v}_{\boldsymbol{a}}^{\boldsymbol{T}} \cdot \boldsymbol{v_a}(1 - \boldsymbol{B})^{-1}$$
$$\Leftrightarrow \boldsymbol{x} = ((1 - \boldsymbol{B})^{-1})' \cdot \boldsymbol{v_a} \tag{1.9}$$

In an effort to link the mathematical formulation of the Leontief and the Ghosh model, Miller and Blair (2009, pp. 547–548) show that the matrices of technological coefficients ($\boldsymbol{A_d}$) and distribution coefficients ($\boldsymbol{B_d}$) are similar. Thus,

$$\boldsymbol{A_d} = \hat{\boldsymbol{X}} \cdot \boldsymbol{B_d} \cdot \hat{\boldsymbol{X}}^{-1} \Leftrightarrow \boldsymbol{B_d} = \hat{\boldsymbol{X}}^{-1} \cdot \boldsymbol{A_d} \cdot \hat{\boldsymbol{X}} \tag{1.10}$$

1.5.3 Objective Functions and Constraints

The optimization problem's objective function expresses the trade balance's deficit. The balance of goods and services $balance \in \mathbb{R}^{1\times 1}$ of an economy is expressed by Eq. 1.11

$$\text{balance} = 1_{\boldsymbol{n}}^{\boldsymbol{T}} \cdot (\boldsymbol{ex} - \boldsymbol{im}) \tag{1.11}$$

The components of final demand $\boldsymbol{f_d}$, are the vectors $\boldsymbol{ex} \in \mathbb{R}^{n\times 1}$,$\boldsymbol{c_d} \in \mathbb{R}^{n\times 1}$, and $\boldsymbol{inv} \in \mathbb{R}^{n\times 1}$, where $\boldsymbol{ex}$ is the vector of the exports, where $\boldsymbol{c_d}$ is the vector of the government and private consumption covered by the domestic production and where $\boldsymbol{inv}$ is the vector of the gross capital formation and change in inventories covered by the domestic production. In Eq. 1.12, the diagonal matrices $\widehat{\boldsymbol{n_1}}, \widehat{\boldsymbol{n_2}}, \widehat{\boldsymbol{n_3}} \in \mathbb{R}^{n\times n}$ are expressing the sectoral shares of $\boldsymbol{ex}$, $\boldsymbol{c_d}$ and $\boldsymbol{inv}$ final demand:

$$\boldsymbol{f_d} = \boldsymbol{ex} + \boldsymbol{c_d} + \boldsymbol{inv_d} = \widehat{\boldsymbol{n_1}} \cdot \boldsymbol{f_d} + \widehat{\boldsymbol{n_2}} \cdot \boldsymbol{f_d} + \widehat{\boldsymbol{n_3}} \cdot \boldsymbol{f_d} \tag{1.12}$$

where, $\widehat{\boldsymbol{n_1}} + \widehat{\boldsymbol{n_2}} + \widehat{\boldsymbol{n_3}} = \boldsymbol{I_n}$

Based on Eq. 1.12, we obtain that the exports of an economy can be determined as:

$$\boldsymbol{ex} = \widehat{\boldsymbol{n_1}} \cdot \boldsymbol{f_d} \tag{1.13}$$

The imports of an economy are the summation of intermediate and final imports.

The vector of intermediate imports $\boldsymbol{im_{im}} \in \mathbb{R}^{n\times 1}$ can be expressed by Eq. 1.14

$$\boldsymbol{im_{int}} = \left(1_n^T \cdot \boldsymbol{Z_m}\right)^T = \boldsymbol{Z_m^T} \cdot 1_n \tag{1.14}$$

The vector of final imports $\boldsymbol{im_f} \in \mathbb{R}^{n\times 1}$ can be expressed by Eq. 1.15.

$$\boldsymbol{im_f} = \boldsymbol{c_{im}} + \boldsymbol{inv_{im}} \tag{1.15}$$

where, $\boldsymbol{c_{im}} \in \mathbb{R}^{n\times 1}$ is the vector of consumption which is satisfied by imports and $\boldsymbol{inv_{im}} \in \mathbb{R}^{n\times 1}$ is the vector of investments satisfied by imports.

Given that the total consumption of an economy is produced by domestic industries or imported, then:

$$\boldsymbol{c_{im}} = \boldsymbol{c} - \boldsymbol{c_d} \tag{1.16}$$

where $\boldsymbol{c} \in \mathbb{R}^{n\times 1}$ is the vector of total consumption and $\boldsymbol{c_d} \in \mathbb{R}^{n\times 1}$ is the vector of consumption covered by domestic production.

Based on Eq. 1.12, we obtain that the vector of consumption covered by domestic production can be determined as:

$$\boldsymbol{c_d} = \widehat{\boldsymbol{n_2}} \cdot \boldsymbol{f_d} \tag{1.17}$$

Finally, from the combination of Eqs. 1.15, 1.16, and 1.17:

$$\boldsymbol{im_f} = \boldsymbol{c} - \widehat{\boldsymbol{n_2}} \cdot \boldsymbol{f_d} + \boldsymbol{inv_{im}} \tag{1.18}$$

Finally, the vector of total imports of an economy $\boldsymbol{im} \in \mathbb{R}^{n\times 1}$ can be defined as:

$$\begin{aligned} \boldsymbol{im} &= \boldsymbol{im_{int}} + \boldsymbol{im_f} \Rightarrow \\ \boldsymbol{im} &= \boldsymbol{Z_m^T} \cdot 1_n + \boldsymbol{c} - \widehat{\boldsymbol{n_2}} \cdot \boldsymbol{f_d} + \boldsymbol{inv_{im}} \end{aligned} \tag{1.19}$$

Using Eqs. 1.13 and 1.19, Eq. 1.11 is transformed as follows:

$$\begin{aligned} \text{balance} &= 1_n^T \cdot (\boldsymbol{ex} - \boldsymbol{im}) \Rightarrow \\ &= 1_n^T \cdot \left(\widehat{\boldsymbol{n_1}} \cdot \boldsymbol{f_d} - \left(\boldsymbol{Z_m^T} \cdot 1_n + \boldsymbol{c} - \widehat{\boldsymbol{n_2}} \cdot \boldsymbol{f_d} + \boldsymbol{inv_{im}}\right)\right) \end{aligned} \tag{1.20}$$

The deficit of the balance of goods and services by sector of economic activity is expressed as

$$\text{deficit} = -\text{balance} \tag{1.21}$$

The first constraint involves the GDP growth rate that the economy should achieveÛy equals the sum of all sectors value-added:

$$gdp = 1_n{}' \cdot \boldsymbol{v_a} \tag{1.22}$$

The second constraint involves the economic complexity, which will be approached using the Krugman Specialization Index. The Krugman Specialization Index (KSI) is a widely used measure of a country's specialization (Krugman, 1991). The index measures the distance between the economic structure of the examined country and a reference group.

$$KSI = \sum \left|S_{i,gr} - S_{i,EU28}\right| \tag{1.23}$$

where, $S_{i,gr}i$ is the exports share of sector i of Greece and $S_{i,EU28}$ is the exports share of sector i of EU28. KSI measures the absolute distance between a sector's relative share between a country and the EU28, and then sums all sectors to create an index. If KSI is equal to zero, then examined country has an industrial structure identical to the EU28 (the country is not specialized). A high value of the index indicates a country with strong sectoral specialization. We should note that the indicator can only be evaluated as a relative one, compared with a group of countries.

In matrix formation, consider a vector $\boldsymbol{s_{gr}} \in \mathbb{R}^{n\times 1}$ is expressed as $\boldsymbol{s_{gr}} = \frac{1}{\boldsymbol{ex}\cdot 1_n{}'} \cdot \boldsymbol{ex}$, while the vector $\boldsymbol{s_{EU28}} \in \mathbb{R}^{n\times 1}$ is defined based on the data of 2015 for EU28 ($\boldsymbol{S_{EU28}}$ is a vector with constant elements). Then $KSI \in \mathbb{R}^{1\times 1}$ is defined as:

$$KSI = \left\|\boldsymbol{s_{gr}} - \boldsymbol{s_{eu28}}\right\|_1 \tag{1.24}$$

1.5.4 The Optimization Problem

The aim of the restructuring problem is to minimize the deficit of the goods and services' balances under specific restriction. The decision variables of the analysis are the matrix of the distribution coefficients $\boldsymbol{B_d}$ and the vector $\boldsymbol{v_a}$ of the sectors' value-added.

$$\text{deficit} = -\text{balance} \tag{1.25}$$

The optimization problem is to define the optimal $\boldsymbol{B_d}$ and $\boldsymbol{v_a}$ in order to minimize $deficit(\boldsymbol{B_d}, \boldsymbol{v_a})$.

The domain of $\boldsymbol{B}_d$ is defined by a lower and an upper matrix $\boldsymbol{B}_1, \boldsymbol{B}_2 \in \mathbb{R}^{n\times n}$, respectively.

$$\boldsymbol{B}_1 \preccurlyeq \boldsymbol{B}_d \preccurlyeq \boldsymbol{B}_2 \tag{1.26}$$

In addition, the domain of $\boldsymbol{v_\alpha}$ is defined by a lower and an upper vector $\boldsymbol{k}_1, \boldsymbol{k}_2 \in \mathbb{R}^{n\times 1}$, respectively, according to Eq. 1.27.

$$\boldsymbol{k}_1 \preccurlyeq \boldsymbol{v_a} \preccurlyeq \boldsymbol{k}_2 \tag{1.27}$$

The symbol $\preccurlyeq$ denotes element-wise inequality.

The GDP of the economy should equal with the GDP projection, as shown in Eq. 1.28:

$$gdp\left(\boldsymbol{B}_d^*, \boldsymbol{v_a}\right) = gdp_{\text{optimum}} \tag{1.28}$$

And the complexity of the economy should increase to

$$ksi\left(\boldsymbol{B}_d^*, \boldsymbol{v_a}\right) = ksi_{\text{target}} \tag{1.29}$$

In summary, the productive restructuring model can be formulated as a constraint optimization problem in Eq. 1.30:

$$\begin{aligned}
&\text{Minimize} && \text{deficit}\left(\mathrm{B_d}, \mathrm{v_a}\right)\\
&\boldsymbol{B}_1 \preccurlyeq \boldsymbol{B}_d \preccurlyeq \boldsymbol{B}_2 &&\\
&\boldsymbol{k}_1 \preccurlyeq \boldsymbol{v_a} \preccurlyeq \boldsymbol{k}_2 &&\\
&\text{subject to:} &&\\
&gdp(\boldsymbol{v_a}) = gdp_{\text{optimum}} &&\\
&\boldsymbol{k}_{\text{si,min}} \leq \boldsymbol{k}_{\text{si}}(\boldsymbol{B}_d, \boldsymbol{v_a}) \leq \boldsymbol{k}_{\text{si,max}} &&
\end{aligned} \tag{1.30}$$

1.6 Future Directions

In this chapter, a theoretical and methodological framework for the formulation of an industrial policy strategy to promote the productive transformation of an economy is introduced.

Firstly, the issues surrounding the definition and the contribution of industrial policy are discussed. In particular, in the first section of the chapter, industrial policy is defined as sector-specific interventions in an economic system toward the productive transformation and the achievement of economic development. This definition emphasizes the vertical nature of industrial policy, given that the process of productive transformation involves targeted interventions.

In addition, productive transformation is analyzed in the theoretical framework of input–output analysis, providing a background to the methodological approach elaborated later in the chapter. In particular, input–output analysis is selected as a methodology capable of reflecting the complexity and complementarity of an economic system and suitable for the formulation of productive transformation as an optimization problem. The literature review highlights the lack of a methodological framework for exploring different aspects (economic, social, and environmental) of productive transformation.

Next, the broad outlines of an industrial policy toward productive transformation is examined. Three complementary aspects are analyzed: The role of industrial sectors, the importance of diversification and sophistication of production, and the contribution of production linkages. The main conclusion of the section is that a successful productive transformation strategy relies on both diversification and sophistication of production and that the improvement of productive linkages is essential to sustain macroeconomic gains.

Finally, a methodological approach is introduced to address the question: which sectors should a productive transformation strategy target to optimize the productive structure, satisfying specific macroeconomic targets in parallel? Furthermore, the mathematical model for the productive transformation of an economy is introduced. The optimization model's objectives and constraints are designed for the Greek economy, a country with structural weaknesses and deep macroeconomic problems. In this case, the objective is minimization of the trade balance deficit. The constraints are achieving a specific growth level with increased economic complexity. The optimal productive structure involves the distribution of final demand between the sectors and the improvement of productive linkages due to import substitution policies.

The novelty of the proposed methodology is that it captures the full economic potential of productive transformation. Furthermore, the intermediate transactions are not considered stable but depend on the growth rates of the sectors they refer to. Thus, the sector's potential role as a consumer of inputs and the producer of intermediate and final products or services is fully documented. In sum, this chapter introduces an in-depth productive transformation that estimates the optimal reallocation of production among the sectors and the optimal level of import substitution.

References

Andreoni, A., & Scazzieri, R. (2014). Triggers of change: Structural trajectories and production dynamics. *Cambridge Journal of Economics, 38*(6), 1391–1408. https://doi.org/10.1093/cje/bet034

Baumol, W. J. (1967). Macroeconomics of unbalanced growth: The anatomy of urban crisis. *The American Economic Review, 57*(3), 415–426.

Belegri, A., Michaelides, P., & Markaki, M. (2011). Labour productivity changes and working time: The case of Greece. *Economic Systems Research, 23*(3), 329–339. https://doi.org/10.1080/09535314.2011.595777

Bresser-Pereira, L. C. (2016). Reflecting on new developmentalism and classical developmentalism. *Review of Keynesian Economics, 4*(3), 331–352. https://doi.org/10.4337/roke.2016.03.07

Cardinale, I., & Scazzieri, R. (2019). Explaining structural change: Actions and transformations. *Structural Change and Economic Dynamics, 51*, 393–404. https://doi.org/10.1016/j.strueco.2018.12.002

Chang, H.-J. (2002). *Kicking away the ladder: Development strategy in historical perspective*. Anthem Press.

Chang, H.-J., & Andreoni, A. (2016). Industrial policy in a changing world: Basic principles, neglected issues and new challenges. Cambridge Journal of Economics, *40*.

Chang, H.-J., & Andreoni, A. (2019). Industrial policy in the 21st century. *Development and Change*.

Chang, H.-J., Andreoni, A., & Kuan, M. L. (2013). International industrial policy experiences and the lessons for the UK. *Economia e Politica Industriale, 43*(4).

Chang, H.-J., Hauge, J., & Irfan, M. (2016). *Transformative industrial policy for Africa*. Economic Commission for Africa.

Chang, N. (2015). Changing industrial structure to reduce carbon dioxide emissions: A Chinese application. *Journal of Cleaner Production, 103*, 40–48. https://doi.org/10.1016/j.jclepro.2014.03.003

Cho, C. J. (1999). The economic-energy-environmental policy problem: An application of the interactive multiobjective decision method for Chungbuk Province. *Journal of Environmental Management, 56*(2), 119–131. https://doi.org/10.1006/jema.1999.0264

Cimoli, M., Primi, A., & Pugno, M. (2006). *A low-growth model: Informality as a structural constraint*. Cepal Review. https://doi.org/10.18356/3995c051-en

De Carvalho, A. L., Antunes, C. H., Freire, F., & Henriques, C. O. (2015). A hybrid input–output multi-objective model to assess economic–energy–environment trade-offs in Brazil. *Energy, 82*, 769–785. https://doi.org/10.1016/j.energy.2015.01.089

Di Tommaso, M. R., Tassinari, M., Bonnini, S., & Marozzi, M. (2017). Industrial policy and manufacturing targeting in the US: New methodological tools for strategic policy-making. *International Review of Applied Economics, 31*(5), 681–703. https://doi.org/10.1080/02692171.2017.1303036

Dietzenbacher, E. (2002). Interregional multipliers: Looking backward, looking forward. *Regional Studies, 36*(2), 125–136. https://doi.org/10.1080/00343400220121918

Economakis, G., & Markaki, M. (2023). Unequal exchange in the EU: The case of trade transactions between Germany, Italy, and Greece. *Science and Society, 87*(1), 21–49. https://doi.org/10.1521/siso.2023.87.1.21

Economakis, G., Markaki, M., & Anastasiadis, A. (2015). Structural analysis of the Greek economy. *Review of Radical Political Economics, 47*(3), 424–445. https://doi.org/10.1177/0486613414542779

Economakis, G., Markaki, M., Androulakis, G., & Anastasiadis, A. (2018). Imperialist exploitation and crisis of the Greek economy: A study. In *Crisis, movement, strategy: The Greek experience* (pp. 40–66). Brill.

Evans, P. (2008). *In search of the 21st century developmental state* (No. 4; University of Sussex Working Paper). University of Sussex.

Fortunato, P., & Razo, C. (2014). Export sophistication, growth, and the middle-income trap. In *Transforming economies–making industrial policy work for growth, jobs & development* (pp. 267–287). ILO.

Ghosh, A. (1958). Input-output approach in an allocation system. *Economica, 25*(97), 58–64.

Hausmann, R., & Klinger, B. (2007). *The structure of the product space and the evolution of comparative advantage*. Center for International Development at Harvard University.

Hirschman, A. O. (1958). Interdependence and industrialization. In *The strategy of economic development*. Yale University Press

Hristu-Varsakelis, D., Karagianni, S., Pempetzoglou, M., & Sfetsos, A. (2010). Optimizing production with energy and GHG emission constraints in Greece: An input–output analysis. *Energy Policy, 38*(3), 1566–1577. https://doi.org/10.1016/j.enpol.2009.11.040

Imbs, J., & Wacziarg, R. (2003). Stages of diversification. *American Economic Review, 93*(1), 63–86. https://doi.org/10.1257/000282803321455160

Kaldor, N. (1967). *Strategic factors in economic development*. Ithaca.

Krugman, P. (1988). *Differences in income elasticities and trends in real exchange rates*. National Bureau of Economic Research.

Krugman, P. (1991). Increasing returns and economic geography. *Journal of Political Economy, 99*(3), 483–499. https://doi.org/10.1086/261763

Lall, S. (2000). The Technological structure and performance of developing country manufactured exports, 1985–98. *Oxford Development Studies, 28*(3), 337–369. https://doi.org/10.1080/713688318

Leontief, W. (1982). Academic economics. *Science, 217*(4555), 104–107. https://doi.org/10.1126/science.217.4555.104

Leontief, W. (1986). *Input-output economics*. Oxford University Press.

Leontief, W. (1991). The economy as a circular flow. *Structural Change and Economic Dynamics, 2*(1), 181–212. https://doi.org/10.1016/0954-349X(91)90012-H

Lin, J. Y. (2011). *From flying geese to leading dragons: New opportunities and strategies for structural transformation in developing countries*. The World Bank.

Lin, P. P., Li, D. F., Jiang, B. Q., Wei, A. P., & Yu, G. F. (2019). Regional input-output multiple choice goal programming model and method for industry structure optimization on energy conservation and GHG emission reduction in China. *International Journal of Computational Intelligence Systems, 12*(2), 1311–1322.

Maneschi, A. (1998). *Comparative advantage in international trade: A historical perspective*. Edward Elgar Publishing.

Markaki, M., & Economakis, G. (2022). International structural competitiveness and the hierarchy in the world economy. *World Review of Political Economy, 12*(2), 195–219. https://www.jstor.org/stable/48676086

Markaki, M., & Papadakis, S. (2021). A modern industrial policy for the Czech Republic: Optimizing the structure of production. *Mathematics, 9*(23), 3095. https://doi.org/10.3390/math9233095

Mazzucato, M., Cimoli, M., Dosi, G., Stiglitz, J. E., Landesmann, M. A., Pianta, M., Walz, R., & Page, T. (2015). Which industrial policy does Europe need? *Intereconomics, 50*(3), 120–155. https://doi.org/10.1007/s10272-015-0535-1

Mi, Z.-F., Pan, S.-Y., Yu, H., & Wei, Y.-M. (2015). Potential impacts of industrial structure on energy consumption and CO_2 emission: A case study of Beijing.

Journal of Cleaner Production, 103, 455–462. https://doi.org/10.1016/j.jclepro.2014.06.011

Milberg, W., Jiang, X., & Gereffi, G. (2014). Industrial policy in the era of vertically specialized industrialization. In *Transforming economies: Making industrial policy work for growth, jobs and development*. International Labour Organization.

Miller, R. E., & Blair, P. D. (2009). *Input-output analysis: Foundations and extensions*. Cambridge University Press.

Ocampo, J.-A. (2005). The quest for dynamic efficiency: Structural dynamics and economic growth in developing countries. In *Beyond reforms: Structural dynamics and macroeconomic vulnerability* (pp. 3–43).

Ocampo, J.-A. (2014). Latin American structuralism and production development strategies. In *Transforming economies. Making industrial policy work for growth, jobs and development* (pp. 41–64). ILO.

Ocampo, J.-A., Rada, C., & Taylor, L. (2009). *Growth and policy in developing countries: A structuralist approach*. Columbia University Press.

O'Donovan, D., & Rios-Morales, R. (2006). *Can the Latin American and Caribbean countries emulate the Irish model on FDI attraction?* Cepal Review.

Oliveira, C., & Antunes, C. H. (2004). A multiple objective model to deal with economy–energy–environment interactions. *European Journal of Operational Research, 153*(2), 370–385. https://doi.org/10.1016/S0377-2217(03)00159-0

Oxford Economics. (2020). *Oxford economics global economic model*.

Papadakis, S., & Markaki, M. (2019). An in-depth economic restructuring framework by using particle swarm optimization. *Journal of Cleaner Production, 215*, 329–342. https://doi.org/10.1016/j.jclepro.2019.01.041

Petralia, S., Balland, P.-A., & Morrison, A. (2017). Climbing the ladder of technological development. *Research Policy, 46*(5), 956–969. https://doi.org/10.1016/j.respol.2017.03.012

Pilat, D., Cimper, A., Olsen, K. B., & Webb, C. (2006). *The changing nature of manufacturing in OECD economies* (STI Working Paper Series). OECD. http://www.oecd.org/science/inno/37607831.pdf

Prebisch, R. (1962). The economic development of Latin America and its principal problems. *Economic Bulletin for Latin America, 7*(1), 1–22.

Reinert, E. S. (2019). How rich countries got rich... And why poor countries stay poor. Hachette UK.

Robinson, J. (2016). *The accumulation of capital*. Springer.

Rodrik, D. (2007). Industrial development: Some stylized facts and policy directions. In *Industrial development for the 21st century: Sustainable development perspectives* (pp. 7–28).

Rodrik, D. (2008). *One economics, many recipes: Globalization, institutions, and economic growth*. Princeton University Press.

Rodrik, D. (2009). Industrial policy: Don't ask why, ask how. *Middle East Development Journal, 1*(1), 1–29. https://doi.org/10.1142/S1793812009000024

Salazar -Xirinachs, J. M., Nübler, I., & Kozul-Wright, R. (2014). Industrial policy, productive transformation and jobs: Theory, history and practice. In *Transforming economies. Making industrial policy work for growth, jobs and development*.

San, J. R. (2010). An environmental/input–output linear programming model to reach the targets for greenhouse gas emissions set by the kyoto protocol. *Economic Systems Research, 22*(3), 223–236. https://doi.org/10.1080/09535314.2010.495709

Sánchez, D. R., Hoadley, A. F., & Khalilpour, K. R. (2019). A multi-objective extended input–output model for a regional economy. *Sustainable Production and Consumption, 20*, 15–28. https://doi.org/10.1016/j.spc.2019.04.009

Savona, M. (2018). *Industrial Policy for a European Industrial Renaissance. A Few Reflections* (SPRU Working Paper Series).

Scazzieri, R. (2018). Structural dynamics and evolutionary change. *Structural Change and Economic Dynamics, 46*, 52–58. https://doi.org/10.1016/j.strueco.2018.03.007

Simoes, A. J. G., & Hidalgo, C. A. (2011). *The economic complexity observatory: An analytical tool for understanding the dynamics of economic development*. Workshops at the Twenty-Fifth AAAI Conference on Artificial Intelligence.

Stiglitz, J. E., Lin, J. Y., & Monga, C. (2013). *The rejuvenation of industrial policy*. The World Bank.

Stöllinger, R., Foster-McGregor, N., Holzner, M., Landesmann, M., Pöschl, J., Stehrer, R., & Stocker-Waldhuber, C. (2013). *A manufacturing imperative in the EU: Europe's position in global manufacturing and the role of industrial policy*. Vienna Institute for International Economic Studies Vienna.

Syrquin, M. (1988). Patterns of structural change. *Handbook of Development Economics, 1*, 203–273. https://doi.org/10.1016/S1573-4471(88)01010-1

Szirmai, A. (2012). Industrialisation as an engine of growth in developing countries, 1950–2005. *Structural Change and Economic Dynamics, 23*(4), 406–420. https://doi.org/10.1016/j.strueco.2011.01.005

Tian, Y., Xiong, S., & Ma, X. (2017). Analysis of the potential impacts on China's industrial structure in energy consumption. *Sustainability, 9*(12), 2284. https://doi.org/10.3390/su9122284

UNIDO, T. (2013). *Sustaining employment growth: The role of manufacturing and structural change*. United Nations Industrial Development Organization Report. United Nations.

Warwick, K. (2013). *Beyond industrial policy: Emerging issues and new trends* (No. 2; OECD Science, Technology and Industry Policy Papers). OECD Publishing.

Yu, S., Zheng, S., Ba, G., & Wei, Y.-M. (2016). Can China realise its energy-savings goal by adjusting its industrial structure? *Economic Systems Research, 28*(2), 273–293. https://doi.org/10.1080/09535314.2015.110271

CHAPTER 2

Greece Toward 2027: Structural Transformation, Industrial Policy, and Economic Development

Maria Markaki and Stelios Papadakis

2.1 Introduction

The Greek Economy was severely affected by the 2008 economic crisis. The roots of Greece's unprecedented crisis should be sought in the country's unfavorable economic structure. The main structural problems of the Greek Economy are limited exports with low diversification; low participation of the manufacturing and technologically advanced sectors in

M. Markaki (✉) · S. Papadakis
Department of Management Science and Technology, Laboratory of Data Science, Multimedia and Modelling, Hellenic Mediterranean University, Heraklion, Greece
e-mail: mmarkaki@hmu.gr

S. Papadakis
e-mail: spap@hmu.gr

P. E. Petrakis (ed.), *Interconnections in the Greek Economy*, The Political Economy of Greek Growth up to 2030, https://doi.org/10.1007/978-3-031-31335-6_2

production and exports; weak linkages among different economic activities; high dependency on intermediate and final imports with high-income elasticity of demand; and specialization in activities of low technological level. The above structural features lead to trade balance deficits and low international competitiveness. Furthermore, the implementation of three Economic Adjustment Programs (2010, 2012, and 2015) formed by the European Union, the International Monetary Fund, and the European Central Bank, and the imposed austerity policies failed to drive the Economy into a growth trajectory and have led to an ongoing recession.

The COVID-19 pandemic and the subsequent economic lockdown triggered a deeper recession, reduced production levels, and increased unemployment. The Greek Economy's peculiar economic structure is emerging as the main obstacle to economic growth and development, and current policies do little to the economic situation. The transformation of the Greek Economy's productive structure through appropriate industrial policies is recognized as the only way to achieve economic development.

In this chapter, the solution to the optimization problem of the economic structure of Greece, introduced in Chapter 1, is analytically discussed. The optimal economic structure is compared to the current one to define the sectors on which industrial policy should focus. Furthermore, the evolution of the backward sectoral linkages is investigated, determining the optimal structure's interconnectedness.

The structure of the chapter is the following: the methodological framework is introduced in the Sect. 2.1. Section 2.2 presents the current sectoral structure of Greece. Then, Sect. 2.3 focuses on the empirical results obtained from implementing the proposed methodology. Finally, Sect. 2.4 discusses policy implementations integrating sectoral and macroeconomic interventions.

2.2 The Sectoral Structure of Greek Economy

As was argued in Chapter 1, the elaboration of an industrial policy plan requires the in-depth knowledge of the Economy's structural features. That is, it relies in no small measure, on the ability to capture the complexity and dynamics of modern economies. Thus, before describing the goal as to how the optimal productive structure is set up, it is helpful to offer some background on the current sectoral structure of the Greek Economy and the country's position within the EU27 member countries. The remainder of this section contains a comparison between the

Greek Economy and the EU27 member countries regarding the sectoral structure of production, the technological features of production and external trade, intersectoral linkages, and the contribution of exports to the value-added generation.

The economic sectors of the Greek Economy are listed in Table 2.1. In the same table is listed the aggregation of the manufacturing sectors according to the technological intensity (Eurostat, 2010).

2.2.1 *Economic structure and the Technological Level of Production*

Table 2.2 shows that the tertiary sector generates a significant share of value-added in all EU27 countries, reaching 72.98% for the EU27 as a whole. The secondary sector (one-digit sectors B, C, D, and F) follows, with its contribution to value-added reaching 25.23% for the EU27, while the primary sector participates in the formation of value-added by only 1.79%. The countries with the largest share of primary sector in value-added are Romania (4.54%) and Greece (4.36%), while the countries with the smallest percentage are Belgium (0.70%) and Luxembourg (0.25%). The countries with the largest share of secondary sectors in value-added are Ireland (37.61%) and the Czech Republic (34.83%), while the countries with the smallest share are Luxembourg (12.48%) and Greece (14.86%). Finally, the countries with the largest share of the tertiary sector in value-added are Malta (85.16%) and Luxembourg (87.27%). By comparison, the countries with the smallest percentage are Ireland (61.41%) and the Czech Republic (63.03%). Although the productive structure is likely to differ among countries, Greece is one of the EU27's most diverse economies; it is at the top of the EU27 regarding the primary sector's contribution and the bottom regarding the secondary sector.

The technological level of the production is highlighted in recent literature as one of the most critical factors determining an economy's competitiveness level (Lall, 2000; Markaki & Economakis, 2020; Petralia et al., 2017). In this respect, the production structure in terms of the sectoral technological level is presented in the following (Table 2.3). Eurostat (2010) classifies the secondary sectors based on their technological features as follows:

- High Technology (HT): C21, C26
- Medium–High Technology (MHT): C20, C27, C28, C29, C30

Table 2.1 Sectoral classification and technological level

Code	*Description*	*Technological level**
A01-03	Agriculture, forestry and fishing	
B	Mining and quarrying	
C10-12	Food, beverages and tobacco products	LT
C13-15	Textiles, wearing apparel, leather and related products	LT
C16	Wood and of products of wood and cork, except furniture; articles of straw and plaiting materials	LT
C17	Paper and paper products	LT
C18	Printing and recording services	LT
C19	Coke and refined petroleum products	MLT
C20	Chemicals and chemical products	MHT
C21	Basic pharmaceutical products and pharmaceutical preparations	HT
C22	Rubber and plastic products	MLT
C23	Other non-metallic mineral products	MLT
C24	Basic metals	MLT
C25	Fabricated metal products, except machinery and equipment	MLT
C26	Computer, electronic and optical products	HT
C27	Electrical equipment	MHT
C28	Machinery and equipment n.e.c	MHT
C29	Motor vehicles, trailers and semi-trailers	MHT
C30	Other transport equipment	MHT
C31_32	Furniture and other manufactured goods	LT
C33	Repair and installation services of machinery and equipment	MLT
35–39	Water supply, sewerage, waste management and remediation	
F	Constructions and construction works	
G45-47	Wholesale and retail trade, repair of motor vehicles and motorcycles	
H49-53	Transportation and storage	
I	Accommodation and food services	
J58-63	Publishing, audiovisual and broadcasting activities, telecommunications, IT and other information services	
K64-66	Financial and insurance activities	
L68	Real estate activities	

(continued)

Table 2.1 (continued)

Code	*Description*	*Technological level**
M69-82	Legal, accounting, management, architecture, engineering, technical testing and analysis activities, scientific research and development, other professional, scientific and technical activities, administrative and support service activities	
O	Public administration and defence services; compulsory social security services	
P	Education services	
Q86-88	Human health services	
R90-99	Arts, entertainment and recreation, other services	

Source Eurostat (2008, 2010)
Note *Technological Level of manufacturing sectors: HT: high technology; MHT: medium–high technology; MLT: medium–low technology; LT: low-technology

- Medium Technology (MT): C19, C22, C23, C24, C25, C33
- Low Technology (LT):C10-C12, C13-C15, C16, C17, C18, C31-C32

Table 2.3 shows the technological structure of the EU27 using the latest available data for the year 2019. The value-added of each technological category is calculated by adding the sectors' value as described above.

Table 2.3 shows that high-tech sectors' contribution reaches 9.33% on average among EU27 member countries, while the corresponding value ranges from 3.32% in Romania, to 34.28% in Denmark. The medium–high-tech sectors' contribution reaches 38.33% on average among EU27 countries, ranging from 4.97% in Ireland, to 52.92% in Germany. Similarly, the medium–low-tech sectors' contribution reaches 26.59%, ranging from 16.14% in Ireland, to 37.04% in Slovakia. Finally, low-tech sectors' contribution reaches 25.75% in the EU27, ranging from 14.30% in Germany, to 57.73% in Lithuania. The Greek Economy is in the 15th place in the ranking of the examined countries regarding the participation of HT sectors in manufacturing, in the 23rd position regarding the share of MHT sectors, in the 6th position regarding MLT's share, and in the 6th position for the LT tech sectors.

A measure of the technologically advanced sector's contribution to an economy is the share of HT and MHT sectors in the production.

Table 2.2 Percentage structure of value-added in EU27 (2019)

	Primary Sector (%)	*Secondary Sector (%)*	*Tertiary Sector (%)*
EU27	1.79	25.23	72.98
BE	0.70	21.42	77.88
BG	3.75	25.05	71.20
CZ	2.14	34.83	63.03
DK	1.52	24.20	74.28
DE	0.80	29.65	69.55
EE	2.87	25.33	71.81
IE	0.97	37.61	61.41
EL	4.36	14.86	80.78
ES	2.88	22.58	74.54
FR	1.80	19.27	78.94
HR	3.56	24.73	71.71
IT	2.14	23.86	74.00
CY	1.99	14.57	83.44
LV	4.28	21.32	74.39
LT	3.59	28.11	68.31
LU	0.25	12.48	87.27
HU	3.96	29.45	66.59
MT	0.80	14.03	85.16
NL	1.85	19.86	78.29
AT	1.21	28.56	70.23
PL	2.67	31.83	65.50
PT	2.38	21.85	75.78
RO	4.54	31.14	64.32
SI	2.29	33.01	64.69
SK	2.76	32.10	65.14
FI	2.67	27.97	69.36
SE	1.63	24.97	73.40

Source Eurostat

This measure is more accurate than the share of HT sectors, because there are only two HT sectors (Basic pharmaceutical products and pharmaceutical preparations and Computer, electronic and optical products). Furthermore, medium–high technology sectors include the "heavy industry", such as the automotive industry, chemical industry, mechanical engineering industry, etc.

Figure 2.1 shows the contribution of the high and medium–high tech (HT & MHT) sectors, cumulatively, to the production of the economies

Table 2.3 Technological structure of EU27* countries, 2019 (%)

	HT (%)	*MHT (%)*	*MT (%)*	*LT (%)*
EU27	9.33	38.33	26.59	25.75
BE	17.02	30.32	26.58	26.08
BG	5.98	23.15	33.25	37.62
CZ	7.79	42.38	30.06	19.76
DK	34.28	26.94	16.99	21.80
DE	10.35	52.92	22.43	14.30
EE	6.54	17.89	29.87	45.70
IE	31.13	4.97	16.14	47.76
EL	7.23	13.93	32.55	46.29
ES	6.62	28.08	29.83	35.46
FR	10.06	30.60	30.57	28.76
HR	9.75	13.05	34.80	42.41
IT	6.67	32.13	29.27	31.93
CY	14.09	5.74	32.20	47.97
LV	6.48	13.24	22.55	57.73
LT	4.66	17.07	21.20	57.07
HU	15.41	38.62	27.16	18.81
NL	8.49	37.17	23.90	30.44
AT	9.50	36.55	29.71	24.24
PL	4.89	23.90	36.99	34.22
PT	4.59	17.42	28.87	49.13
RO	3.32	28.43	26.37	41.89
SI	14.48	29.76	35.09	20.68
SK	3.69	38.34	37.04	20.93
FI	14.61	31.74	26.59	27.06
SE	4.18	44.05	26.19	25.58

Source Eurostat
Note *No data is available for Luxembourg and Malta. For Ireland, Lithuania, and Sweden, the data refers to 2018

concerned. The HT & MIT sectors account for 47.67% of the manufacturing output for the EU27. By contrast, for Germany, Denmark, Hungary, the Czech Republic, Sweden, Finland, and Belgium, the HT & MHT sectors reach or exceed 50% of the industrial production. On the other hand, Greece is in the 23rd place among the examined countries, as the share of HT & MHT sectors in manufacturing is 21.16%. Cyprus ranks in the penultimate position with 19.84% and Estonia is in the last position with 19.72%. Based on the above analysis, Greece's inferior position in the share of the technological advance sectors is mainly due to

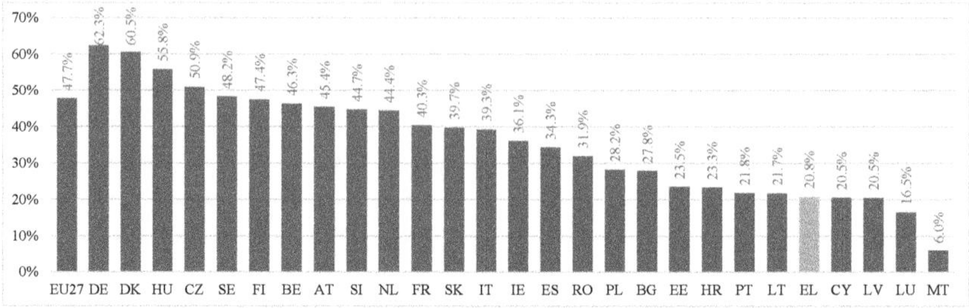

Fig. 2.1 Share of HT & MHT in value-added for EU27 countries, 2018 (%) (*Source* Eurostat and author's calculations)

the non-specialization of the Economy in the so-called "heavy industry" sectors.

2.2.2 *External Trade and Technological Level of Imports and Exports*

The literature on industrial policy focuses on the importance of the manufacturing sector as the driving force of economic growth. Recent studies argue that the technological structure of exports largely determines a country's position in international competition, as technologically advanced products, are characterized by higher-income elasticity of demand (Economakis & Markaki, 2014; Lall, 2000). Cohen and Zysman (1988) found a link between a country's export performance and technology's efficient use and dissemination across sectors. This view is also supported by Petralia et al. (2017), who points out the importance of technology in determining a country's level of development. Specifically, more developed countries tend to specialize in producing complex products using complex and less concentrated technologies than less developed ones.

In Greece, the share of high and medium–high technology products in exports is relatively low compared to the rest of the EU27 countries. Economakis and Markaki (2020) showed that in 2016, Greece was ranked last among EE countries in the share of HT and MHT products in total exports. The share in question was 24.3% for Greece, while in the top of the ranking was Ireland with a share of 85.5% and the median was Spain with a share of 55.5%. In the same research, the authors found a similar output when the technological level of imports is considered. The percentage of HT and MHT products in the Greek Economy's imports is 44.77% (third-lowest). By comparison, the corresponding value varies from 70.66% in Ireland to 35.1% in Cyprus, with a median of 56.5% in Austria. The technological levels of imports and exports are related. Imports include final and intermediate products and the latter are used in the production process. The technological level of intermediates reflects the technological level of output; thus, a low share of HT & MHT imports, as in Greece, indicates that domestic production tends to produce lower technology products. This is confirmed by the technological level of Greek exports of goods within the Euro Zone (Economakis et al., 2018).

Furthermore, Hausmann et al. (2014) determined that the economic complexity of a country (measured by the Economic Complexity Index—ECI) depends on the diversity of its exports and their ubiquity (the number of the countries able to produce them and those countries' complexity). Thus, countries that can maintain a diverse range of sophisticated and unique productive know-how, can produce a wide diversity of goods, including complex products that only a few other countries can produce (Markaki & Economakis., 2022; Simoes & Hidalgo, 2011).

As shown in Fig. 2.2, the Economic Complexity Index (ECI) for 2018 brings Greece in the last position within the EU27 countries. This output implies that Greece is a country that exports only a few range of products which (i) are also products of relatively high ubiquity and (ii) are exported by not very diversified countries.

In summary, the above analysis documents a divergence between Greece's production and trade structure and the rest of the EU27 countries, leading to the conclusion that Greece is facing unfavorable terms of trade within the European economies. Greece's productive structure indicates an economy with low production and export diversification, specializing in less technological advance products.

2.2.3 *Economic Linkages and Sectoral Structure*

The sectoral structure of an economy's production and exports is critical for identifying industrial policy objectives. However, policymakers cannot overlook that each sector's production process is based on the supply of products and services from other branches. A change in the production level of a sector will increase the demand for intermediates

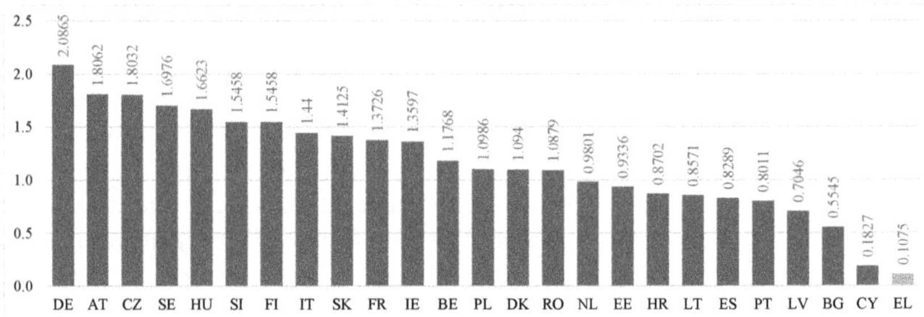

Fig. 2.2 Economic Complexity Index (ECI) for the EU27* (2018) (*Source* The Growth Lab at Harvard University [2019] and *Note* *No data available for Luxembourg and Malta)

from the sector supplying industries; thus, sectoral changes are not independent. The economic interdependencies, or linkages, that develop in an economic system diffuse a change in production structure throughout the Economy. The impact of the change depends on the intensity of the linkages. A sector strongly linked with other sectors in the production network can potentially cause broader and most significant effects on the extension of production than those caused by a sector with weak links. The backward linkages of the sectors are a measure of the level of their economic interdependencies and are widely used for the investigation of the productive structure of an economic system (national, regional, local) and for the evaluation of economic and social policies as well as forecasts at macroeconomic and sectoral level (Belegri-Roboli et al., 2010, 2011; Economakis & Markaki, 2023; Economakis et al., 2015; Miller & Blair, 2009; Suh, 2009).

The inquiry into the question of the strength of backward linkages of the Greek Economy will be based on two considerations. Firstly, the literature does not provide specific values that define a strong, average, or weak level of backward linkages. Therefore, estimating the strength of backward linkages is based only on evidence from comparative studies. Thereby, the strength of the Greek Economy's backward linkages will be investigated based on comparison within the EU27 countries. Secondly, although strong backward linkages indicate that the sector significantly impacts the Economy, backward linkages measure the total change in the Economy's production when a unit change occurs in the sector's demand. Thus, the sector's size should also be taken into account; a large sector with relatively high backward linkages is more likely to have a significant output increase which will have a high multiplying effect on the whole Economy. On the contrary, in the short term, a small sector cannot extend its production to a level that will create a critical multiplying effect, even if the sector shows relatively high backward linkages.

In Fig. 2.3, the backward linkages of the Greek Economy and a comparison with EU27 countries are depicted based on the WIOD data (Timmer et al., 2015). Greece's backward linkages are lower than the median of EU27 member countries for primary and most tertiary sectors. By contrast, for the secondary sectors, the opposite picture emerges. In particular, Greece has higher sectoral links than the median of EU27 member countries for most secondary sectors (specifically sectors C13_C15, C16, C20, C21, C22, C26, C27, C29, C31_C32). However, these sectors with relatively high interconnections produce only 2.03% of the Greek Economy's product, so their impact as multipliers of the existing dynamics is limited. Thus, the findings shown, result from either the production of different output types by the same sector (as in the case of C29) or the existing ones of a small and dynamic sector (as in the case of C21).

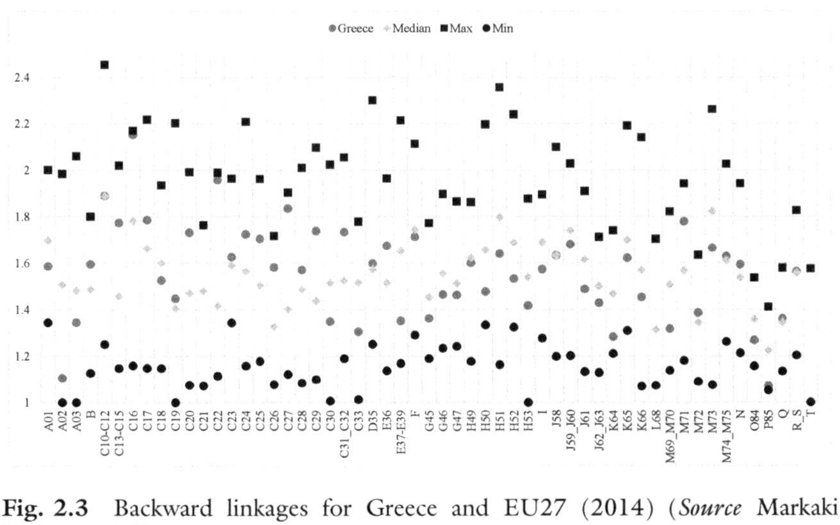

Fig. 2.3 Backward linkages for Greece and EU27 (2014) (*Source* Markaki [2019, p. 79])

For a complete assessment of the Greek Economy's level of interconnectedness, the sectors with significant contributions to value-added (2.5% of the total value-added or more) are isolated, and their backward linkages are examined. Of the 15 sectors contributing more than 2.5% to the Greek production, only two, Q (Activities related to human health and social care) and R_S (Arts, entertainment, and other service activities), have shown backward linkages greater than the median of EU27 member countries. In contrast, the rest of the sectors (i.e., A01, C10-C12, F, G46, G47, H50, I, J61, K64, L68, M69_M70, O84, P85) show lower values.

The corresponding results for the case of EU27 countries are presented in Fig. 2.4, where a significant variation is evident. Greece ranks in the penultimate position with Cyprus, Luxembourg, Malta, and the Netherlands. In other words, it appears that the dynamics of the relatively large sectors in the Greek Economy are significantly lower than those of most EU member countries.

The subordinate position of the Greek Economy's interconnectedness to the EU27 countries indicates that Greece is characterized by a different production technology to the average technology of the EU27. The non-homogenous production of a sector and diversified technology can lead to various backward linkages within the EU27 countries. This study shows that the Greek Economy's production technology creates a network of lower-intensity transactions than in most EU27 countries.

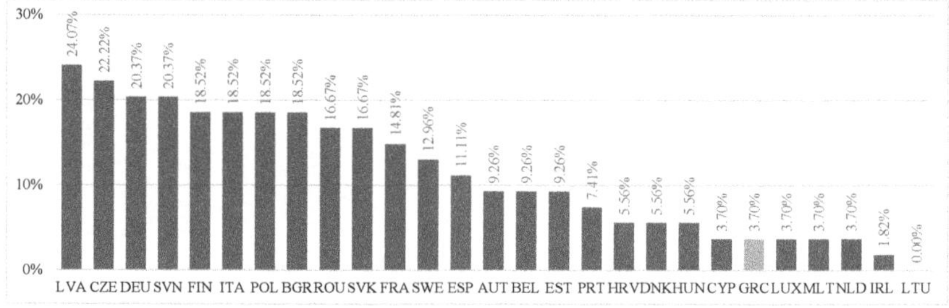

Fig. 2.4 Share of large sectors with high backward linkages (2014) (*Source* Markaki [2019, p. 79])

2.2.4 *Domestic Value-Added in Exports and Technological Level of Exports*

The Domestic Value-Added in Exports (DVX) expresses the domestic value-added, created to satisfy exports' demand. DVX depends on both the export structure and the production structure of the Economy under investigation. It is a measure that can reflect the contribution of exports to an economy or show how a country's position in international competition affects its productive potential (Hummels et al., 2001; Koopman et al., 2012).

Figure 2.5 depicts the unit DVX for all EU27 countries. The unit DVX expresses the new value-added created in each domestic Economy when exports show an increase of one unit. The estimation of the unit DVX includes all economic sectors, irrespective of whether the sector is exporting or has linkages with the exporting sectors. The unit DVX ranges between 0.714 in Germany and 0.323 in Luxembourg. Greece is found in the 9th position within the EU27 countries, with a value equal to 0.669. Greece's exporting activities generate value-added mainly in the tertiary sector, while the participation of the secondary sector is relatively low.

The results show an extensive diversification between EU27 member countries, due both to differences in the structure of exports and economic interdependencies. The EU27 countries demonstrate differentiated integration into the international competition, and therefore

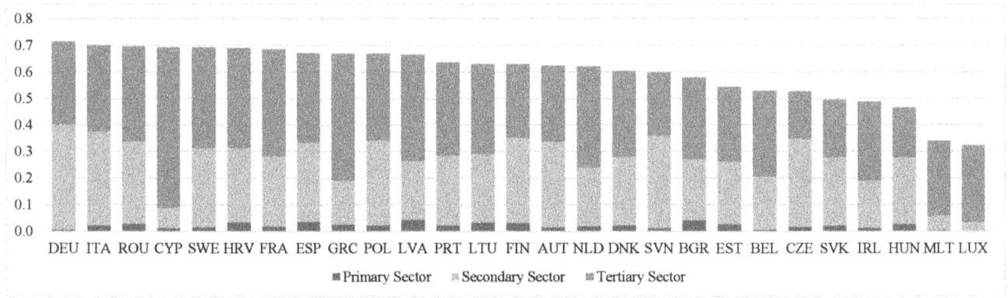

Fig. 2.5 Unit domestic value-added in exports, EU27 (2014) (*Source* WIOD and authors' calculations)

different levels of benefits from international trade. The benefit of countries in the top five of the ranking is, on average, 65% greater than that of countries in the last five positions.

Although Greece shows a relatively high unit DVX, when attention turns to the technological level of the generated value-added, the findings are not encouraging.

Figure 2.6 shows the HT & MHT sectors' contribution to the unit DVX for the EU27 countries. The contribution of technologically advanced sectors (HT and MIT sectors) ranges from 66,97% in Germany to just 17.25% in Greece, with an average value of 43.52%. This finding confirms that the integration of European countries into international competition creates conditions conducive to developing technologically advanced sectors in some countries (e.g., Germany, Hungary, Sweden) and makes it difficult for others (Latvia, Lithuania, Greece).

The technologically advanced sectors include the high-tech sectors C21 (Basic pharmaceutical products and pharmaceutical preparations) and C26 (Computer, electronic, and optical products) as well as the medium–high-tech sectors C20 (Chemicals and chemical products), C27 (Electrical equipment), C28 (Machinery and equipment n.e.c.), C29 (Motor vehicles, trailers, and semi-trailers), C30 (Other transport equipment). Conclusively, it becomes clear that the growth of those sectors and their interconnection with the rest of the economic network contribute significantly to the highly competitive position and the converse. Therefore, we conclude that strengthening the production system's coherence is an additional important aspect of industrial policy.

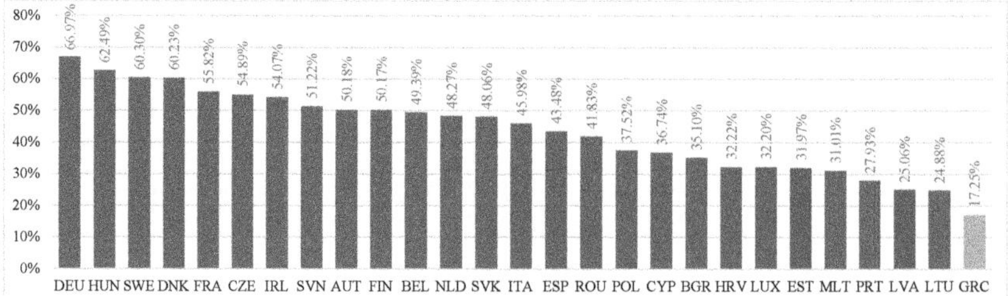

Fig. 2.6 Share of HT & MHT sectors in unit DVX, EU27 (2014) (*Source* WIOD and authors' calculations)

2.2.5 Summary

The survey findings highlight the need to implement an industrial policy that will lead to the structural transformation of the Greek Economy. In Greece's case, industrial policy should aim at (1) the reallocation of production to favor industrial and technologically advanced sectors and 2) the strengthening of sectoral linkages, leading to an increased multiplying effect of the economic system. In addition, such an industrial policy will positively impact the labor market by creating new jobs or redistributing workers to higher-productivity jobs.

2.3 Defining the Parameters of the Optimization Problem

Section 2.2 has demonstrated that, in the case of Greece, industrial policy should favor the country's development and competitiveness through an increase of the manufacturing share in production, the enhancement of the exporting orientation, the promotion of technological advances in the various sectors, and an improvement in sectoral linkages. Therefore, it is now necessary to explain the optimization model's formulation and the restructuring/transformation targets that could be empirically applied to the Greek Economy.

As was analytically discussed in Chapter 1, the Greek Economy's structural transformation aims to reduce the trade balance deficit, which is achieved by reallocating production within the economic sectors and import substitution in the intermediate demand. The parameters of the optimization problem are: the domain of the matrix of the distribution coefficients ($\boldsymbol{B}_1$ and $\boldsymbol{B}_2$) and the domain of the value-added vector ($\boldsymbol{k}_1$ and $\boldsymbol{k}_2$).

The proposed methodology is grounded on the theoretical model of input–output analysis. Thus, the application of the model requires the availability of an input–output table. The most recent one for Greece is the 2015 input–output table following the NACE Rev. 2 sectoral classification (Eurostat, 2008).

The definition of the $\boldsymbol{B}_d$ domain (i.e., the lower limit $\boldsymbol{B}_1$ and the upper limit $\boldsymbol{B}_2$) will also define the level of import substitution in intermediate demand. Presuming that the production technology remains as is, the lower limit of $\boldsymbol{B}_d$ is the current one and the upper limit is the matrix of the distribution coefficients $\boldsymbol{B}$. If the optimal matrix $\boldsymbol{B}_d^* = \boldsymbol{B}_{d,current}$

then, there is no substitution in intermediate imports and if $\boldsymbol{B}_d^* = \boldsymbol{B}$, then, there is a full substitution of intermediate products. The second case is not valid since a modern economy does not produce all types of products domestically. In this study, the lower limit of $\boldsymbol{B}_d$ is set to $\boldsymbol{B}_{d,current}$. In this case, the structural transformation will be based on the reallocation of production within the sectors, not import substitution. The upper limit $\boldsymbol{B}_2$ is defined by the equation $\boldsymbol{B}_2 = \boldsymbol{A}_{d,current} + \boldsymbol{S}_{max} \cdot \boldsymbol{A}_{m,current}$, where $\boldsymbol{S}_{max} \in \mathbb{R}^{n \times n}$ is a diagonal matrix whose diagonal elements $s_{i,max} \in [0,1]$. $s_{i,max}$ expresses the i sector's maximum coefficient of substitution and captures the maximum possible level of sector i to produce intermediate inputs for other sectors, substituting intermediate imports from the corresponding sectors abroad. If $s_{i,max} = 0$, then, there is no possibility for intermediate import substitution for sector i, while if $s_{i,max} = 1$, then the substitution of intermediate imports is full. Thus, the optimal intersectoral structure $\boldsymbol{B}_d^*$ is connected with the estimation of the optimal coefficient of substitution, s_i^* for each sector ($0 \leq s_i^* \leq s_i$). The coefficient of substitution, s_i applied in this research is presented in Table 2.4. For the sector not included in Table 2.4, the s_i equals zero.

Vectors $\boldsymbol{k}_1$ and $\boldsymbol{k}_2$ are defined on the basis of Oxford Economics projections (Oxford Economics, 2020). Figure 2.7 presents the percentage change in gross value-added expected from 2019 to 2027, according to the Basic and the Plus scenarios of Oxford Economics. In this research, the low level of value-added ($\boldsymbol{k}_1$) equals the projection of the Basic Scenario and the upper level of value-added ($\boldsymbol{k}_2$) is set by the authors. The determination of the maximum possible change of value-added is based on the current dynamics of the sectors.

Table 2.4 Substitution rate

Sector	*Substitution coefficient*
A01-03, C10-12, C13-15, C17, C18, C32, C33	0.6
C20, C21, C22, C23, C24, C25, C27	0.4
C26, C28, C30	0.2

Source Authors' creation

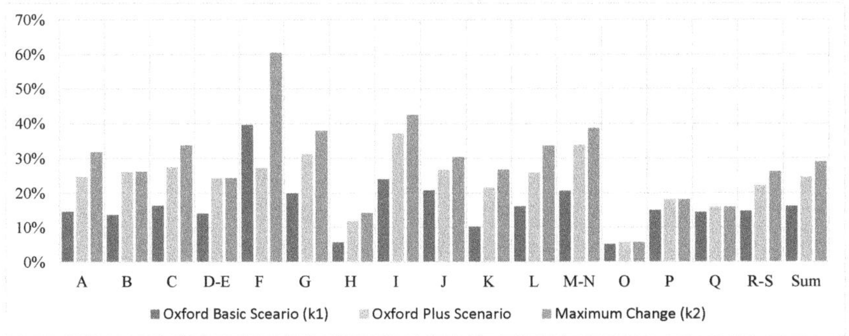

Fig. 2.7 Rate of change of value-added from 2019 to 2027 (*Source* Oxford Economics [2020] and author's own estimations)

2.4 The Optimization Algorithm

The discipline of computational intelligence includes tools and methodologies which allow solving problems that are difficult or even impossible to solve by traditional methods.

One of the key pillars of computational intelligence is algorithms able to optimize the parameters of a system toward achieving a clearly defined goal. This optimization is achieved with evolutionary optimization algorithms inspired by nature. The concept of optimization is a general concept, which may include either the evolution of a system's structure to meet specific objectives or the determination of the values of the parameters of a system's predefined architecture by formulating its behavior as a parameterized function with respect to its parameters (function optimization).

In this work, the concept of optimization focuses on defining the parameters of a system's clearly defined architecture. That is, we deal with function optimization.

Although most evolutionary algorithms can be appropriately designed for structure and function optimization problems, two subfields of computational intelligence are more appropriate, more efficient, and more easily applicable for facing function optimization problems. (a) Genetic Algorithms (GA), which are inspired by the evolution of species through natural selection and (b) particle swarm optimization (PSO), which is inspired by the social behavior and cooperation of flocks while seeking food. Especially in the field of function optimization, it has been empirically shown that PSO is more efficient than Genetic Algorithms, as it provides a clearer ability to adjust for exploration and exploitation power. The balance between exploration and exploitation capacity is a key concept for every optimization process. This balance is regulated through the emphasis that each particle gives to its individual and social behavior and addresses one of the inherent problems of Genetic Algorithms, which effectively attains the optimal region but has difficulties in accurately locating it (for an analytical presentation of nature-inspired evolutionary optimization algorithms, see: Papadakis & Markaki, 2019; Markaki & Papadakis, 2021).

The problem we treat in this work falls into the category of function optimization. The objective function, which is to be optimized, is nonlinear and the computation of its derivatives is quite difficult. Moreover, the objective function is non-continuous due to some min., max. operators involved in the constraints, which an accepted solution must satisfy. Thus, a PSO algorithm is employed for the solution of the optimization problem.

2.5 The Structural Transformation of the Greek Economy

The optimal economic structure for the Greek Economy is obtained with the solution of the optimization problem. After presenting the basic macroeconomic results, a comparative analysis of the optimal structure against the current one will focus on (1) the industrial structure, (2) the economic linkages, and (3) the domestic value-added in exports. The descriptive evidence presented in the previous section has shown that the subordinate position of the Greek Economy among EU27 countries is due to technological and structural weaknesses. Thus, potential improvements in the Economy's technological and structural features resulting from the optimal structural transformation are also investigated.

The Greek Economy's structural transformation will lead to a trade balance of goods equal to -8.6% of GDP, a significant improvement compared to the respective value of 2019, which reaches −12.45% of GDP. Furthermore, the trade balance of goods and services is estimated at −1.32% of GDP. However, this value does not include the travel balance, as the input–output table only exports goods and services. Therefore, the balance of goods and services could rise to as much as 5% of GDP in 2027, assuming a travel balance equal to the level of 2019.

2.5.1 *The Structural Change of Production*

Table 2.5 compares the Greek Economy's current structure for 2019 with the optimization problem's output for 2027. The Economy's structural transformation will potentially increase the share of secondary sectors (sectors with codes B, C, D, and E at the NACE Rev. 2 classification) in value-added production from 14.86% in 2019 to 18.16% in 2027. Notably, the share of secondary sectors in the optimal structure is more significant than in the Basic and the Plus Scenarios of Oxford Economics estimation (15.92% and 16.39%, respectively). Furthermore, a part of the increase in secondary sectors is identified in the manufacturing sector (C), whereas the rest mainly concerns construction sector (F).

Moreover, the findings show a considerable reduction of the tertiary sector and a slight increase in the primary sectors. As a result, the primary sector (A) share in the optimal structure reached 4.52% of the total value-added, showing a slight increase compared to 2019, where the respective share was 4.36%. By contrast, the percentage of tertiary sectors is 77.32% in the optimal structure, lower than in 2019, when the respective share was 80.78%.

As shown in Table 2.6, the technological structure of manufacturing sectors exhibits significant improvement. The percentage of high-tech and medium–high-tech sectors is significantly increased, while the share of medium–low and low-tech sectors is decreased. As a result, the cumulative share of HT and MHT sectors will reach 29.43%, improving the Greek Economy's position in the EU27 countries compared to 2019 (see Fig. 2.1).

Table 2.5 Current Structure (2019) and Optimal Structure (2027)

	2019 (%)	*2027 (%)*
Primary Sectors (A)	4.36	*4.52*
Secondary Sectors (B, C, D, F)	14.86	*18.16*
Of which Manufacturing (C)	9.85	*10.86*
Tertiary Sectors	80.78	*77.32*

Source Authors' calculations

The analytical structure of manufacturing at the sectoral level is depicted in Fig. 2.8. The economic sectors are listed in the vertical axis based on their technological level. Furthermore, Fig. 2.9 presents the manufacturing sectors' share change from 2019 to 2027. The five larger sectors for Greece in the optimal structure are C10-C12, C20, C21, C24, and C25. These sectors produce 66.23% of the total manufacturing value-added. All these sectors indicate an increase in their participation in production. Notably, sector C19 was included in the larger five sectors in 2019, but the participation, as shown in the optimal structure decreased its importance.

The evidence presented in Fig. 2.9 suggests that the Greek Economy's optimal productive structure will potentially increase the participation of HT and MHT sectors, except sectors C29 (Motor vehicles, trailers, and semi-trailers) and C30 (Other transport equipment). This finding is expected, as the expansion of the aforementioned sectors implies significant scale capital investments. Moreover, the majority of MLT and LT sectors show a decrease in their participation in value-added generation, with the exceptions of sectors C24 (Basic metals), C25 (Fabricated metal products), and C10-C12 (Food, beverages, and tobacco products). These findings regarding sectors C24 and C25 agree with the concept of import substitution, as both sectors play an essential role in the Greek Economy as producers of intermediates. Moreover, sector C10-C12 is the larger manufacturing sector and a significant exporter and contributes to the productive network of tourism activities.

2.5.2 *The Structural Change of Economic Linkages*

Figures 2.10 and 2.11 illustrate the backward linkages of the optimal structure and the percentage change between the optimal structure and the last available input–output table, respectively. As Fig. 2.10 shows, the backward linkages of the manufacturing sectors are, in most cases, higher than those of the services sectors. Furthermore, the process of structural transformation, as Fig. 2.11 indicates, leads to a strong positive impact on backward linkages in all the economic sectors.

The more significant increase of backward linkages (more than 15%) is located in sectors C22 (Rubber and plastic products), C13-C15 (Textiles, wearing apparel, leather, and related products), C17 (Paper and paper products), and C26 (Computer, electronic, and optical products). Following that, sectors C24 (Printing and recording services),

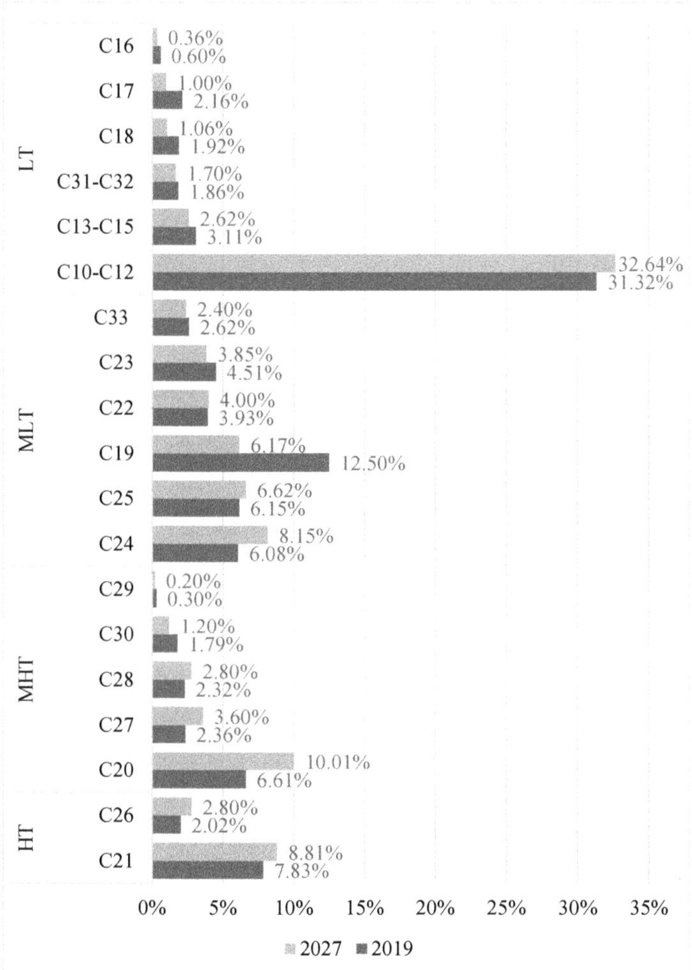

Fig. 2.8 Structure of manufacturing (2019 and Optimal Structure 2027) (*Source* Authors' calculations)

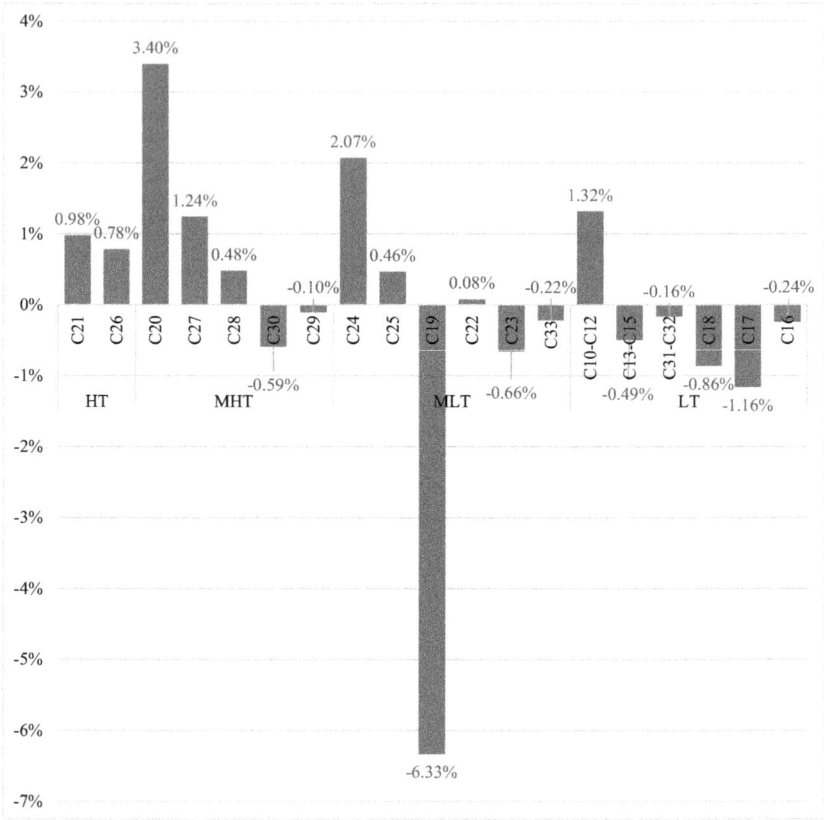

Fig. 2.9 Change of the manufacturing sectors' share from 2019 to 2027 (*Source* Authors' calculations)

Table 2.6 Technological structure of manufacturing sector (2019 and optimal structure 2027)

	2019 (%)	*2027 (%)*
HT	9.85	11.61
MHT	13.39	17.82
MLT	35.79	31.20
LT	40.96	39.37

Source Authors' calculations

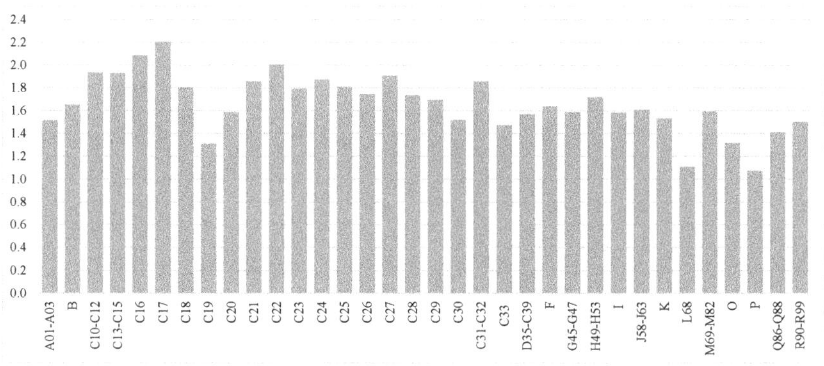

Fig. 2.10 Backward Linkages with the optimal structure, 2027 (*Source* Authors' calculations)

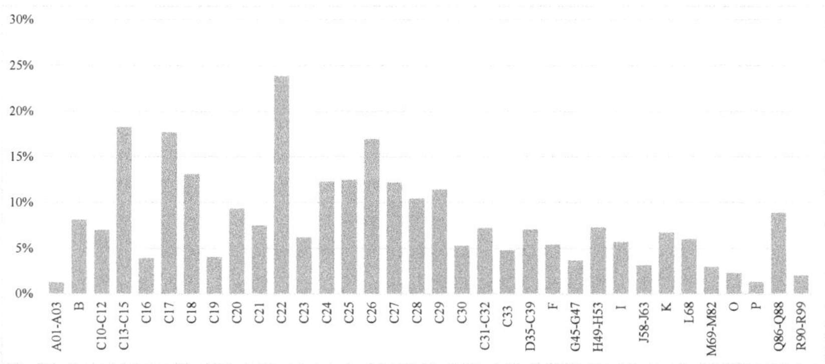

Fig. 2.11 Percentage change of backward linkages, 2015–2027 (*Source* Authors' calculations)

C25 (Fabricated metal products, except machinery and equipment), C27 (Electrical equipment), and C28 (Machinery and equipment n.e.c) show an increase in backward linkages of 10% to 15%. The increase is lower in the rest of the sectors.

The improvement of the backward linkages results from (i) the import distribution in intermediates and (ii) the reallocation of production within sectors. On the one hand, import substitution develops a more robust network of linkages, as domestic sectors satisfy a much larger part of the

Table 2.7 The domestic value-added in exports before and after the restructuring process

	2014	*2027*
DVX (Total Economy)	0.669	0.741
Manufacturing DVX	0.165	0.227
Share of Manufacturing DVX	24.73%	30.71%

Source Authors' calculations

intermediate demand for products and services. On the other hand, the reallocation of production diversifies the economic system's internal structure, as the distribution of intermediate demand (and supply) within the sectors also changes. Therefore, the effect of structural transformation is diffused throughout the Economy.

2.5.3 *The Improvement of the Domestic Value-Added in Exports*

The domestic value-added per unit of exports (Table 2.7) increased by 10.74%, from 0.069 in 2014 to 0.741 in 2019. For the same period, the contribution of the secondary sectors increased from 24.7 to 30.71%

The technological change of the DVX is presented in Fig. 2.12. As shown in Fig. 2.12, the contribution of HT and MHT sectors increases and MLT and LT's contribution decreases. As a result, the cumulative percentage of HT and MHT sectors rises from 17.25 to 21.45%, improving the country's competitive position among the EU27.

The empirical findings discussed in Sect. 2.4 show that the Greek Economy's structural transformation can improve the country's productive structure, increase manufacturing contribution in the value-added generation, and increase the share of technologically advanced products. As a result, the value-added generated by imports is significantly increased, improving the Greek Economy's terms of trade.

2.6 Policy Interventions

In this research, an optimization methodology based on input–output analysis is introduced. The proposed methodology aims to define the Greek Economy's optimal structure to maximize the impact of structural transformation policies. Furthermore, this approach traces a growth trajectory based on a robust economic and mathematical model that

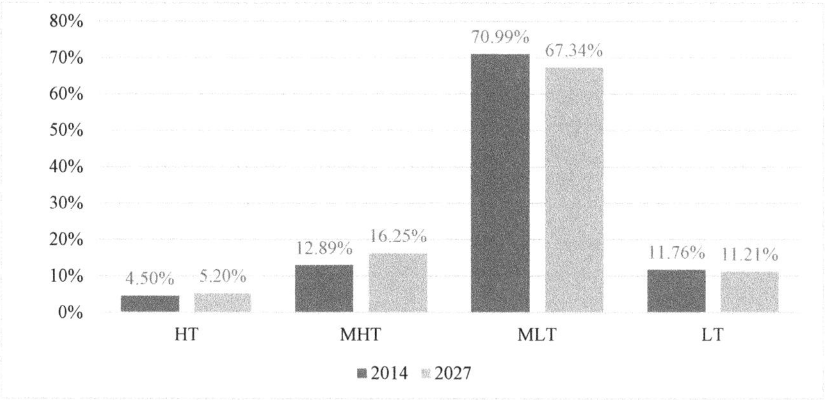

Fig. 2.12 Percentage change of backward linkages, 2015–2027 (*Source* Authors' calculation)

goes beyond the descriptive information usually found in industrial policy studies.

Taken together, the research findings suggest that the Greek Economy's structural transformation can lead to an increased GDP growth rate and, simultaneously, achieve a relatively low deficit in the balance of goods and services along with increased interconnectedness of the economic activities. Moreover, based on the optimal productive structure, policymakers can pursue a mix of structural policies, integrating sectoral and macroeconomic interventions.

Besides the fact that sectoral-specific policy interventions are necessary for achieving the reallocation of production within the sectors, this research highlights the dependency of the country's total economic performance on the diffusion of structural change throughout the economic network. Thus, sectoral interventions should be planned as a coherent whole rather than as individual sectoral policies. In this context, different policy interventions, such as export promotion, import substitution, public procurement policies, encouraging foreign direct investment, R&D development, and promotion of technologically advanced sectors, can be crucial for economic development. Finally, the importance of horizontal policies cannot be overlooked, especially concerning labor market policies (skills and education policies, training subsidies).

References

Belegri-Roboli, A., Markaki, M., & Michaelides, P. (2010). *The intersectoral relations of Greek Economy*. INE/GSEE.

Belegri-Roboli, A., Markaki, M., & Michaelides, P. G. (2011). Labour productivity changes and working time: The case of Greece. *Economic Systems Research, 23*(3), 329–339. https://doi.org/10.1080/09535314.2011.595777

Cohen, S. S., & Zysman, J. (1988). Manufacturing innovation and American industrial competitiveness. *Science, 239*(4844), 1110–1115. https://doi.org/10.1126/science.239.4844.1110

Economakis, G., & Markaki, M. (2014). Extraversion and crisis of the Greek Economy: A study. *Bulletin of Political Economy, 8*(2), 175–204.

Economakis, G., & Markaki, M. (2020). *Structural characteristics of the Greek Economy, crisis and productive reconstruction* (INE/GSEE).

Economakis, G., & Markaki, M. (2023). Unequal exchange in the EU: The case of trade transactions between Germany, Italy, and Greece. *Science & Society, 87*(1), 21–49. https://doi.org/10.1521/siso.2023.87.1.21

Economakis, G., Markaki, M., & Anastasiadis, A. (2015). Structural analysis of the Greek Economy. *Review of Radical Political Economics, 47*(3), 424–445. https://doi.org/10.1177/0486613414542779

Economakis, G., Markaki, M., Androulakis, G., & Anastasiadis, A. (2018). Imperialist exploitation and crisis of the Greek Economy: A study. In *Crisis, movement, strategy: The Greek experience* (pp. 40–66). Brill.

Eurostat. (2008). *NACE Rev. 2–statistical classification of economic activities in the European Community*.

Eurostat. (2010). *Aggregations of manufacturing based on NACE Rev. 2*. https://ec.europa.eu/eurostat/cache/metadata/Annexes/htec_esms_an3.pdf

Hausmann, R., Hidalgo, C. A., Bustos, S., Coscia, M., Simoes, A., & Yildirim, M. A. (2014). *The atlas of economic complexity: Mapping paths to prosperity*. MIT Press.

Hummels, D., Ishii, J., & Yi, K.-M. (2001). The nature and growth of vertical specialization in world trade. *Journal of International Economics, 54*(1), 75–96. https://doi.org/10.1016/S0022-1996(00)00093-3

Koopman, R., Wang, Z., & Wei, S.-J. (2012). Estimating domestic content in exports when processing trade is pervasive. *Journal of Development Economics, 99*(1), 178–189. https://doi.org/10.1016/j.jdeveco.2011.12.004

Lall, S. (2000). The Technological structure and performance of developing country manufactured exports, 1985–98. *Oxford Development Studies, 28*(3), 337–369. https://doi.org/10.1080/713688318

Markaki, M. (2019). *The production structure of the Greek Economy, employment, professional specialties and skills: Input-output analysis, 2000–2018*. National Institute of Labour and Human Resources. https://lmd.eiead.gr/wp-content/uploads/2019/01/%CE%9C%CE%B1%CF%81%CE%BA%CE%B1%CE%BA%CE%B7%CE%95%CE%99%CE%95%CE%91%CE%94.pdf

Markaki, M., & Economakis, G. (2020, August 14). *Measuring the international structural competitiveness and the hierarchy of national economies: The case of the European Union*. PREPRINT (Version 1). Available at Research Square. https://doi.org/10.21203/rs.3.rs-60232/v1

Markaki, M., & Economakis, G. (2022). International structural competitiveness and the hierarchy in the world economy. *World Review of Political Economy, 12*(2), 195–219. https://www.jstor.org/stable/48676086

Markaki, M., & Papadakis, S. (2021). A modern industrial policy for the Czech Republic: Optimizing the structure of production. *Mathematics, 9*(23), 3095. https://doi.org/10.3390/math9233095

Miller, R. E., & Blair, P. D. (2009). *Input-output analysis: Foundations and extensions*. Cambridge University Press.

Oxford Economics. (2020). *Oxford economics global economic model*.

Papadakis, S., & Markaki, M. (2019). An in-depth economic restructuring framework by using particle swarm optimization. *Journal of Cleaner Production, 215*, 329–342. https://doi.org/10.1016/j.jclepro.2019.01.041

Petralia, S., Balland, P.-A., & Morrison, A. (2017).Climbing the ladder of technological development. *Research Policy, 46*(5), 956–969. https://doi.org/10.1016/j.respol.2017.03.012

Simoes, A. J. G., & Hidalgo, C. A. (2011). *The economic complexity observatory: An analytical tool for understanding the dynamics of economic development*. Workshops at the Twenty-Fifth AAAI Conference on Artificial Intelligence.

Suh, S. (2009). *Handbook of input-output economics in industrial ecology* (Vol. 23). Springer Science & Business Media.

The Growth Lab at Harvard University. (2019). *Growth projections and complexity rankings, V2* [Data set]. https://doi.org/10.7910/dvn/xtaqmc

Timmer, M. P., Dietzenbacher, E., Los, B., Stehrer, R., & Vries, G. J. (2015). An illustrated user guide to the world input–output database: The case of global automotive production. *Review of International Economics, 23*(3), 575–605. https://doi.org/10.1111/roie.12178

CHAPTER 3

A Regional Analysis Of Inputs-Outputs Of The Greek Economy: A Baseline Depiction Of Interconnections In Greece

Pagiavla Georgia and Pisinas Yorgos

3.1 Introduction

The economic structure, productive capacities, technologies, localization factors, and behavior of economic agents are essential in the implementation of any policy. Tables of inputs and outputs are usually drawn at regular intervals at national level and are used by researchers and economic/industrial policymakers to find solutions to various issues and make recommendations. However, when it comes to regional economic policy, National Tables of Inputs-Outputs (NIOTs) may provide particularly important information, but they are unable to fully describe sectoral

P. Georgia
Panteion University, Athens, Greece

P. Yorgos (✉)
University of Patras, Patra, Greece
e-mail: y.pisinas@gmail.com

P. E. Petrakis (ed.), *Interconnections in the Greek Economy*, The Political Economy of Greek Growth up to 2030, https://doi.org/10.1007/978-3-031-31335-6_3

interconnections. Thus, while IOTs represent the product flows between the different sectors of the economy, through the ultimate demand or exports, the answers provided by analysis in terms of the Regional Tables of Inputs-Outputs (RIOTs) provide essential information on the operation of regional economies. Research interest has recently shifted from the national to the regional level, given that the economy is not a non-spatial entity and that interregional trade features greatly in the relationship between the periphery and the center. However, research and policy questions in regional economic analyses often call for improvements in how RIOTs are estimated. The aim of the present chapter is to introduce a methodology by means of which input–output tables can be generated for Greece's several regions and which can then be used to create a basic outline of the sectoral/regional interconnections that occur in the country.

The structure of the chapter is the following: Sect. 3.2 presents the theoretical significance and limits of IOTs and emphasizes their wide range of applications and points of relevance for economic policy. Then (Sect. 3.3) the theoretical framework of IOTs is presented. The next Sect. 3.4 presents why should a regional Input–Output model be favored in place of the econometric models for studying a regional economy. In Sect. 3.5, the construction processes of regional I-O tables are presented and reference is made to the most important and widely applied techniques. The next Sect. 3.6 presents the RIOTs in Greece provided by the App-RegMIP, a one-of-its-kind software program that allows the regionalization of a national input–output table. Then (Sect. 3.7) are presented the assessments which have been based on the input–output table for Greece and provide a full picture about sectoral interconnections within the main regions of the Greek economy. Finally, Sect. 3.8 presents the main conclusions of this chapter.

3.2 Input–Output Tables And Sectoral Interconnections: Theoretical Significance And Limits Of IOTs

Input–output tables are a particularly useful macroeconomic tool which, since its appearance in the middle of last century (Leontief, 1936), rapidly became central to economic analysis (Ten Raa, 2006). The reason for this is the range of possibilities they have, combined with their strong grounding in economic reality, with Romanoff (1974) being among the first to elaborate the connection between the model of the economic base and the analysis of inputs-outputs. An IOT is comprised of the immediate economic data collected from an economy in terms of the exchanges of the various production units among themselves. In its simplest form, it assumed that each sector produces a consistent product to which end inputs are required by other sectors of the economy while, in turn, it also fuels production in other sectors.[1] In more refined forms, the sectors are considered to produce a multitude of products without, however, this altering the core analytic framework of IOT analysis (Ten Raa, 2006).

3.2.1 *Policy Ramifications And Applications Of IOTs*

IOTs have a wide range of applications and points of relevance for economic policy. In essence, their main feature is that they highlight an economy's interconnectedness. By definition, IOTs record sectoral interconnections so that, in a table's horizontal reading, the sales are recorded of a particular sector to an economy's various industries and, in a vertical reading, the purchases are seen which an industry requires to generate its product. The ramifications of this information for the exercise of economic policy are enormous. To start with, if we expect the demand for some product to rise in an economy, then the table can forewarn us about demands for other products in order to be able to meet this new demand. These are called backward linkages and they concern a sector's needs in primary or auxiliary materials and equipment. Correspondingly, if for some reason, a sector's market price goes up, then the tables can let us know about the anticipated impact of the remaining sectors on the market price. These are known as forward linkages, since they concern the product's utilization by the other sectors of the economy.[2]

In addition, the tables also have application across a range of matters of international trade, analyses of economic dependence or autonomy, and

[1] Normally, a table has 4 parts (Ü & Hewings, 2013); here, we focus on the 1st part which refers to the sectoral exchanges for intermediate products and makes up the nucleus of the table, with the remaining parts corresponding to ultimate demand, imported intermediates together with the added value of the contributing factors and the imported final goods.

[2] For these two kinds of basic information, different type of tables need to be used, respectively Leontief and Ghosh (1958) types is the proper type providing us with this information (cf. Markaki & Papadakis, 2023a, 2023b; Oosterhaven & Hewings, 2013).

the macroeconomic stability of the various economies. Examining one of the main uses of the input–output analysis, Miller and Blair (2009) estimated the effects on the economy of the change in one element and studied a variety of summary measures that are referred to as multipliers and may be calculated with the use of the reverse Leontief table.[3] Sometimes, these applications may lead in initially unexpected directions, such as their ramifications for environmental issues (Leontief, 1970) which nowadays is a main field of analysis (Suh & Kagawa, 2009; Ten Raa, 2006). This last development becomes possible through the translation of sectoral interconnections into ecological footprints, for example, translating production needs in energy/materials (backward links) into coal emissions for an analysis of the environmental impact. Similar analytical ramifications could also be elaborated in terms of demands in human capital, since it is possible to go from a picture of the productive structure, into the analysis of human capital (Pisinas, 2022a, 2022b; Lopez & Ferreira do Amaral, 2013). It is therefore, clear that the potential of I-O tables is not restricted to interconnections but extends into most issues involving political economy. In this context, the lack of regional I-O tables, renders the country's regional policy weak. At all events, in the post-COVID era, the value of analyses based on I-O tables ought to be upgraded as they have to do with all the aspects that are adversely affected (demand, disruption of chains of value, disruption of international trade, the impact of the economy on ecological quality, etc.).

3.3 The Theoretical Framework Of IOTs

The analysis of the interconnections among various economic sectors in the prevailing economic thinking entails the so-called analysis of general equilibrium. As per the Walrasian general equilibrium, the state in which all sectors are simultaneously in equilibrium is examined and, so, the state in which a change in one of them is bound to have an economy-wide effect.

Therefore, analysis in terms of inputs-outputs is often read as an analysis of general equilibrium (Szabó, 2015; Ten Raa, 2006; Oosterhaven & Hewings, 2013). Yet, the hypotheses necessary for the construction of

[3] Leontief's reverse table provides a measure of the impact on the economy when a sector's ultimate demand rises by one unit. This is known as multiplier of the sector (Holt, 2017, p. 12).

IOTs do not necessarily correspond to those of the Walrasian equilibrium which presupposes a series of strict hypotheses in order to comprise an analytical framework (Fine, 2016). The input–output tables are constituted directly out of an economy's stylized facts without the intervention of aggregate functions of production, hypotheses about consumer preferences or the behaviors of economic agents according to the prevalent models of economic thought. As a result, it has been suggested that the analysis of IOTs' circuits be read in a pluralist manner (Akhabbar & Lallement, 2010). Nevertheless, for the sake of a practical approach that avoids the methodological contradictions of a pluralist eclecticism, it is noted that the technical reading of production on the basis of IOTs, is methodologically incompatible with the Walrasian theory of general equilibrium which is founded on marginal productivity (Reyes, 2016).

The hypotheses supporting an IOT are the following[4]:

Homogeneous products, which also imply the use of a single technique of production per sector.

- Absence of restrictions in the use of production factors.
- Stable technological factors. This is the models' most restrictive hypothesis.[5]

Moreover, as argued by Markaki (2018), IOTs presume the absence of externalities in production although this needs to remain an open question for further investigation. To the extent that IOTs are not constituted within a Walrasian theory of the market, the question of externalities should not come up. Insofar as IOTs are founded on empirical data, they ought to be able to fully represent reality. So, if we take into consideration climatic conditions as the largest externality with an impact on

[4] See Markaki 2018 (Cf. also Leontief, 1991; Livas, 1994).

[5] From an economic standpoint, this hypothesis appears excessively strict as it means the inability to substitute inputs. However, as argued by Leontief (1966, 49) this is particularly sensible from a technical point of view, and, also, empirically observable. To produce a cake, one could replace sugar (with honey, glycoprotein, stevia, or some synthetic sweetener) which is of enormous value for an economist, but ultimately, a cake needs to have a minimal amount of sweetness and every confectioner is aware that these proportions are not to be played with. As economists, we need to hold on to the fact that the use-values of products play an irreplaceable part in production which Leontief (1966, 9) had in mind when he noted the value of "experts with practical experience in each field".

agricultural production, a table of 2020s should refer to the conditions of production of 2020s as would a corresponding table of 1950s. Thus, the former would need to take into consideration the cumulative climate change, as a result of the production during this 70-year-long period. On the other hand, of course, any projections we make on the 2020s table for 2090s, will be based on the conditions of production of 2020s. The emphasis of IOTs on use values,[6] renders them a tool useful not only for internal economic analysis but also for important matters of externalities such as the ecological footprint of production or industrial relationships, as has been noted by the sector of Industrial Ecology (Suh, 2009).

3.4 National And Regional Tables: Regional Policy

Tables of inputs and outputs are usually drawn at regular intervals at national level and are used by researchers and economic/industrial policymakers to find solutions to various issues and make recommendations. National Tables of Inputs-Outputs (NIOTs) already provide particularly important information, however, they are unable to fully describe sectoral interconnections. According to Miller and Blair (2009), there are two specific characteristics that are linked at the regional level whereby the distinction between national and regional input–output models is rendered visible and necessary. First, the production technology is specific in each region and can be similar or, on the contrary, very different to the one recorded on the national table of inputs-outputs. For example, the age of regional industries, the features of the input markets or the level of training of the workforce and the directly accessible primary materials, are important factors affecting the regional technology of production which may diverge from the national one. Second, the smaller the economic entity under study is (whether a region or a national economy), the more it is dependent on the external world, making all the more important the exported and imported elements of demand and supply, respectively. It should be noted that these elements correspond not just to international trade but also to the trade between regions and the country to which the region belongs (Sargento, 2009).

[6] See footnote 5.

Thus, while IOTs represent the product flows between the different sectors of the economy, through the ultimate demand or exports, the answers provided by analysis in terms of the Regional Tables of Inputs-Outputs (RIOTs) concern the effect of the appearance of a new business in the regional economy under investigation, the economy interconnections between regions, the means of achieving a balance between different regions and, finally, the ramifications for a region if an input is, for some reason, obstructed (Hewings, 1985). The study of the regional economic system as a system of extended interdependence, provides essential information on the operation of regional economies. On account of this, it has attracted the interest of many researchers among whom, Isard (1951) (the founder of the sector of Regional Science), Tiebout (1957, 1969), Chenery (1962), Miernyk (2020), and Miller and Blair (2009), even though respective studies of the Greek economy are few and mostly focused on subjects of special interest (Bellas et al., 2017; Rovolis et al., 2016).

The question arises of why should an Input–Output model be favored in place of the econometric models which are based on chronological series, i.e., data from multiple moments in time. The answer is that such data is not always available at a regional level. Thus, in the service of describing an economy's structure, the use of RIOTs seems to be the best alternative (Rovolis et al., 2016). The most widely employed regional models of input–output are those where a particular region is in the place of the country, (one considered "isolated" from the economic structure of the rest of the country) and those where many regions are investigated simultaneously, which are divided into models of "interregional" analysis and models of "multiregional" analysis. So, then, the choice of input–output analysis for studying a regional economy, is based on the special significance of inter-sectoral exchange, the importance, that is, of the multiplicative dynamic which the interconnections between the sectors of economic activity can bring about (Bellas et al., 2017).

Input–output models provide a static picture of the regional economy and make it relatively easy to calculate the effects of changes in some sectors on the rest of the regional economy but have certain limitations which need to be pointed out (Rovolis et al., 2016). Firstly, the collection of statistical data on a region, though easier than the data required for econometric outcomes, is, nevertheless, still a fairly demanding process. It is characteristic that central governments undertake sample studies in order to arrive at RIOTs so as to measure relationships between the various sectors. Secondly, the role of imports in a regional economy is underestimated, i.e., an expenditure's "leak" in the regional economy is underestimated and, therefore, its multiplicative effect on the regional economy is overestimated. In Greece, certain regions are under a status of inner periphery as they are the least developed of all the regions, while Greece itself is one of the least developed countries out of the EU's 27. This two-fold lagging behind in relation to the national and the European average, gives rise to a sense of abandonment, resulting in talk about the "State of Athens" which appears indifferent to the fate of such regions (Petrakos & Psycharis, 2004). Athens, where the largest growth is concentrated, is a node in an S-shaped axis which starts in Patras and ends in Kavala, via Athens and Thessaloniki, as can be seen in (Fig. 3.1). It is characteristic that 50% of the population is concentrated in Athens, while, also, 50–55% of the labor force, 65% of services, 50% of doctors and hospital beds, 55% of higher education graduates, 45% of employment in industry, and 85% of companies, are to be found within the wider area of Attica (Polyzos, 2019). In other words, the country shows pronounced inequalities at regional level. Regional analysis indicates an increased interest in the input–output models as a result of increased economic integration in the European Union, with related efforts to reduce regional inequalities within each country and between member countries. This necessitates the use of a reliable logistic system helpful in locating regional ramifications and interregional spillover effects, which it will then be possible to use in the monitoring of regional policies (Sargento, 2009) (Fig. 3.1).

Moreover, the tertiary sector is significantly more developed than the primary and secondary sectors of the economy in all Greek regions. Despite that, there are pronounced differences between regions regarding the specialization of production, with Eastern Macedonia stronger in the Primary sector and the Peloponnese in the Secondary sector (Polyzos, 2019). As for the use of the input–output models at a regional level, the Greek economy lags significantly behind in terms of the growth needs of a healthy regional growth policy, able to recognize both the internal interconnections of the regions so as to strengthen their self-sufficiency and resilience, and the interconnections for the regions' development, viewing the national economy as a synergistically evolving system (Oosterhaven & Hewings, 2013).

To locate the growth dynamics and potential benefits from investigating entrepreneurship in the economy of the region of Western Greece,

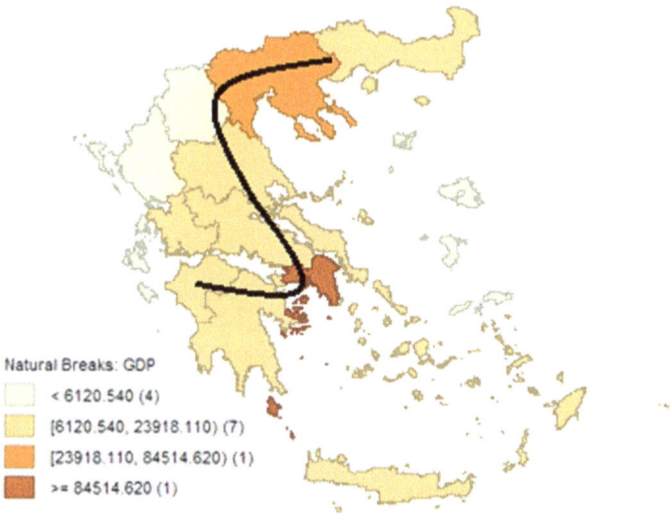

Fig. 3.1 The growth axis S and regional GDP (2015) (*Source* Eurostat. Processed by the authors)

Bellas et al. (2017), link the particular traits of entrepreneurship with the region's productive structure. The productive structure, the relations between sectors, and the regional employment structure are investigated with, among others, the use of inputs-outputs.

In the study by Rovolis et al. (2019), the input–output model was employed for the design and budgeting of a transition plan into the post-coal (lignite) period, in the Western Macedonia Region (WMR). The study was based on the alternative economic activities that have been suggested from time to time by organizations of Western Macedonia, in order to explore the possibilities they offer for regional growth (internal sectoral interconnections). Alternative scenarios were presented of "mild", "median", and "intense" growth, with estimated job positions, the locally added value, and the investments required for their implementation during a fifteen-year period, where the temporal-classic expansion was calculated of the multiplicative outcomes for the WMR.

3.5 The Construction Processes Of Regional I-O Tables

All of the above indicates that the fields of application of input–output analysis are, among others, the economics of growth, the economics of labor, regional economics, the economics of energy and the environment. As regards regional economics, the analysis of inputs-outputs presupposes the compiling of RIOTs. Many different methods of regionalizing are found in the international literature (Szabó, 2015) and researchers are trying to agree on those common rules that will enable the comparison of regional economic structures in time and space (Jensen et al., 1986). In this section, reference will be made to the most important and widely applied techniques.

The compiling of RIOTs through sampling is possibly the most accurate procedure. In this case, the companies in the sample provide information on sales (to other companies and consumers) and on their markets (other companies) inside and outside the region. Industries in different areas may produce different products or make use of different inputs in their production processes. Sampling studies can help researchers take into consideration the particular regional characteristics so that a precise picture is drawn of the technological and commercial structure of the region under study, even though it has certain important disadvantages (Szabó, 2015). Firstly, it is a procedure that requires a great deal of time and money to carry out. Consequently, by analogy to the recommendations by Leontief (1970) regarding national tables, the even more demanding compilation of RIOTs requires the systematic engagement of the state's official economic organizations. Secondly, the management of data is particularly critical, as any errors at this stage may lead to significant distortions at the final outcomes precisely because of the highly relative importance of business data in a regional context which tends to increase the smaller the region is. Finally, often the data collected by companies are not balanced and the findings of the methods for balancing them do not converge, especially in the case of smaller samples.

The non-survey techniques which are applied to RIOTs can be generally defined as a set of procedures that aim to compile the data of a regional table based on the figures included in a similarly constructed national table (Jensen, 1990). These techniques are also known as up-to-down methods, since they use the values of the entire national economy as departure points and then apply specific regional indices for the process of their regionalization. The indices used depend on the data available at a regional level, with the most common ones being employment and income. However, the differences between the regional industrial mix and the national one, may cause errors in the tables, since national structures are applied to regional industries where the percentage of each of the participating sectors is different to the national one.

The literature points out that the issues of technology and external trade are the most important sources of error in the use of national indices for regionalization (Sargento, 2009). More specifically, the technological index in the RIOTs is considered equal to the corresponding national one. In other words, technology is considered as spatially neutral. In terms of the regionalization of inputs internal to the sector, the table of exchanges is usually compiled using the sector's total median consumption of every region as a basic index for regionalization. This means that only the markets are regionalized. In other words, every column of the national table of exchanges internal to every sector, is divided into as many columns as the number of regions. Finally, the accuracy of RIOTs is determined by the methods used for the estimation of the region's external trading (with other countries and other regions). Nevertheless, the calculation of the trade flows inside regions is fairly difficult due to the scarcity of empirical data.

The most widely applied manner for estimating regional quotients is the regionalization of the national table of inputs-outputs, using Location Quotients (LQs). The LQ methods are based on the admission that technology at a regional level is exactly the same as on a national one and that the regional trade quotients differ from the national input quotients to the extent that goods and services are imported from other regions. Essentially, LQs provide the ability to compare activities at regional level with reference to national figures. In sum, the basic assumptions of this procedure are (González et al., 2022):

- Identical technologies between the region and the national economy.
- The regions prefer to consume products which they themselves produce.
- Positive regional exports after meeting the regional demand.

The Location Quotient (LQ) of production is given by the formula:

$$LQ = \frac{\frac{A_{ir}}{A_r}}{\frac{A_{in}}{A_n}}$$

where,

A_{ir}= the production of sector i in region r,

A_r = the total production in region r,

A_{in} = the production of sector i throughout the country, and.

A_n = the production in the country.

The next step is to estimate the national technological quotients against the participation quotients. The usual practice is, if the LQ quotient is equal to or greater than 1 (basic activity), then, the national technological quotient is multiplied by one.[7] If the LQ quotient is smaller than 1,[8] then, the national value is multiplied by the value of the LQ quotient. The outcome of this process, however, is not the technical quotient of the region, which is considered stable, but a trade quotient (Oosterhaven & Hewings, 2013).

Among the initial ramifications of LQ is the cross-industry location quotient (CILQ), comparing the quota of sales of the regional sector's product to the national level, to the regional sector's purchases to the national level. Subsequently, a new formula was suggested where the λ parameter was adjusted.[9] The critical hypothesis on which the FLQ is based, is that a region's tendency to import from other regions is correlated conversely and non-linearly to its relative size. By incorporating the adjustment for local size, the FLQ should be a more accurate assessor of

[7] If the value of the participation quotient is equal to 1, the economic activity (i.e., the sector) under examination is balanced (an alternative phrasing would be that the particular region is "self-sufficient" in terms of the sector under examination) while, if the value of the LQ ratio is greater than 1 (or greater than 1,25 according to a different view), the activity ought to be considered as basic, i.e., there will be a surplus in the sector and this surplus will be exported interregionally or abroad.

[8] If this value is smaller than 1 (there is also the view that it should be smaller than 0,75 but in most empirical applications, the unit is used as a "boundary"), this activity is considered as "non-basic" and this means that for this activity, there will be pure imports (For more details, cf. Rovolis et al., 2016).

[9] The λ parameter which concerns the relative size of the regional economy, is given by the formula $\lambda = [\log_2(1 + x_r/x_n)]^{\delta}$ and it is a parameter controlling the degree of convexity in the equation so that, the greater the value of δ, the lower is the value λ and the greater the margin for more regional imports.

the regional input quotients and, therefore, of the multipliers also. Alongside other, non-investigative methods, the FLQ aims to provide regional researchers with a means with which they can compile regional tables that reflect as much as possible, each region's economic structure (Flegg et al., 2021).

3.6 Riots In Greece

The assessments which will be presented in the next chapter have been based on the input–output table in basic values for Greece for 2015, which is posted on the webpage of the Greek Statistical Service. It includes 65 different products which represent the contribution of industries and correspondingly, 65 sectors of production which represent the industries or the industries' consumption. For the implementation of the regionalization, the gross added value per sector was utilized for the 13 Greek regions for the same time period also available at the Greek Statistical Bureau (see Table 3.1). It is worth noting that we had to downsize group the 65 sectors to 10 through NACE coding. However, for the analysis, we focus on 3 out of the 13 regions and specifically Attica, Western Greece, and Central Macedonia, since they are the most important regions as nodes on the developmental S-shaped axis, as has been previously mentioned in greater detail.

To extract the results, the App-RegMIP was used, a one-of-its-kind software program that allows the regionalization of a national input–output table. This particular program calculates the FLQ which, as mentioned, assumes a corrective quotient λ that represents the regional figure compared to the national. The program allows the selection of an LQ method (FLQ or AFLQ) and a value for the δ parameter.

This program was chosen because, on the one hand, it is easy to use, thus, it is easy to reproduce the evaluations of other studies and confirm their validity, but mainly because there is agreement in the literature on the validity of the FLQ outcomes in relation to the rest of the available sources (Flegg et al., 2021).

3.7 Results

The three tables below present the results after the regionalization for Attica, Central Macedonia, and Western Greece (Table 3.2, 3.3 and 3.4).

Table 3.1 Relative size of sectors in Greece, Attica, Central Macedonia, and Western Greece

	Greece		*Attica*		*Central Macedonia*		*Western Greece*	
	Added Value	*Percentage A.V*	*Added Value*	*Percentage A.V*	*Added Value*	*Percentage A.V*	*Added Value*	*Percentage A.V*
k1	6,816.13	4.40	347.43	0.47	1,340.15	6.40	747.68	10.65
k2	7,445.18	4.81	1,780.20	2.43	617.36	2.95	310.99	4.43
k3	14,627.52	9.45	5,865.86	8.00	2,605.99	12.44	605.97	8.63
k4	3,494.55	2.26	1,313.72	1.79	481.32	2.30	196.39	2.80
k5	38,659.57	24.97	17,704.68	24.13	5,259.39	25.10	1,584.68	22.57
k6	7,866.69	5.08	5,294.80	7.22	794.34	3.79	223.16	3.18
k7	28,027.84	18.11	16,487.71	22.48	3,015.89	14.40	1,175.70	16.74
k8	7,683.43	4.96	5,303.24	7.23	803.46	3.84	195.71	2.79
k9	30,894.08	19.96	13,692.87	18.67	4,881.98	23.30	1,590.60	22.65
k10	9,288.89	6.00	5,567.02	7.59	1,150.34	5.49	390.93	5.57
TOTAL	154,804.00	100.00	73,357.53	100.00	20,950.20	100.00	7,021.81	100.00

Source Greek Bureau of Statistics. Processed by authors

Table 3.2 RIOT evaluations for the Attica region

Sector	*k1*	*k2*	*k3*	*k4*	*k5*	*k6*	*k7*	*k8*	*k9*	*k10*
k1	0.02	0.00	0.01	0.00	0.00	0.00	0.00	0.00	0.00	0.00
k2	0.04	0.06	0.10	0.01	0.01	0.00	0.00	0.01	0.01	0.01
k3	0.26	0.07	0.31	0.85	0.29	0.02	0.03	0.08	0.14	0.08
k4	0.00	0.00	0.00	0.28	0.03	0.01	0.05	0.01	0.02	0.03
k5	0.14	0.03	0.20	0.30	0.48	0.02	0.03	0.12	0.21	0.22
k6	0.05	0.01	0.03	0.07	0.06	0.16	0.04	0.04	0.06	0.08
k7	0.00	0.03	0.02	0.10	0.19	0.05	0.02	0.18	0.02	0.28
k8	0.01	0.02	0.05	0.38	0.09	0.07	0.01	0.11	0.06	0.09
k9	0.00	0.01	0.01	0.02	0.01	0.09	0.00	0.01	0.25	0.02
k10	0.00	0.01	0.01	0.04	0.05	0.07	0.01	0.07	0.06	0.32

Source Greek Bureau of Statistics. Processed by authors

Table 3.3 RIOT evaluations for the Central Macedonian region

Sector	*k1*	*k2*	*k3*	*k4*	*k5*	*k6*	*k7*	*k8*	*k9*	*k10*
k1	0.20	0.00	0.08	0.00	0.02	0.00	0.00	0.00	0.00	0.00
k2	0.01	0.05	0.06	0.01	0.01	0.00	0.00	0.01	0.01	0.02
k3	0.26	0.07	0.34	0.80	0.34	0.02	0.04	0.08	0.14	0.14
k4	0.00	0.00	0.00	0.28	0.03	0.01	0.05	0.01	0.02	0.04
k5	0.12	0.03	0.14	0.18	0.42	0.02	0.03	0.12	0.14	0.25
k6	0.02	0.01	0.01	0.02	0.02	0.06	0.02	0.04	0.02	0.04
k7	0.00	0.03	0.01	0.04	0.11	0.05	0.01	0.18	0.01	0.19
k8	0.00	0.02	0.01	0.12	0.04	0.06	0.01	0.04	0.02	0.05
k9	0.00	0.01	0.01	0.02	0.01	0.09	0.00	0.01	0.25	0.02
k10	0.00	0.01	0.01	0.02	0.04	0.07	0.01	0.07	0.03	0.30

Source Greek Bureau of Statistics. Processed by authors

3.7.1 *Intraregional Interconnections*

Having extracted the RIOTs for the country's main economic regions, we are able by means of a series of transformations on the tables, to obtain important data about each region, the significance of the various sectors for them, and the level of their autonomous development. The processing of this data regarding their transformations, the solving of equations of linear algebra, as well as the extraction of all remaining data, took place through the Mathematica computational program.

Table 3.4 RIOT evaluations for the Western Greece region

Sector	*k1*	*k2*	*k3*	*k4*	*k5*	*k6*	*k7*	*k8*	*k9*	*k10*
k1	0.24	0.00	0.12	0.00	0.03	0.00	0.00	0.00	0.00	0.00
k2	0.01	0.07	0.12	0.01	0.02	0.01	0.00	0.02	0.01	0.02
k3	0.10	0.07	0.23	0.41	0.23	0.02	0.03	0.08	0.09	0.08
k4	0.00	0.00	0.00	0.28	0.03	0.01	0.05	0.01	0.02	0.04
k5	0.06	0.03	0.17	0.12	0.36	0.02	0.03	0.12	0.11	0.20
k6	0.01	0.01	0.01	0.01	0.02	0.05	0.02	0.04	0.01	0.03
k7	0.00	0.03	0.01	0.04	0.13	0.05	0.02	0.18	0.01	0.20
k8	0.00	0.01	0.01	0.07	0.03	0.04	0.00	0.03	0.01	0.03
k9	0.00	0.01	0.01	0.02	0.01	0.09	0.00	0.01	0.25	0.02
k10	0.00	0.01	0.01	0.02	0.04	0.07	0.01	0.07	0.02	0.29

Source Greek Bureau of Statistics. Processed by authors

The tables, which were the product of the process of regionalization, were Leontief tables which express the interregional quotients. As has been noted, however, this type of tables allows interconnection analysis only as far as backwards interconnections are concerned. For a full analysis of interregional interconnections, these tables needed to be turned into one of absolute values. For this to happen, the data is still needed of the ultimate demand for each region. Unfortunately, due to the wider scarcity of regional information, we were unable to procure full data regarding regional consumption levels. In order to overcome this obstacle, we assumed that the country shows uniform consumption behavior and extracted the ultimate demand for each region by allocating the total consumption on the basis of regional incomes as shown in the input–output tables we have compiled. We can then extract the forward interconnections, following Ghosh's methodology (1950) through linear algebraic transformations and operations in the matrices.

We now have a full picture about sectoral interconnections within the main regions of the Greek economy, as these emerge from its total regional model. Based on this data, we can examine the sectoral interconnections regarding their significance and the role they play in Greek economy. For the analysis of the interconnections between sectors, we follow the method of Rasmussen (1956). Two basic indices are used here: the power of dispersion index (PD) and the sensitivity of dispersion index (SD).

The PD index is defined as the relative area s to which an increase in ultimate demand for the products of a sector i is dispersed through the entire economic system, and it is calculated as follows:

$$PD_i = \frac{\left[\left(\frac{1}{n}\right)\Sigma_j(l_j, i)\right]}{\left[\left(\frac{1}{n^2}\right)\Sigma_j(\Sigma_i(l_j, i))\right]},$$

where l expresses the quotients of the Leontief table. If there is a sector where its value is greater than 1, then, the need for an increase of intermediate inputs to more than one unit in the ultimate demand of that sector, will be greater than average. That sector has a great significance backwards. By contrast, for a sector with PD_i < 1, then, the sector is of relatively little import to the economy.

The index SD describes the corresponding area in terms of forward interconnections:

$$SD_j = [(1/n)\sum_g (l_i, j)]/(1/n^2)\sum_i (\sum_j (g_j, i)],$$

where g expresses the quotients of the Ghosh table. As before, if in a sector we have SD > 1, the area which affects an increase in the sector's production is going to be greater than average. By contrast, for SD < 1, the sector will be of little import in terms of forward interconnections, compared to the rest.

Having the values for PD and SD, we can classify the sectors according to Rasmussen's proposal (1965) in four categories:

- Key sectors, comparative high forward and backward effect. (SD>1 and PD>1)
- strategic sectors, have a comparative small effect on other sectors but are greatly affected by the (SD > 1)
- pushing sectors, of great import for other sectors. (PD>1)
- independent sectors, relatively independent ones compared to the interconnections of the rest of the economy. (SD<1 and PD<1)

Presentation and analysis of findings (Table 3.5, 3.6 and 3.7).

In terms of key sectors, sector k5 (Wholesale and retail, transport and storage, activities of service provision in accommodation and food) is seen to be the key sector of the economy in all three regions with a

Table 3.5 Rasmussen classification and backward-forward multipliers for the region of Attica

Sector	*Multipliers* Backward	Forward	PD	SD	Classification
s1	4.00	1.05	0.68	0.48	Independent
s2	2.04	1.40	0.34	0.64	Independent
s3	5.18	4.24	0.88	1.93	Strategic
s4	14.67	1.58	2.48	0.72	Independent
s5	8.69	4.04	1.47	1.84	Key
s6	3.62	1.75	0.61	0.80	Independent
s7	2.46	2.31	0.42	1.05	Strategic
s8	4.21	2.22	0.71	1.01	Strategic
s9	6.49	1.52	1.10	0.69	Pushing
s10	7.76	1.82	1.31	0.83	Pushing

Source Processed by the authors

Table 3.6 Rasmussen classification and backward-forward multipliers for the region of Central Macedonia

Sector	*Multipliers* Backward	Forward	PD	SD	Classification
s1	3.33	1.41	0.88	0.74	Independent
s2	1.69	1.26	0.45	0.66	Independent
s3	3.49	4.16	0.92	2.19	Strategic
s4	7.68	1.52	2.03	0.80	Pushing
s5	5.43	3.16	1.44	1.67	Key
s6	2.39	1.27	0.63	0.67	Independent
s7	1.86	1.69	0.49	0.89	Independent
s8	2.95	1.41	0.78	0.74	Independent
s9	3.50	1.48	0.92	0.78	Independent
s10	5.49	1.61	1.45	0.85	Pushing

Source Processed by the authors

percentage of added value 24,13 for Attica, 25,1 for Macedonia, and 22,5 for Western Greece. Beyond that, only the region of Western Macedonia has another key factor, k3 (Processing) with a percentage of added value 8,63. It is worth noting that both sectors have strong backward and forward multipliers.

Table 3.7 Rasmussen classification and backward-forward multipliers for the region of Western Greece

	Multipliers				
Sector	*Backward*	*Forward*	*PD*	*SD*	*Classification*
s1	2.04	1.43	0.77	0.87	Independent
s2	1.54	1.32	0.58	0.80	Independent
s3	2.82	2.62	1.07	1.58	Key
s4	4.14	1.51	1.57	0.91	Pushing
s5	3.69	2.55	1.40	1.54	Key
s6	1.96	1.19	0.74	0.72	Independent
s7	1.49	1.65	0.56	1.00	Strategic
s8	2.42	1.24	0.92	0.75	Independent
s9	2.57	1.46	0.97	0.89	Independent
s10	3.75	1.55	1.42	0.94	Pushing

Source Processed by the authors

Sector k10 emerges as a pushing sector in all three regions (Arts, entertainment, recreation, other service provision activities, activities of households as employers, diverse household activities relating to the production of goods and services for own use, activities of extraterritorial organizations and agencies, news coverage and communication) with a percentage of added value of 7,59 in Attica, 5,49 in Central Macedonia, and 5,57 in Western Greece. Also, pushing sector located in Attica, is sector k9 (Public administration and defense, mandatory social insurance, education, activities to do with human health and social welfare) which is explained by the concentration of these mechanisms in Athens, while in Central Macedonia and Western Greece pushing sector is k4 (Constructions).

The economy's independent sectors that were identified in all three regions are k1, k2, k6 (Agriculture, forestry, and fishing; mines, quarries, industry, provision of electricity, natural gas, steam, air-conditioning and water, processing of sewage, refuse management and sanitation; fiscal and insurance activities) with a sum total of added value 10,2 in Attica, 13,14 in Central Macedonia, and 18,26 in Western Greece. In the Attica region, k4 is found to be independent, and in Central Macedonia and Western

Greece two more independent sectors are found, k8 and k9 which have mostly to do with service provision.

Finally, the strategic sectors in the economy of Attica are k3 and k7 (Management of real estate), in the economy of Central Macedonia, k3, and in the economy of Western Greece k7, with k7 having over double the percentage of added value of k3, in which, however, fairly high values are obtained for both backward and forward multipliers.

3.8 Conclusions

Input–output tables have a wide range of applications and outcomes for economic policy and they highlight an economy's interconnectedness. Although they are fairly widely used at a national level, Greek economy lags significantly behind in the use of input–output tables at regional level. The particularity of regional analysis is that it requires the extraction of regional data and, in the case of input–output tables, requires the regionalization of the national tables. To this end, utilizing the App-RegMIP instrument, we have carried out the regionalization of the three more important regional economies of Greece (Attica, Central Macedonia, and Western Greece). Next, using Rasmussen's criterion, we classified the 10 sectors of the three regional economies into key, pushing, independent and strategic, based on the significance of each for the economy and the interconnectedness characteristics they possess. In this process, key sectors were those relating to commerce, such as trade, transport and storage and services of accommodation and food provision, while for Western Greece, a key sector is that of Processing. By contrast, the relatively independent sectors are primary ones (agriculture and mining) and the production of energy and financial services, as these are sectors which systematically do not form high interconnections with the rest of the economy. On the contrary, other sectors which appear as independent, such as constructions in Attica, appear as pushing in the rest of the regions.

Appendix

See Table 3.A1

Table 3.A1 Presentation of the Sectors' coding

Code	*NACE Code*	*Analytic Description*
k1	A	Agriculture, forestry and fishing
k2	B + D + E	Mines, quarries, industry, provision of electricity, natural gas, steam, air-conditioning and water, processing of sewage, management of refuse and sanitation
k3	C	Processing
k4	F	Constructions
k5	G + H + I	Wholesale and retail, repair of engine driven vehicles, transport and storage, activities for the provision of accommodation and food
k6	K	Fiscal and insurance activities
k7	L	Management of real estate
k8	M + N	Vocational, scientific and technical activities, administrative and supporting activities
k9	O + P + Q	Public administration and defense, mandatory social insurance, education, activities to do with human health and social welfare
k10	R + S + T + U + J	Arts, recreation, entertainment, other service provision activities, activities of household as employers, diverse household activities to do with the production of goods and services for own use, activities of extraterritorial institutions and agencies, news coverage and communication

References

Akhabbar, A., & Lallement, J. (2010). Wassily Leontief and Léon Walras: The Production as a Circular Flow. Working Paper Centre Walras-Pareto—UNIL.

Bellas, N., Kanellakis, M., Markaki, D., Sardelianos, N., & Pappas. (2017). The socioeconomic impact of the Rio-Antirrio Bridge, Monitoring Centre of Arterial Routes in Western Greece and the Peloponnese—POADEP.

Chenery, H. B. (1962). Development Policies for Southern Italy. *The Quarterly Journal of Economics, 76*(4), 515–547.

Fine, B. (2016). *Microeconomics*. University of Chicago Press Economics Books.

Flegg, A. T., Lamonica, G. R., Chelli, F. M., Recchioni, M. C., & Tohmo, T. (2021). A new approach to modelling the input–output structure of regional economies using non-survey methods. *Journal of Economic Structures, 10*(1), 1–31.

Ghosh, A. (1958). Input-output approach in an allocation system. *Economica, 25*(97), 58–64.

González, S. N., Romero, C. A., Ramos, M. P., Negri, P. A., & Marino, M. (2022). The App-RegMIP: An open access software for regional input-output tables estimation. *International Journal of Computational Economics and Econometrics, 12*(3), 284–302.

Hewings, G. J. D. (1985). *Regional input-output analysis*. Reprint. (Ed.), Grant Ian Thrall. WVU Research Repository, 2020.

Holt, J. (2017). *Approaches to estimating regional input-output tables*. NZ Transport Agency research report (No. 619).

Isard, W. (1951). Interregional and regional input-output analysis: A model of a space-economy. *The Review of Economics and Statistics, 33*(4), 318–328.

Jensen, R. C., West, G. R., & Hewings, G. (1986). Explorations in the comparison of regional economic structure with input-output models. In *Modeling and Simulation, Proceedings of the Annual Pittsburgh Conference* (pp. 245–249). ISA.

Jensen, R. C. (1990). Construction and use of regional input-output models: Progress and prospects. *International Regional Science Review, 13*(1–2), 9–25.

Leontief, W. (1936). Quantitative input and output relations in the economic systems of the United States. *The Review of Economic Statistics*, 105–125.

Leontief, W. (1966). *Input-output economics*. Oxford University Press.

Leontief, W. (1970). Environmental repercussions and the economic structure: An input-output approach. *The Review of Economics and Statistics*, 262–271.

Leontief, W. (1991). The economy as a circular flow. *Structural Change and Economic Dynamics, 2*(1), 181–212.

Livas, P. (1994). *Analysis of inputs-outputs*. Stamoulis.

Lopes, J. C. & Ferreira do Amaral, J.(2013). *The Structure and Evolution of Production, Employment and Human Capital in Portugal: An Input-Output Approach*, Working Papers Department of Economics 2013/24, ISEG - Lisbon School of Economics and Management, Department of Economics, Universidade de Lisboa.

Markaki, M. (2018). Changes in the country's social structure as a result of technological shifts in the sectors of economic activity, vocational specializations and skills: Analysis of Inputs-Outputs (2000–2016), National Institute of Labor and the Workforce.

Markaki, M. & Papadakis, S. (2023b) Greece towards 2027: Structural Transformation, Industrial Policy and Economic Development. In Petrakis, P. (Ed.)

Interconnections in the Greek economy: Between macro- and microeconomics. Palgrave Macmillan.

Markaki, M. & Papadakis, S. (2023a). Industrial Policy and Productive Transformation: An Optimization Approach based on Input-Output Analysis. In Petrakis, P. (Ed.) *Interconnections in the Greek economy: Between macro- and microeconomics*. Palgrave Macmillan.

Miernyk, W.H. (1965). *The elements of input-output analysis*. Reprint. Edited by Randall Jackson. WVU Research Repository, 2020.

Miller, R. E., & Blair, P. D. (2009). *Input-output analysis: Foundations and extensions*. Cambridge University Press.

Oosterhaven, J. & Hewings, G. J. (2013). Interregional input-output models. *Handbook of regional science*, 397–423.

Petrakos, G., & Psycharis, G. K. (2004). *Regional development in Greece*. Kritiki.

Pisinas, Y. (2022b). Production Structure, Technological Change and Requirements in Human Capital. In P. E. Petrakis (Ed.), *Human capital and production structure in the Greek economy: Knowledge, abilities, skills*. Palgrave Macmillan.

Pisinas, Y. (2022a). Human Capital and Structural Economic Transformation. In P. E. Petrakis (Ed.), *Human capital and production structure in the Greek economy: Knowledge, abilities, skills*. Palgrave Macmillan.

Polyzos, S. (2019). *Regional Development*. Kritiki.

Rasmussen, P. N. (1956). *Studies in inter-sectoral relations* (Vol. 15). E. Harck.

Reyes, F. A. (2016). Equilibrium and economic policy in W. Leontief's theory. *Cahiers d'economie Politique,* (2), 203–217.

Romanoff, E. (1974). The economic base model: A very special case of input-output analysis. *Journal of Regional Science, 14*(1), 121–129.

Rovolis, A., Kalimeris, P., Prodromou, M., & Mantzaris, N. (2016). Roadmap for the transition of the Western Macedonia Region to a post-lignite era. WWF Economic Technical Assessment.

Sargento, A. L. M. (2009). Regional input-output tables and models: interregional trade estimation and input-output modelling based on total use rectangular tables (Doctoral dissertation, Universidade de Coimbra (Portugal)).

Suh, S., & Kagawa, S. (2009). Industrial ecology and input-output economics: a brief history. In *Handbook of Input-Output Economics in Industrial Ecology* (pp. 43–58). Springer, Dordrecht.

Suh, S. (Ed.). (2009). *Handbook of input-output economics in industrial ecology*. Springer.

Szabó, N. (2015). Methods for regionalizing input-output tables. *Regional Statistics, 01*, 44–65.

Ten Raa, T. (2006). *The economics of input-output analysis*. Cambridge University Press.

Tiebout, C. M. (1957). Regional and interregional input-output models: An appraisal. *Southern Economic Journal, 24*(2), 140–147. https://doi.org/10.2307/1054417

Tiebout, C. M. (1969). An empirical regional input-output projection model: The State of Washington 1980. *The Review of Economics and Statistics, 51*(3), 334–340. https://doi.org/10.2307/1926567

PART II

Relations in the Greek Industries

CHAPTER 4

Networks in Ownership and Management Structures

Giorgos Vasilis

4.1 Introduction

In general, a network is a system consisting of many similar parts that are connected together to allow movement or communication between or along the parts, or between the parts and a control center (Cambridge Dictionary, n.d). Networks can develop at several levels: individual (social network), organizational, cross-organizational (a system between organizations), and international. According to Castells (1996), a network is "that specific form of enterprise whose system of means is constituted by the intersection of segments of autonomous systems of goals" (p. 171), a definition that applies to all networks. But what is, overall, the role of networks? We may consider the action or the process of interaction with

G. Vasilis (✉)
Center of Continuing Education and Lifelong Learning (E-Learning), National and Kapodistrian University of Athens, Athens, Greece
e-mail: gvasilis@uoa.gr

P. E. Petrakis (ed.), *Interconnections in the Greek Economy*, The Political Economy of Greek Growth up to 2030, https://doi.org/10.1007/978-3-031-31335-6_4

others in the service of exchanging information and developing professional or social contacts as a network's main function which can thus be defined as the act of generating or establishing a group of organizations with the aim of exchange, action, or production between the organization's members (Alter & Hage, 1993).

For the purposes of this overview, a network may be defined as a set of autonomous organizations which come together to attain goals that they cannot attain separately (Chisholm, 1998). Chisholm (1996) explains that the organizations/members belong to networks in order to be able to handle the meta-problems that lie behind many problems and understanding which is essential to finding a solution. In terms of systems theory, an individual organization's commitment to a higher aim or goal, is considered to affect the entire system. The network is thought of as an organizational innovation apt to be quickly adopted because it offers a competitive advantage (Alter & Hage, 1993; Jarillo, 1993). Networks are not characterized by centralized power but, rather, they are by definition decentralized forms of organization (Chisholm, 1998), structured usually horizontally, and not vertically. At the same time, they contribute to the distribution of labor among the contracting parties (Alter & Hage, 1993), thus ensuring the valuable contribution of each member, as well as creating interdependent relationships.

The bibliography concerning the study of networks covers a wide range of scientific fields, including, among others, sociology, the political and administrative sciences, information and systems science, biology, et al. In this case, we look to the bibliography concerning the application of networks to the field of economics, i.e., corporate networks and, especially, those created and developed between companies through board and ownership interlocks.[1] Corporate networks of this kind are not a novel phenomenon. They appeared during the Second Industrial Revolution and the creation of modern corporations, and they were analyzed since the end of the nineteenth century, with the academic community and governments initially focusing on the danger implicit in the strength

[1] Corporate networks may assume many forms such as, for instance, the interconnections formed between organizations by means of trade (Wilhite, 2001), inter-organization loaning (Battiston et al., 2016), or the relationships with the suppliers (Choi &Wu, 2009).

and power corporations assumed due to their size (trusts) and the elimination of completion which this entailed (David & Westerhuis, 2014). At the center of such considerations was also the crucial role of financial institutions in the formation of corporate networks (Hilferding, 1910; Jeidels, 1905).

So, then, the present chapter initially focuses on corporate networks as smallworlds (Sect. 4.2). Next (Sect. 4.3), we focus on the bibliography relating to board interlocks as a crucial form of corporate networks. In Sect. 4.4, we look at the connection between companies that assumes the form of ownership interlocks, also known as ownership networks. In Sect. 4.5, reference is made to the institutional environment and how it affects the interlocking behavior of companies. In the sequel (Sect. 4.6), there is specific reference to the empirical studies concerning Greek enterprises. Finally, in Sect. 4.7, the challenges for future research are presented, which relate to ownership and board interlocks.

4.2 Corporate Networks as Small-Worlds

Since the 1960s, technical developments, particularly the development of graph theory,[2] have allowed for the better modeling and visual rendering of the relationships and bonds which develop in corporate networks. More recent developments in computer graphics have introduced new techniques for the exploration of networks with a complex structure. Corporate networks created through board- or ownership interlocks have been extensively treated in the bibliography as graphs comprised by a set of elements: nodes, otherwise known as vertices—usually the corporations—and the edges[3]—usually the directors or owners—which make for a link[4] connecting two nodes. Certainly, both directors and owners may be considered as a type of node, while a link may signify different types of relationships.

[2] In mathematics, graph theory is the study of graphs, i.e., mathematical structures used to produce models of the relationships between objects.

[3] A node's linked part is that part of the graph comprised by the node itself and all the other nodes that it may reach through paths delineated along the edges. The distance between two nodes is the number of edges connecting them, while the shortest path connecting two nodes (in the sense of crossing the fewest edges) is known as geodesic.

[4] When the links approach the maximum number of connections between the nodes, then the network is designated as thick, otherwise as sparse.

The analysis of social networks constitutes a crucial methodology for the analysis of the relationships between the actors (Burt, 1992). Inside the social network that is structured as a graph, certain nodes (companies or individuals) may exert a stronger influence or have higher status, data which can be measured by certain indicators of the centrality[5] of the node's position. This has attracted wide research interest (Larcker et al., 2013; Mariolis & Jones, 1982; Pfeffer & Salancik, 1978; Takes & Heemskerk, 2016) mostly in investigating the powerful or, at least, advantageous position of an organization inside the network or the correlation between the position of an organization inside the network and its performance, without, however, this being considered as always positive (Andres et al., 2013).

Corporate networks as graphs develop in formations and patterns (clique, pyramid, star, circle, et al.) that may differ from country to country, implying a different structure and relationship between the organizations inside the network (Windolf & Beyer, 1996). Due to the fact that cliques are subgraphs where every node is connected to every other node (full connectivity), it comes as no surprise that there are many approaches/methods of community detection in corporate networks, based on the investigation of cliques (Heemskerk & Takes, 2016; Piccardi et al., 2010; Vitali & Battiston, 2014), as more information is thus available at the topical level of connections.

In the research of boards and corporate interlocks, the network is mostly made up of one type of node, corporations, which are linked by one type of connection, the directors who sit on two or more boards (Bizjak et al., 2009; Davis, 1991; Edling & Sandell, 2001; Haunschild, 1993). The network consisting of one type of node (corporations, or their owners in the case of ownership interlocks) is called 1-mode network or unipartite graph. Insofar as the interlocks may be due to the corporations' strategy, this appears normal. However, this is not the only possible mapping of the interconnections. Another possible network transformation is if it is approached as a network of directors (or owners in the case

[5] Such indicators are, the degree of centrality, closeness of centrality, betweenness centrality, and eigen vector centrality. The first concerns the sum total of tips that are connected inside a node; the second, the average length of the smallest route between the node and all the other nodes in the graph; the third defines the times when a node operates as a bridge along the shortest route between two other nodes; and the last one measures a node's influence in the network, defined by the value of the nodes to which it is connected.

of ownership interlocks) who are linked via the organizations (Battiston & Catanzaro, 2004; Burris, 2005; Carroll, 2004; Davis et al., 2003). In all cases, however, the unipartite graph cannot fully account for the complex ties that develop simultaneously among the companies and those among the directors or owners.

Moreover, it is possible to analyze the network as a graph made up by both directors (or owners) and a company as nodes[6] (Newman et al., 2001; Robins & Alexander, 2004; Wang et al., 2009), with the connection between a director and a corporation meaning that the director is a board member of that particular company. A network with two different types of nodes is called a 2-mode network or bipartite graph.[7] A network's downgrade, in terms of the approach to it, from 2-mode to 1-mode, always implies a loss of information (Bohman, 2012). In this case also, the connections are generated between nodes of different types. The analysis of the three levels is more complex but provides additional information about the relationships that evolve within the network.

A particular type of mathematical graph is the small-world network which possesses certain attributes.[8] The small-world may be considered as a social network where many dense grids of actors are characterized by relationships that operate as conduits of control and information

[6] In the mathematical field of graph theory, this constitutes a bipartite graph whose vertices can be divided into two separate and independent sets so that each edge connects a summit of one set with a summit of the other.

[7] In this type of network, the connections are generated always between nodes of a different type, but it is also possible, through the analysis of two distinctive unipartite graphs, to more fully depict the ties that develop inside the network: between corporations, or between directors (or owners) but also between the two.

[8] The two main qualities that characterize a small-world, according to the Watts-Strogatz model (Watts & Strogatz, 1998), which is a specific category of small-world networks of random graphs, are the concepts of the mean path length—which is to say randomly selected pairs of nodes that turn out to be unexpectedly close to one another—and high clustering—the tendency for nodes of the network to be in the same "neighborhood". By contrast, according to the Erdős-Rényi model (Erdos & Renyi, 1959), the Poisson random graphs show a small index of clustering—inconsistent with the observed real social networks (Watts & Strogatz, 1998).

(Milgram, 1967; White, 1970).[9] As, for instance, from people's friendship relationships at the micro-level of a social system, we are able to observe a small-world structure at the (macro) level of a social system (Watts & Strogatz, 1998), so have corporate networks been extensively analyzed in the bibliography as small-world networks in relation to the sum total of the corporate large-world. In such a network, a relatively large number of organizations can be connected to others through a small number of ties. Many studies in the recent bibliography of board and ownership interlocks investigate whether corporate networks meet the small-world requirements (Davis et al., 2003; Heemskerk & Takes, 2016; Kogut &Walker, 2001; Robins & Alexander, 2004). These studies are usually empirical and their analysis covers specific geographical parameters. The study by Kogut and Walker (2001) of German corporations was the first to introduce a topological analysis of ownership networks.

4.3 Board Interlocks and Corporate Networks

Corporate networks assuming the form of board interlocks, otherwise known [as] interlocking directorate or overlapping directorships, have monopolized research interest on the networking of companies. At all events, interconnected directors in the United States (US) are an established practice of companies listed at the stock exchange, since the beginning of the twentieth century (Mizruchi, 1982), and globally, too, this is the rule rather than the exception among big companies (Davis & Greve, 1997). The bibliography on the use of corporate interconnections starts at the beginning of the past century, flourishes in the 1970s and 1980s and further intensifies in the 1990s (Mizruchi, 1996), and continues to the present with renewed impetus, provided by further developments in graph theory at the beginning of 2000s.

Alongside the increased interest, the criticism leveled at this research has also intensified. The main objections center on the inability of the analysis of corporate interconnections to predict corporate behavior

[9] Renowned psychologist Stanley Milgram (1933–1984) was the first to analyze the issue of the small-world (Milgram, 1967) through the mean number of connections between two individuals randomly selected from a population. From this research, the idea emerged that any two people (in the United States) could be connected through a chain of six contacts (at an average). An important offshoot of this work is the investigation of several sets of random graphs (Newman et al., 2001).

and correlate those ties with corporate performance, or even record the complexity and composition of the corporate interlock networks (Mizruchi, 1996; Zajac, 1988).

Nonetheless, despite such criticism, interlocks remain a powerful indicator of the interrelationships between companies (Mizruchi, 1996). Although in the United States, the anti-monopoly legislation of 1914 (Clayton Antitrust Act) forbids board interlocks between companies in the same sector (Fennema & Schijf, 1978)—as this would mean a potential alliance, especially among the larger organizations and, hence, a violation of anti-monopoly legislation—at least one in eight of overlapping directorships in the United States is between companies that are supposed to be in competition (Wardrip-Fruin & Montfort, 2003, p. 480).

Board interlocks can efficiently interconnect unconnected companies (Kang, 2008), leading to inter-corporate ties via the creation of social networks. Hallock (1997) points out that the prevalence of such ties is too pronounced to be accidental and probably reflects essential mechanisms of organization. One reason why interconnections between boards are so popular, is that they represent a reliable and low-cost conduit of information and communication between companies (Haunschild, 1993).

We have board interlocks when a member of a company's directorial board also sits on another board, or several (Mizruchi, 1996; Pennings, 1980). They are thus defined in their simplest form, as the relationship created between two boards when they share at least one member, with the network of those relationships (board interlocking network) comprising the total of the companies' boards, along with all the existing interconnections entailed therein (Mizruchi, 1996). Two companies have an immediate interconnection (direct interlock) if a member of the directorial board of one simultaneously sits on the directorial board of the other, and indirect interconnection (indirect interlock) if at least one member on the directorial board of each company sits on the board of a third (Green & Semple, 1981; Salinger, 2005). Although this distinction is not commonly made in the bibliography, indirect interconnection may be an even more important form of connection which, moreover, does not fall under the legal restrictions that apply to direct interconnection (Green & Semple, 1981).

What is it, however, that has caused the prevalence of board interlocks and what is their role? There have been a number of explanations as to the reasons for the emergence and spread of the phenomenon, as there have been attempts to analyze its implications beyond the economic realm, at a political and social level. Bibliography on board interlocks is now fragmented, as it draws from several scientific disciplines and uses a variety of theoretical perspectives without a unified understanding of how the finds of the bibliography fit together.

The first unified approach is by Mizruchi (1996) and, as he explains, a central issue in the research on the interconnections of corporations has been and continues to be, what interconnections do. Mizruchi (1996) distinguishes five basic determining factors which explain the formation of board interlocks: collusion, cooptation and monitoring, legitimacy, career advancement, and social cohesion. These factors (see below) have prevailed in the explanations offered in the bibliography on the emergence of the phenomenon. Additionally, a frequent distinction in the bibliography is between the factors responsible for the formation of board interlocks into those concerning the companies' activity or pursuit and those concerning the behavior or motives of the individuals-directors.

As an initial approach, the inaugural theories (Dooley, 1969; Hilferding, 1910; Jeidels, 1905) argued that it was the banks' pivotal position in the financial system that led to the creation of such ties between financial institutions and companies. Financial institutions exerted influence on non-financial institutions aiming to control them, which created relationships of power and interdependency. Besides, companies with great capital requirements tend to interconnect with banks (Mizruchi & Stearns, 1988; Pfeffer, 1972), while financial institutions try to get a representative on a company's board so as to better monitor the company's financial state of affairs (Eisenhardt, 1989; Mizruchi, 1982). Dooley (1969) ascertains that five distinct factors are responsible for the appearance of board interlocks: (1) the size of the company, (2) the extent of control by the management, (3) the company's financial connections, (4) the relationship with the competitors, and (5) the presence of topical financial interests.

A large part of the relevant bibliography interprets board interlocks as attempts at inter-corporate control and supervision (Allen, 1974, 1978; Burt, 1983; Gulati & Westphal, 1999; Kotz, 1978; Mizruchi, 1982; Zeitlin, 1974). The interconnections in this case result from companies wishing to gain control over others by accessing positions in their directorial boards, though with unsound corporate governance and collusion as possible consequences. A more positive version of the control theory is that companies strive for control through collaboration, and interlocks are merely manifestations of the companies' interdependency (Pfeffer & Salancik, 1978). These are seen as non-competitive interactions, beneficial to all parties involved. Within this analytic framework, the corporate elite promotes cooptation, and interlocks represent companies' attempts to predict unexpected events in their environment and consolidate their relationship with other companies (Allen, 1974). Nevertheless, the inability to locate dense networks in many cases (Scott, 1997) weakened the argument for coordinated action, favoring alternative interpretations of the phenomenon of board interlocks (Useem, 1984).

Thus, through a wide range of analysis, it has been suggested in the bibliography that board interlocks are created because they contribute to a social structure that supports the cohesion of the corporate elite (Chu & Davis, 2016; Heemskerk & Takes, 2016; Palmer, 1983; Useem, 1982; Zeitlin, 1974). The directors frequently come from higher social classes, having similar educational backgrounds and shared channels of contacts, resulting in the creation of a social "inner circle". In this context, ties between companies may be interpreted in terms of the existence of a hegemonic class (Koenig & Gogel, 1981), the social class approach (Ornstein, 1984) or, also, the directors' social affinity (Yue, 2012) and the theory of social networks (Bohman, 2006, 2012).

Another frequently addressed matter concerning directors' motives that is thought to account for the interconnections of directorial boards, has to do with the prospects of professional advancement and the benefits (higher salary and status) these ties can offer to directors (Westphal & Stern, 2006) and managing directors (Kramarz & Thesmar, 2013). These interconnections work to signal the extensive networks of some directors, leading to higher social capital, and offering them greater flexibility and access (Johnson et al., 2011). This may be explained for by the fact that well-connected directors have a great many conduits for disseminating information and exercising control (Coleman, 1990), thus availing themselves of the opportunity to connect companies which could not otherwise be connected (Burt, 1992).

Thus, board interlocks are considered beneficial as the interconnected members carry their experience to other companies that are called on to make similar decisions (Davis, 1996), and provide valuable information for the consideration of other managing directors (Lorsch & Maclver, 1989; Useem, 1984). The motive for incorporating someone who belongs to the directorial board of another company, may also have to do with the person's special traits and abilities (their human capital) which, however, does not have a direct bearing on the company itself. In general, a great part of the relevant bibliography argues that board interlocks help the interconnected companies overcome their dependency on resources (resource dependence theory) through formulating a set of strategies (Burt, 1978; Hillman et al., 2009; Ong et al., 2003; Shrader et al., 1991; Simoni & Caiazza, 2012). Those managing the company are motivated to ensure its survival and reinforce their own autonomy, while maintaining stability in the organization's transactions (Pfeffer & Salancik, 1978).

Moreover, board interlocks are useful as the company's quality signaling, highlighting its position in its environment (Certo, 2003; Connelly et al., 2011; Kang, 2008) and aiding in the better dissemination of the company's reputation, both positive (Certo, 2003) and negative (Kang, 2008). If a company becomes interconnected with another of "good" reputation, it sends out a signal of high quality to interested parties (such as stock holders and investors) who are assessing it, thus taking advantage of a spillover effect due to the board interlocks.

Beyond the companies' motives for connecting through board interlocks, research interest has also focused on the impact these ties have on companies. Many previous studies have shown that these actions help interconnected companies to manage the uncertainty in their environment (Martin et al., 2015; Mizruchi & Stearns, 1988; Ong et al., 2003; Shrader et al., 1991; Stearns & Mizruchi, 1986; Useem, 1984), while also making available information which would not otherwise be accessible (Haunschild & Beckman, 1998). When companies operate in conditions of high uncertainty, they often perform better if they have developed more board interlocks (Boyd, 1990). These ties reduce uncertainty because they improve access to higher up channels of information and communication (Hillman et al., 1999). Useem (1984) argues that the greater a company's centrality is in the network, the more access to information it has.

At the same time, board interlocks are thought to allow the dissemination of new practices of corporate governance (Davis, 1991; Larcker et al., 2013; Palmer et al., 1993; Shropshire, 2010; Tuschke et al., 2014), while they may also facilitate strategic choices such as alliances, merges and buy-outs or the listing of companies in the stock exchange (Gulati & Westphal, 1999; Moore et al., 2012; Rousseau & Stroup, 2015). Davis

(1991) has shown that the network of interconnections can contribute to the process of a company's strategic defense against threats of a buy-out (poison pills). At the same time, however, buy-outs and mergers can disseminate inside the network through mimetic practices (Haunschild, 1993). Mimetic behaviors inside the network are more likely to occur when there is a high level of uncertainty and ambiguity and there is a dearth of alternative sources of information (Haunschild & Beckman, 1998).

As a result of the above factors, board interlocks have real consequences and are capable of affecting the performance and behavior of the interconnected companies (Beckman & Haunschild, 2002; Cai & Sevilir, 2012; Haniffa & Hudaib, 2006; Harris & Shimizu, 2004). The acquisition of the necessary resources and information operates as a basis for this to occur (Davis & Cobb, 2010). Interconnections of this type, aided by the process of learning and dissemination (Davis & Cobb, 2010; Hillman et al., 2009), boost research and growth, thus improving the performance of companies (Davis, 1991; Gronum et al., 2012). Moreover, the interconnections of directorial boards facilitate access to capital (Stearns & Mizruchi, 1993) and a company's loaning (Mizruchi, 1996), as well as the formation of corporate alliances (Gulati & Westphal, 1999), aspects that bolster the company's position. Nevertheless, certain studies indicate that board interlocks may also be related to a decline in performance (Fligstein & Brantley, 1992; Stokman et al., 1985). The negative correlation between the ties of directorial boards and companies' performance may be explained by the fact that the connected members may be loyal to their social circle (elite) rather than their corporate boards, with the result that they are more interested in social cohesion rather than financial outcomes (Burris, 2005), or that occupying multiple positions on a number of directorial boards may adversely affect their efficacy in tending to the company's management (Andres et al., 2013; Harris & Shimizu, 2004).

4.4 Corporate Networks of Interlocking Ownership

A significant part of the bibliography has focused on the other type of interconnection between companies that we are looking at, namely, ownership interlocks, otherwise known as ownership networks. Ownership interrelatedness, in its simplest form, creates a network where two companies are connected if one owns a certain percentage of the other (Vitali & Battiston, 2014; Vitali et al., 2011). This type of connection between companies has proven extremely important in, among others, understanding corporate control and flows of value globally (Glattfelder & Battiston, 2009; Vitali et al., 2011). Another possibility is the ownership bond due to the connection between two companies by means of the same owner (indirect connection) with, generally, companies also able to connect through more than one owner.

Stockholders in a company may be entities that cannot belong to others (e.g., natural persons, families, associations, and public agencies) or other companies. Thus, a distinction is made between primary owners (individuals) and secondary owners (companies). Direct ownership in a sector can be easily ascertained from the records of the distribution of shareholding, however, due to cross-shareholding,[10] the true ownership structure may be hidden behind a composite or not readily visible network of indirect relationships and interdependent owners. This scenario concerns forms of indirect ownership, i.e., ownership through another entity (company) which generate indirect interests among shareholders, whether these are individuals or companies.[11]

These composite structures of ownership form patterns of corporate networks (Almeida & Wolfenzon, 2006; Rungi et al., 2017; Wolfenzon, 1999) and their analysis bears on a wide range of issues, such as, for instance, patterns that relate to companies' tax evasion (Richardson et al., 2016). According to Levy and Szafarz (2016), there are four reasons which can motivate the existence of composite ownership systems: (1) the boosting of cooperation between companies which own one another, (2) a silent alliance and the increase of market power, (3) the attraction of external stock holders, and (4) corporate control which can be beneficial, although at the expense of the minority of stockholders (tunneling).

Although a great many studies exist of ownership structures, a comparatively small number focus on indirect ownership or issues to do with cross-partnerships. In the bibliography, indirect ownership has been

[10] These concerns ownership structures such as pyramid shareholding, one-sided shareholding, reciprocal shareholding, and cyclical shareholding.

[11] As a simple example of composite ownership structure, individual A owns part of the stocks of Company B, which is also the part owner of Company C. Even though A is not a shareholder of (so not directly interested in) Company C, he is an indirect "owner" and, thus, benefits from its revenue because of Company B.

linked to great benefit for the shareholders (Dietzenbacher et al., 2000; Flath, 1992, 1993). Nevertheless, the connection is not necessarily positive for the performance indices of the connected companies, with empirical outcomes being usually dubious or contradictory (Flath, 1993; Lichtenberg & Pushner, 1994; Morck et al., 2000; Yafeh & Yosha, 2003), which is also the case for the impact of composite ownership structures on the remunerations of managing directors (Allen, 1981).

Ownership networks have also been studied to ascertain the transmission of economic distress from one or more companies to the network (financial contagion effect) and the consequent ramifications (Bardoscia et al., 2017; Dastkhan & Gharneh, 2019; Elliott et al., 2014). In addition, ownership links have proven decisive in locating offshore fiscal hubs (Garcia-Bernardo et al., 2017; Rungi et al., 2017) or for the ability of multinational companies, due to the centrality of their place in the network, to affect public policy (Compston, 2013). More generally, the position of a crucial company in the network, is an indicator of the influence it may exert on restructuring practices (such as buy-outs and mergers) inside the network (Kogut & Walker, 2001).

Cross-shareholdings can potentially lead to silent collusions with the aim of increasing the power of companies (O'Brien & Salop, 2000). Companies may have reduced motives for competition due to ownership ties, resulting in high prices and low production (Azar et al., 2018). Research shows that this is dependent on the sector's structure and that, though such practices do exist in companies related by ownership, they are not necessarily the rational choice (Alley, 1997; Gilo et al., 2006; Reitman, 1994).

In studying the architecture of the global ownership network, Vitali et al. (2011) attempt to gather and process all the observable structures of ownership around the world, using the concepts of composite networks. The research shows that the main part of the existing ownership and (flows of) value in global markets is monopolized by a small group of shareholders, with the centralization of control resulting in the formation of many "hyper-entities" which control the largest part of companies worldwide, thus raising issues of financial stability and competition at a global level.

The fact that the control of companies is dispersed among many shareholders, particularly in Anglo-Saxon countries, makes it look like that there is a crowd of shareholders owning a small number of stocks in some companies. By contrast to this impression, however, Glattfelder and

Battiston (2009), looking at the stock markets of 48 countries, show that through composite ownership networks, a local distribution of control is linked to a global concentration of control and input—a fact which had not been systematically addressed previously. In a larger sample, Rungi et al. (2017) examine the patterns formed by ownership networks in 208 countries and come across a high concentration of corporate power, as less than 1% of the parent companies—which have over 100 subsidiary companies—are responsible for more than 50% of sales globally.

The ties of shared ownership are a particular kind of inter-corporate relationships and indubitably represent a vested interest in having a say in the control of company decisions. Nevertheless, only a small portion of the bibliography includes ownership networks in its study of areas relating to corporate control, its flow (Battiston, 2004; Chapelle & Szafarz, 2005; Davallou et al., 2015; Dorofeenko et al., 2007; Glattfelder & Battiston, 2009) and concentration (Brancaccio et al., 2018; Vitali et al., 2011). Games theory has been used as a method for analyzing the quantification of corporate control through voting systems, though this is a fairly heterogeneous body of research, differing in both their aims and their field of analysis (Aminadav et al., 2011; Karos & Peters, 2015; Levy, 2009; Levy & Szafarz, 2016; Rungi et al., 2017).

By contrast, the demarcation between ownership and company control is a frequent subject of analysis in the bibliography on composite ownership networks (Ben-Nasr et al., 2015, Claessens et al., 2000; Laeven & Levine, 2008; Lemma & Negash, 2016; Lingmin, 2016; Napoli, 2018; Paligorova & Xu, 2012). By and large, the above studies concern statistical approaches and their main contribution consists in the introduction of a rule aiming to demarcate ownership from rights to control (Claessens et al., 2000), the so-called weakest link principle[12] which, however, has disadvantages and limitations (Dietzenbacher & Temurshoev, 2008). Because of cross-shareholdings and the ownership patterns that emerge (such as pyramids) the rights to control (vote) many times exceed the rights of the dividends (Claessens et al., 2000; La Porta et al., 1999). More recently, problems relating to ownership networks and issues of control have been methodologically approached through some models of optimization (Di Giacomo & Cenci, 2018; Martins & Neves, 2017; Romei et al., 2015).

[12] This rule can be summed as follows: if company A owns 10% of company B's shares and company B owns 20% of company C, then, company A controls 2% of company C.

4.5 Institutional Environment and Comparative Study

Because research on ownership and board interlocks limits itself to the interconnections that develop at a national level and/or the analysis of a small time period, it enhances our understanding only partially, due to each country's particular characteristics, and the change occurring in networks over more long-term periods. Any comparative studies of corporate networks between countries only concern small time periods while studies concerning the long-term development of corporate networks focus at the national level.

The first full and systematic cross-country comparative study is by Stokman al. (1985). Their book focuses on corporate interconnections between the 200 largest companies in 10 Western European countries and explores company interconnections across countries and their effects on company performance, highlighting structural differences between countries. Scott (1991) was among the first to explain that differences in the countries' structural background that are due to cultural and historical factors that can lead to a different structure and development of corporate networks, making a distinction between Great Britain and the United States, and between mainland Europe and Asian countries.

Institutional divergence and differences in ideological and economic background influence the pattern and distribution of ownership ties among the largest companies, shaping different corporate bonds in different countries. For example, in the United States a negative attitude toward large companies has led to aggressive restrictions in the ability of financial institutions and organizations to control public companies (Fligstein, 1990), while, at the same time, as also happens in Great Britain, pension funds, mutual trusts and distinct individual shareholders are the main owners of large companies (Useem, 1996). By contrast, in Germany, banks and large companies have prevailed as owners of large enterprises (Jurgens et al., 2000).

The presence of powerful institutions affects corporate structuring. Rungi et al. (2017) correlate decisions of strategic inter-corporate control with the institutional environment. Among other things, they show that the pyramidal structures of ownership networks that operate as channels of control at a global level, are less likely to develop in countries with powerful economic institutions and a staunch adherence to contracts as these reinforce more transparent forms of corporate governance.

Franks and Mayer (1997) locate two ownership structures, internal and external systems, on the basis of which, US and British companies are distinguished from French and German ones. An internal system entails certain small companies listed in the stock market, which are characterized by a few interactions and represent a complex corporate ownership network. By contrast, an external system involves many large companies in the stock market, with more interaction between the companies but less ownership ties. The research outcomes indicate that French and German companies mainly follow the ownership structure of the internal system, while US and British ones, that of the external system.

Windolf and Beyer (1996), studying the corporate networks formed by ownership and board interlocks in the 623 largest companies of Germany and the 520 largest companies of Britain, conclude that Germany reflects a system of "cooperative capitalism", while Britain is an instance of "competitive capitalism". In Germany, by contrast to Britain: (1) ownership (stocks) is particularly concentrated, allowing owners to dominate the company; (2) the network of board interlocks is closely tied to the capital network, i.e., serves the reinforcement of the owners' power; and (3) both networks are amassed within the same sector (horizontal interconnections), i.e., connections between competitors are very likely.

Following the distinction between "varieties of capitalism" made byHall and Soskice (2001),[13] van Veen and Kratzer (2011) focus on the structural aspects of board interlocks between fifteen European countries (see Sect. 4.6). Their results show great quantitative differences in the network's denseness within the countries closely associated with the prevalent capitalist system in each country, whereas at the level of a European network, the countries occupy completely different positions. This happens because a country's international position depends significantly on the network's structure and the duration of the country's membership in the EU (van Veen & Kratzer, 2011).

[13] The distinction concerns liberal market economies (LME) versus the coordinated market economies (CME). In LME, companies plan their activities mainly based on markets and hierarchies, while in CME, they are more dependent on the relationships outside the market. Also, in LME, companies turn to financial markets for investment capital and, as a result, transparency is important and stock prices are a primary criterion of company performance. By contrast, in CME, companies are funded by debt and banks play an important role, while there are close-knit ties between banks and industrial companies. In this case, reputation and trust, rather the price of stocks, are important criteria of company performance.

Research into corporate networks has nevertheless shown that the categorization of countries isn't straightforward. Kogut (2012) has shown that the dichotomy between the free market and the coordinated market economies is rather blurred. By collecting data to do with ownership and board interlocks on 22 countries around the world, he found among others, that there are significant differences between the Anglo-Saxon countries (the United States, Great Britain, and Canada) while, behind these differences, certain continuities persist, such as the adherence of small-world attributes to corporate networks (Kogut, 2012).

Using data from 2005 on the corporate networks in 12 countries, Cardenas (2012) contributes another distinction to the one concerning the varieties of capitalism, one which is based on the joint influence of the financial system, state intervention, ownership structure, and the globalization of the creation of corporate networks in every country (Cardenas, 2012, pp. 315–316). Classifying the countries in two groups, corporate networks in the first group may be described as cohesive: the power structure is located in unity, concentration, and control. The cohesive network in Italy, France, Germany, and Spain is consistently explained by the combination of the economy structure which is centered around banks, the interventionist state, the concentrated ownership, and the small financial internationalization. The networks of the second group of countries (Canada, Australia, Switzerland, the United States, and Great Britain) are described as dispersed, as they are fragmented, decentralized, and with more unified ties due to the combination of non-interventionist state, the market-centered structure of the economy and decentralized ownership.

Collecting data from the largest companies in 208 countries, Heemskerk and Takes (2016) examine the topological attributes of a global corporate network—made of 968,409 companies interconnected through board interlocks—in which are included all personal interconnections, both at the level of tip management and directorial boards. The detection of community reveals that peripheral clusters play a fundamental part in the architecture of the network of global political economy. The article shows that transatlantic connections remain particularly powerful: Europe and North America remain interconnected through a dense network of members sitting on the same boards, while a separate Asian cluster—geographically isolated—is developing and gaining economic and political power, although Asia by and large remains outside the field of networks of the established global (i.e., Northern Atlantic) corporate elite.

4.6 Application to Greek Companies

As we conclude the survey of the bibliography, it is worth noting that research on the formation of corporate networks, structured by the ownership and board interlocks of Greek companies, is fairly limited, with the four cases identified below presented in chronological order of publication.

Using a historical approach to the analysis of social networks, Dritsas et al. (1996) compare three small economies of the interwar period, Austria, Greece, and Sweden and, specifically, the structure and defining factors of the formation of board interlocks and the place (centrality) of the banks in each country's corporate network. With 1938 as the reference year, they use data on Greece mainly available from the Bank of Greece on corporate unions, budgets, and the composition of directorial boards and, also, from the press of the Athens Stock Exchange, the government gazette, and the posts of the association of member companies, with the sample consisting of 52 companies (large companies in operation for at least 15 years) including nine banks and two insurance companies. Their findings on Greece show that the interconnections of the boards, though not as pronounced as in other European countries, concerned 38 companies which, in the interwar period, had developed ties with at least one other company. The ten more central companies in the network were connected to another nine, while the highest degree of centrality belonged to Chemical Products and Fertilizers Ltd. Three of the large banks, the Commercial Bank, the Ionian and Popular Bank, and the National Bank of Greece, were among the ten most central companies with their boards connected both with industrial companies as well as among themselves.

In a sample of the 27 richest economies (with high stock exchange values) on the basis of the per capita income for 1993, La Porta et al. (1999) utilize data (mainly from the World Scope database) on ownership structures aiming to define the ultimate stock owners of the companies with high capitalization. They find that, aside from the economies with very effective protection of the stock holders, relatively few companies in the sample possess a wide range of ownership. On the contrary, they are usually controlled by families or the state. The owners also usually have control rights over the companies that significantly exceed cash flow rights, mainly through pyramidal structures and participation in management. The data for the Greek ownership structures (deriving primarily from Bloomberg Financial Systems) indicate that the large Greek companies are characterized by a very small dissemination of company control.

The most thorough approach to corporate networks which include Greek companies is found in the article by van Veen and Kratzer (2011). They investigate the structural aspects of board interconnections in the 15 countries that joined the European Union (EU) during the first four waves of accession (EU-15), showing the differences between the countries. The analysis is based on graph theory and in particular, the use of the degree of centrality and the concept of network density in order to highlight the companies' position in the network (at a local and global level) and the networking of board members. The sample selection, with a different number of companies in every country, refers to the year 2006 (January 1st) and was based on large and usually multinational companies in the stock exchange—362 in number, with 20 Greek ones among them—with financial capitalization as a basic choice criterion, while the data concerning the board members—6,115 positions in total, out of which 256 concern Greek companies—were mainly drawn from the annual corporate reports. The collection of additional data was made through other sources on the web, while complementary data was drawn from "Google Finance" (finance.google.com), "Zoom Info" (www.zoominfo.com), and "Top Management" (www.topmanagement.net).

The findings show great quantitative differences in network density outside the countries (van Veen & Kratzer, 2011). These differences are significantly related to the "variety of capitalism" (Hall & Soskice, 2001) prevalent in each country. Also, the cross-country analysis of corporate ties reveals a European network inside which the different countries occupy a completely different place while, as was mentioned, a country's international position closely correlates to the duration of its EU membership. Specifically, for the (20) Greek companies, the findings show a low network density, as they show the least number (after Portugal) of interconnections globally (14 out of a total of 1132, with 246 interconnections of the 38 French companies being the largest number) but also locally, after Luxembourg and Portugal (12 connections out of a total of 688, with the greatest number, 145 connections, once more being to the 38 French companies). As a consequence, they are also characterized by a small degree of centrality in the European network (two connections with European companies out of a total of 444 connections, 101 of those by French companies). Another interesting finding is that the board members of Greek companies have positions on up to two boards simultaneously, with the largest percentage (93.8%) corresponding to only one.[14]

The study by Pastra et al. (2015) concerns another case where a more general analysis is made of the structure and characteristics of corporate boards in Greek shipping, without, however, focusing on the corporate networks that form in the industry, while emphasis is given to the (significantly low) percentage of women therein and the concomitant benefits of their presence. Nevertheless, drawing data from the Athens Stock Exchange for the shipping industry for the period 2002–2012, Pastra et al. (2015) found 305 board formations, with 84 of those numbering a total of 38 members with positions on two or more boards of listed companies. 30 out of those 38 (78.9%) held positions simultaneously on two different boards and eight (21.1%) respectively on three.

Finally, in the most recent research on networks that include Greek companies, Andrikopoulos et al. (2019), on the basis of data from Bloomberg's webpage on board members and key executives, use graph theory to find out the key nodes in the network of personal and corporate interconnections in a sample of 110 shipping companies, listed in the stock market, 10 of which were based in Greece. The study involves looking into the social networks that had formed—in a specified period—by means of the ties developed simultaneously by the leadership interlocks and the board interlocks in the shipping industry, the econometric appraisal of the factors determining those interconnections (company size, board size, profitability, and leverage), and the effects of the leadership interlocks on agent conflicts. The research findings indicate that the network of leaderships is denser than that of companies, that interconnections of directorial boards have a positive effect on profit and

[14] The most characteristic case of "big linker" is that of the German Cromme G. who has a position on the boards of nine companies simultaneously.

leadership interlocks have a negative effect on internal costs that occur due to the competitive interests of shareholders (agency costs).

4.7 Further Research

A literature review highlights the existence of a narrow research sample, as most of the published research on corporate networks of the form that concerns us is geographically focused on the United States. An even greater gap in the bibliography of board interlocks has to do with the investigation of international board interlocks, i.e., interconnected companies located in different countries. These types of interconnections have attracted next to no academic interest despite indications that they may actually be the most prevalent (Staples, 2007). For instance, Staples (2007) ascertained that in 2005, 75% of the 80 largest international companies had non-nationals sitting on their boards. Further study of international company interconnections is deemed important as it is able to highlight cross-country and intercultural consequences of the formation of such company ties.

Research on ownership and board interlocks as forms of company networks is extensive. Yet, only a few studies jointly analyze the two types of company interconnections (Bohman, 2012). In a study of the Japanese keiretsu networks, Lincoln et al. (1992) concluded that company link-ups through their directors is not a common phenomenon, yet the existing such links follow ownership links. Besides, broken ties between boards regenerate to a greater degree if the companies have simultaneously ownership ties (Ornstein, 1984). It has moreover been shown that in the United States, the participation of banks in non-financial companies is a powerful predictor of board interlocks (Kotz, 1978; Mizruchi, 1982). Thus, the high correlation between the two forms of corporate interconnection highlights the importance of including ownership structures in the bibliography on board interlocks, since the interests of shareholder-owners may significantly affect the real consequences of the interconnectedness of the boards.

Every type of tie that develops between two or more corporations, particularly if they belong to the same sector, is potentially a factor for collusion. This understandably incites interest in whether the ties investigated among competitors are motivated by attempts at collusion, whether they are effective in facilitating the collusion or, whether, ultimately, there is no correlation. Although the possibility of collusion through ownership interlocks has indeed been investigated (Alley, 1997; Azar et al., 2018; Gilo et al., 2006; O'Brien & Salop, 2000; Reitman, 1994), the role of board interlocks in the promotion and dissemination of collusion has not. Nevertheless, the data on this issue is hard to locate because there is no systematic research on the motives of companies to form ties through joint directors. Also, whereas market power appears to be related to and facilitate ties between companies in the same sector, the few large companies in sectors of high concentration have no need of such ties in order to regulate prices (Mizruchi, 1996). There are, then, few indications that interconnections of this type are necessary in order to control competition. It is however not known whether, for instance, a company that improves its performance as a result of related illicit practices will promote such practices to other companies through board interlocks or whether collusions will be limited once a company forms ties with other companies which do not engage in such practices.

Moreover, as has been pointed out, many studies focus on the diffusion of corporate strategies through board interlocks (Davis, 1991; Palmer et al., 1993; Shropshire, 2010) and restructuring practices through ownership interlocks (Kogut & Walker, 2001) without, however, investigating whether these ties also contribute to a restraint on corporate behaviors. Thus, yet another extension in the research of corporate governance would be to investigate whether corporate interconnections also facilitate the withdrawal of strategic actions. One such example would be the strategic decision to withdraw investment in a company following its link up with another.

Finally, one other subject not covered in the bibliography and seems promising for future research, is the correlation of the corporate interconnections we are considering with entrepreneurship. Both large companies (Dooley, 1969) and small to middle ones (Gronum et al., 2012) develop corporate ties. However, research has not focused on understanding the ways in which corporate interconnections are likely to differ depending on a company's age or the extent to which companies at initial stages of their development form comparable bonds.

The review of the bibliography shows that the comparison of the structural characteristics of institutions in different countries can contribute to a fuller understanding of the causes and ramifications of corporate networks in the form of ownership and board interlocks (Cardenas, 2012; Fligstein, 1990; Franks & Mayer, 1997; Kogut, 2012; Scott, 1991; van Veen & Kratzer, 2011; Windolf & Beyer, 1996). Though it is known that institutions play a vital role in the formation of corporate bonds (Aguilera & Jackson, 2003), comparative institutional analysis (institutional changes and their great complexity) of corporate networks is consistently scarce. Thus, an important matter for further research is how the operation of interconnections differs in different parts of the globe. The perception that the global corporate elite operates in distinct peripheral communities (Heemskerk & Takes, 2016) and the fact that institutional robustness may effectively contribute to better corporate governance, may mean that it's necessary to take into account peripheral-topical aspects of the corporate environment, if we are to grasp the ways in which corporate power is generated and accumulated. This research need requires an approach of multiple methodologies where the methods of network analysis are complemented in depth by qualitative studies. In other words, the research on the global corporate elite needs to be "denser".

Appendix

Table 4.A1 Synopsis of empirical research articles on board* and ownership** interlock networks (*Source* Author's own creation)

Article	*Methodology*	*Country*	*Period*	*Main Findings*
Allen (1974) *	Sociometric analysis	United States	1935, 1970	Increasingly more widespread and full cooperation among large companies (cooptation) in which financial institutions are increasingly occupying central positions
Allen (1978) *	Sociometric analysis	United States	1935, 1970	The structure of the corporate elite is largely organized around a series of distinct and cohesive interconnected groups in which many companies jointly share a number of directors
Alley (1997) **	Econometric analysis	United States, Japan	1979–1994	Although collusion appears to prevail in the Japanese car industry, it is more competitive than in the American car industry
Andres et al. (2013) *	Social network & econometric analysis	Germany	2003–2006	Companies with closely interconnected boards show lower performance and pay their executive members significantly more
Andrikopoulos et al. (2019) *	Social network & econometric analysis	Global analysis	2006	Leadership interlocks are denser than the network of shipping companies, the interconnections of boards impact profit-making positively and leadership interlocks have a negative impact on costs due to the competing interests of shareholders

Article	*Methodology*	*Country*	*Period*	*Main Findings*
Azar et al. (2018) **	Econometric analysis	United States	2016	Shared ownership interlocks (specifically in the US aerospace industry) generate powerful anti-competition motives while the high density of ownership interlocks entails higher costs
Bardoscia et al. (2017) **	Social network analysis	Global analysis	2013	Processes widely believed to stabilize the financial system i.e., market integration and diversification, can actually lead to instability as they contribute to the generation of cyclical structures that tend to reinforce economic hardship thus subverting systemic stability and increasing the likelihood of large crises
Battiston (2004) **	Social network analysis	United States, Italy	2002	The study of the topological structure in the relationships of the ownership interlocks in the Italian stock exchange and in two major US stock markets shows that the former is made up of different interest groups, while the US markets are characterized by very large owners who control the mutually overlapping subsets of reserves

(continued)

Table 4.A1 (continued)

Article	*Methodology*	*Country*	*Period*	*Main Findings*
Battiston and Catanzaro (2004) *	Social network analysis	United States (Italy)	1999, (1982, 2002)	The extensive comparative analysis of the statistical attributes of board interlocks for the largest by revenue 1000 US companies and the companies of the Italian stock market, shows many common statistical attributes in the data groups, despite the fact that they refer to different countries and different years, thus implying an underlying mechanism not sufficiently accounted for by the existing network models
Beckman and Haunschild (2002) * **	Social network & Econometric analysis	United States	1986–1997	Findings show that companies connected to others possessing a related heterogeneous previous experience, tend to pay less for their buy-outs and have better performance. A company also pays less insurance fees when the companies linked to its network (1) have closed deals of differing sizes, (2) possess rare information (2), and (3) are of different size. In addition, in the corporate network, experience affects the quality of company decisions
Ben-Nasr et al. (2015) **	Econometric analysis	France	1998–2013	There are strong indications that companies with many large shareholders present less duration of debt

Article	*Methodology*	*Country*	*Period*	*Main Findings*
Bizjak et al. (2009) *	Econometric analysis	United States	1996 –2002	Board interlocks facilitate the exchange of information and the diffusion of corporate policy in the network. Specifically, it appears that these ties are products of the dissemination of the dubious practice of backdating stock options
Bohman (2006) * **	Econometric analysis	Sweden	2000–2003	Share repurchases are not just related to specific economic features of the companies but also to social influence through board interlocks. The argument of social embeddedness holds even when ownership networks are taken into consideration
Bohman (2012) * **	Social network analysis	Sweden	1990–2005	The joint examination of owners' networks, companies and board members show that board interlocks depend to a large degree on ownership interlocks. The findings provide a new way of understanding the mechanisms behind the formation of board interlocks. Moreover, the correlation between types of interconnections suggests that the ownership network can potentially generate some of the phenomena attributed to the board interlocks

(continued)

Table 4.A1 (continued)

Article	*Methodology*	*Country*	*Period*	*Main Findings*
Boyd (1990) *	Econometric analysis	United States	1980	Developing a structuring model to ascertain whether directorial boards respond to different types of environmental uncertainty, it was seen that in a more uncertain environment, these tend to be of a smaller size while they simultaneously develop an increased number of interactions. This correlation was higher in companies with a high performance
Brancaccio et al. (2018) **	Social network analysis	Global Analysis	2001–2016	The global network control is especially concentrated: the percentage of large owners who cumulatively own 80% of the global value of companies, is considered in the sample to always be below 2%. Also, investigating the phenomenon's dynamic, an increase is observed in the concentration of ownership: this tendency acquires a more systematic and general character as of the beginning of the economic crisis in 2007, with an increase of over 20%

Article	*Methodology*	*Country*	*Period*	*Main Findings*
Burris (2005) *	Sociometric analysis	United States	1980	The social ties created through common participation in corporate boards contribute more to the cohesiveness of political behavior than to shared economic interests, such as those that relate to activity in the same sector or the same geographical location
Burt (1978) *	Input–Output analysis	United States	1967	The suggested theory explains where the board interlocks should appear between sectors of the economy, where they ought not to appear and what the profitability is of effective interconnection
Cai and Sevilir (2012) *	Econometric analysis	United States	1996 –2008	Examining the transactions of mergers and buy-outs in the presence of a board interlock between the buyer-company and the target companies, it is shown that buyers get an information advantage on the real value of the target companies, allowing them to acquire low performing companies at an attractive price
Cardenas (2012) **	Social network analysis & Fuzzy-set qualitative comparative analysis	Global Analysis	2005	This study analyzes national corporate networks with interlocks, defines two main types of corporate networks in twelve developed countries and traces the causal conditions (financial system, state intervention, ownership structures and globalization) that prevail in each country and influence the corresponding structure of corporate networks

(continued)

Table 4.A1 (continued)

Article	*Methodology*	*Country*	*Period*	*Main Findings*
Chapelle and Szafarz (2005) **	Matrix methodology	Global Analysis	2003	On the basis of the rule of the majority, a model is provided designed to assess the ratio of the control (full control vs full ownership) by the ultimate owners of a group of companies. This ratio is determined per share, per company and per shareholder
Chu and Davis (2016) *	Social network & sociometric analysis	United States	1997– 2010	The findings show that the network of board interconnections in the US has changed in fundamental ways. What used to be the case for board interlocks for 100 years, changed within 10 years. The American corporate interconnection network suffered an impressive reduction of corporate ties among board members
Claessens et al. (2000) **	Weak-Link & Game Theory Approach	Inter-national Analysis	1996	Due to cross-shareholdings and to the ownership patterns that form (such as pyramids) the control rights (voting) often exceed those of dividends. More than two thirds of companies are controlled by only one shareholder, with older companies typically controlled by the family. Also, a significant portion of corporate wealth in Eastern Asia is concentrated in some families

Article	*Methodology*	*Country*	*Period*	*Main Findings*
Dastkhan and Gharneh (2019) **	Simulation modeling	Iran	2010–2015	Results show that the suggested simulation model and the network of crossover participation are appropriate for the analysis of the systemic danger and its spread to financial systems. The structural characteristics of financial networks play an important part in the dissemination of shock and financial crisis
Davallou et al. (2015) **	Social network analysis	Iran	2014	The results of analysis of the ownership network of the Teheran stock market show that over 86% of all observable ownership relationships have formed through indirect ownership and with the presence of at least one intermediate owner. Also, the study of the degree of concentration shows that over 60% of the market's total value belongs to only 10% of shareholders

(continued)

Table 4.A1 (continued)

Article	*Methodology*	*Country*	*Period*	*Main Findings*
Davis (1991) *	Econometric analysis	United States	1984–1989	The findings support a prospect of social structuring in the purchase of corporate control in which the network of interconnections provides a social framework which favors continued administrative dominance. The findings are also more consistent with models of structural cohesion rather than ones of structural equivalence (two nodes are considered structurally equivalent if they have the same adjacent areas) as responsible for the social, structural mechanism of diffusion
Davis and Greve (1997) *	Diffusion model	United States	1980, 1986	The authors compare the difference between two innovative practices of corporate governance that were adopted in response to the wave of buy-outs during the 1980s: poison pills (which spread quickly due to a process of diffusion from board to board) and golden parachutes (which spread slowly via geographical proximity)
Davis et al. (2003) *	Social network analysis	United States	1982, 1990, 1999	The level of connectedness among hundreds of large US companies and the thousands of board members is highly consistent with time's passage

Article	*Methodology*	*Country*	*Period*	*Main Findings*
Di Giacomo and Cenci (2018) **	Optimization approach	Multi-national analysis (Europe)	2015	In this article, a linear model of programming is introduced, namely, the cheapest control problem, that contributes to both descriptive analysis and the optimization approach. The solutions to the problem allow the estimation of three indices that measure the ease with which a company can be controlled, on the basis of the ownership relationships
Dietzenbacher et al. (2000) **	Micro-economic analysis	Holland	1995	In every case, competition is reduced due to ownership interconnections. Comparing the case of shareholding with the no-shareholding case, the cost-price margins were found to be 2% higher in a Bertrand market and 13% higher in a Cournot market
Dietzenbacher and Temurshoev (2008) **	Input–output analysis	Czech Republic	1997	The methodology applied allowed for a picture to emerge of "secret ownership structures" in the banking sector. The complexity of the network of relationships between primary and secondary owners which was quantified, and the relevant ownership chains which were mapped, showed that indirect ownership relationships play a decisive role in the banking sector

(continued)

Table 4.A1 (continued)

Article	*Methodology*	*Country*	*Period*	*Main Findings*
Dooley (1969) *	Descriptive analysis	United States	1935, 1965	Comparing the years 1935 and 1965, it seems that the frequency of board interlocks is pretty similar
Dorofeenko et al. (2007) **	Matrix methodology	Germany	2000	In cross-over forms of ownership, the rights of control and ownership can be completely separated and there may exist multiple balances in the economy
Dritsas et al. (1996) *	Social network analysis	Austria, Greece, Sweden	1938	The study shows that the three countries present similar patterns of board interconnections, the intensity and density of which accorded with the overall level in each country's economic development. Austria had the largest number of banks in a central position in the network, followed by Sweden and then Greece
Edling and Sandell (2001) **	Econometric analysis	Sweden	1997	The strategic choices of industrial and economic organization as corporate behaviors, such as the transfer from primary to secondary markets examined here, may be predicted by the social influence exerted by board interconnections

Article	*Methodology*	*Country*	*Period*	*Main Findings*
Flath (1993) **	Econometric analysis	Japan	1981	Banks and insurance companies in Japan have the tendency to own, directly and indirectly, stocks in clients who borrow more intensively than themselvesı while some banks are also more inclined to keep stocks in companies with larger overall leverage
Fligstein and Brantley (1992) * **	Sociometric analysis	United States	1969, 1969–1979	The existing power relations within the company, the perception of control that prevails in the actions of the company and those of its competitors, play a part in the economic actions undertaken by large companies, despite differences in management, ownership, bank control or the presence in the banks of board interlocks
Franks and Mayer (1997) **	Descriptive analysis	France Germany, United Kingdom, United States	1990	French and German companies mainly follow the ownership structure of the internal system (small companies characterized by few interactions) while British and US ones follow ownership structure of the external system (a lot of large companies with interactions but fewer ownership ties amongst the companies)

(continued)

Table 4.A1 (continued)

Article	*Methodology*	*Country*	*Period*	*Main Findings*
Garcia-Bernardo et al. (2017) **	Social network analysis	Multi-national analysis (global)	2015	In analyzing the ownership network across countries on the basis of global chains of corporate ownership, it becomes clear that there is a geographical specialization in the offshore network and the greatly significant role for global economy is revealed of Holland and the United Kingdom, as dominant country-channels in international chains of corporate ownership
Glattfelder and Battiston (2009) **	Social network analysis	Multi-national analysis (global)	2017	In Anglo-Saxon countries, corporate control tends to be diffused amongst many shareholders and is seen to be very concentrated at a global level, i.e., in the hands of very few important shareholders. The exact opposite is observed to be the case for European countries
Green and Semple (1981) *	Spatial analysis	United States	1978	The research shows that companies do indeed make use of the interconnections of directorial boards and that the network that has been created has topical differentiations and can affect peripheral stability

Article	*Methodology*	*Country*	*Period*	*Main Findings*
Gronum et al. (2012) **	Econometric analysis	Australia	2005	Strong heterogeneous bonds improve innovation in small to middle-sized companies. However, the relationship between network ties and corporate performance is more complex, as the positive relationship is formed through the innovation
Gulati and Westphal (1999) *	Econometric analysis	United States	1995	This study shows that board interlocks can have qualitatively different ramifications for the creation of new strategic alliances between companies and alliances of companies, depending on the behavioral processes that make up the base for the companies' ties, while these outcomes of cohesion are in turn mitigated by ties developed with third parties
Hallock (1997) *	Econometric analysis	United States	1992	Interconnected board members enjoy at an average, significantly greater remunerations than not-interconnected ones
Haniffa and Hudaib (2006) * **	Econometric analysis	Malaysia	1996–2000	As regards board interlocks, which is a common phenomenon in Malaysian economy, the findings suggest that these ties do not add to corporate performance, with the market considering multiple ties as not healthy

(continued)

Table 4.A1 (continued)

Article	*Methodology*	*Country*	*Period*	*Main Findings*
Harris and Shimizu (2004) *	Econometric analysis	United States	1981–1989	There is a positive relation between the percentage of overly taxed board members (sitting on multiple boards simultaneously) and excessive performances while there is no evidence that such individuals miss meetings. Moreover, the findings suggest that the "busy" members have not a detrimental but, rather, a favorable impact on the company's basic strategic decisions (such as buy-outs) as they are significant sources of knowledge
Haunschild (1993) *	Econometric analysis	United States	1981–1990	Corporate directors imitate the buy-out practices of those companies with which they are interconnected through board members
Haunschild and Beckman (1998) *	Social network & Econometric analysis	United States	1981–1990	We measured the effect of alternative sources of information on the relationship between board interlocks and corporate buy-outs. The findings show that most of the alternative sources reduce the impact of the ties between directorial boards except for one, the coverage of the company by the press, which increases it

Article	*Methodology*	*Country*	*Period*	*Main Findings*
Heemskerk and Takes (2016) *	Social network analysis	Multi-national analysis (global)	2013	The transatlantic connections remain particularly strong: Europe and North America remain interconnected in a dense network of joint board members, while the separate Asian complex is developing and gaining financial and political power, although Asia, nevertheless, remains by and large outside the field of the established global (Northern Atlantic) corporate elite
Johnson et al. (2011) *	Econometric analysis	United States	1993–2000, 2000–2007	The hypothesis that higher remunerations relate to the admission of board members with high status or multiple ties does not appear to hold. However, the company's complexity relates to the ability to add members with a strong social fund and the prestige of the current directorial board is connected with the ability to bring on new members of high prestige
Kang (2008) *	Econometric analysis	United States	1998–2002	Important penalties to do with corporate reputation were found in 45 (out of 244) companies linked through board interlocks with 30 companies accused of financial fraud in the United States. Also, companies had greater chances of experiencing important reputational penalties when the interconnected members occupied supervisory or government positions

(continued)

Table 4.A1 (continued)

Article	*Methodology*	*Country*	*Period*	*Main Findings*
Kogut and Walker (2001) **	Social network analysis	United States	2007–2010	A network's small-world attributes have an impact on innovative performance of the company complex
Kramarz and Thesmar (2013) *	Econometric analysis	France	1992–2003	There is a strong interconnection between the network of chief executive officers and that of directors. Social networks are associated with multiple benefits for the executive directors but have detrimental effects on corporate governance
La Porta et al. (1999) **	Econometric analysis	Multi-national analysis (27 rich countries)	1995, 1996	Apart from economies where the shareholders are well protected, comparatively few companies in the sample have a wide range of ownership. On the contrary, they are primarily controlled by families or by the state. Also, the owners usually have control rights which significantly exceed cash flow rights, mainly through using pyramidal structures and their participation in management

Article	*Methodology*	*Country*	*Period*	*Main Findings*
Laeven and Levine (2008) **	Econometric analysis	Multi-national analysis (13 European countries)	1996–1999	It is ascertained that (1) one third of the companies introduced into Europe have more than one big owner, (2) the market value of companies with many big owners differs to that of other companies, and (3) the relationship between the evaluation of companies and the distribution of rights over dividends to many big owners, are in accordance with the predictions of recent theoretical models
Larcker et al. (2013) *	Social network & Econometric analysis	United States	2000–2007	In total, the findings suggest that corporate networks formed out of board interlocks provide financial benefits that are not directly reflected in the stock prices
Lemma and Nevash (2016) **	Econometric analysis	Multi-national analysis (deve-loping countries)	1996–2010	In the countries of the sample, the concentration of ownership and/or the existence of big stockholders in non-financial companies increases with the structuring of debt at corporate level, the levels of the industry's regulation, a country's level of corruption and the real per capita gross national product, while it diminishes with the basic capital structure, the size of the company and the orientation of a country's financial system

(continued)

Table 4.A1 (continued)

Article	*Methodology*	*Country*	*Period*	*Main Findings*
Levy (2009) **	Social network analysis, Weak-Link Approach, Matrix Methodology & Game Theory Approach	Beligum	2005	The article compares existing methods for ascertaining a company's owners in a pyramidal structure without crossover ownership. These are applied to the Colruyt company, citing the different results in the corporate inspection which each method generates
Levy and Szafarz (2016) **	Game Theory Approach	Germany	1998	Taking into consideration ownership interlocks, it appears that managers can obtain indirect voting rights and thus insulate their companies from external control
Lichtenberg and Pushner (1994) **	Econometric analysis	Japan	1976–1989	Ownership by financial institutions of their own funds in Japan can effectively replace the defunct foreign market of buy-outs, resulting in the surveillance and intervention which minimize the risk of loss of productivity. At the same time, high levels of inter-corporate ownership, distance companies from the management of their problems, at the expense of their performance

Article	*Methodology*	*Country*	*Period*	*Main Findings*
Lincoln et al. (1992) * **	Econometric analysis	Japan	1980	Studying the Japanese keiretsu networks, researchers conclude that corporate connections through the directors are not commonplace, but the existing such ties follow the ties of ownership
Lingmin (2016) *	Econometric analysis	China	2003–2012	Companies with the widest divergence between final control rights and rights over dividends have a significantly higher level of leverage of capital structuring. Also, leverage is an increasing motive for owners as, with the risk of confiscation that is prevalent in Chinese economy, debt increase is a tool for them to maintain control over funds and corporate decisions
Mariolis and Jones (1982) *	Social network analysis	United States	1962, 1964, 1966	Examining the reliability and stability of centrality in corporate interlock networks, it is ascertained that measurements of centrality are highly reliable and stable. Moreover, out of three measurements that were investigated (number of interlocks, non-directional centrality, and directional centrality), the number of board interlocks is slightly more reliable or stable than the other two. Lastly, the findings indicate that the central position of banks is more stable in relation to that of companies

(continued)

Table 4.A1 (continued)

Article	*Methodology*	*Country*	*Period*	*Main Findings*
Martin et al. (2015) *	Econometric analysis	United States	2001–2009	Companies are likely not to form board interlocks necessarily in order to reduce uncertainty but in order facilitate adaptability and improve performance when they are faced with uncertainty
Martins and Neves (2017) **	Social network analysis & Optimization approach	Multi-national analysis (20 European countries)	2015	A series of solutions is examined which reveals alternative strategies of corporate control, using a wide range of companies in the European stock exchange. Strategies for control usually differ in whether they allow mutual cross-shareholding structures or not
Mizruchi and Stearns (1988) *	Econometric analysis	United States	1956 –1983	Decreasing solvency, reduced profit margin, increased demand for capitals at diminishing interests, and the matching of increased demand for capital with the stages of shrinkage of the business cycle, correlate with the existence of board interlocks
Moore et al. (2012) *	Econometric analysis	United States, United Kingdom	2002–2006	Characteristics of the external network, such as board interlocks, are important factors for predicting the external capital market choice from a foreign market, by a company of initial public offering

Article	*Methodology*	*Country*	*Period*	*Main Findings*
Morck et al. (2000) **	Econometric analysis	Japan	1985, 1986, 1987	Ownership of its capital by a bank and corporate value are negatively associated in Japan. Also, middle levels of ownership significantly increase a bank's power to appropriate surplus funds of client-companies. Ownership ties with banks also appear to affect the company's value through influence on the investment policies of client-companies while introducing loose economic restrictions which allow companies to take up more marginally acceptable investment opportunities
Napoli (2018) **	Econometric analysis	Italy	2017	A more favorable framework is created for strategic change and innovation when a company extends membership to the directorial board or the top management team, to individuals outside the dominant families, in order to gain access to funds controlled by associates
Ong et al. (2003) *	Econometric analysis	Singapore	1997	Market capitalization, board size, total assets, return on assets, return on sales, profit before tax and nature of the company (financial or non-financial) are significantly correlated with board interlocks

(continued)

Table 4.A1 (continued)

Article	*Methodology*	*Country*	*Period*	*Main Findings*
Ornstein (1984) *	Econometric analysis	Canada		Approximately half the interlocking directorates reflected corporate imperatives and half reflected class solidarity. Interlocks involving executives or between corporations with two or more interlocking directors were more likely to be reconstituted in cases of the retirement of directors, but the effects of location, industry, and foreign ownership were more likely to be reconstituted in cases of the retirement of directors, but the effects of location, industry, and foreign ownership were weak
Paligorova and Xu (2012) **	Econometric analysis	Multi-national analysis (G7 countries)	2003–2006	Companies in networks of a pyramidal form have significantly higher leverage and the use of debt in pyramids is associated with the risk of expropriation. Findings indicate that the capital structure of pyramids is affected by the expropriation activities of ultimate owners that have excess control rights

Article	*Methodology*	*Country*	*Period*	*Main Findings*
Palmer (1983) *	Econometric analysis	United States	1962, 1964, 1966	This article presents evidence regarding the continuity of board interlocks that have been accidentally disrupted by such events as death or retirement, a fact which reveals something of the extent and manner in which different types of ties facilitate formal coordination
Pastra et al. (2015) *	Descriptive analysis	Greece	2001–2012	Drawing data on the Greek shipping industry from the Athens Stock Exchange, 305 board formations were found, out of which 84 included a total of 38 members who, during their term, occupied positions on two or more boards of listed companies. 30 out of the 38 (78,9%) held positions on two boards, and 8 (21.1%) on three boards simultaneously
Piccardi et al. (2010) * **	Social network analysis & Optimization approach	Italy	2008	The main finding is that both the board and ownership networks of the Italian companies examined exhibit a strong community structure and, moreover, the two structures overlap significantly. This is due to several factors such as pyramidal groups and members on multiple boards. Overall, this means that the small-world of listed companies is actually split into well identifiable communities

(continued)

Table 4.A1 (continued)

Article	*Methodology*	*Country*	*Period*	*Main Findings*
Richardson et al. (2016) **	Econometric analysis	China	2005–2010	There is an important, non-linear relationship between ownership concentration and tax avoidance. Also, a significantly positive association is found between pyramidal ownership structure and tax avoidance due to the entrenchment effect, i.e., the managers' use of the company to promote their own interests rather than those of the shareholders
Robins and Alexander (2004) *	Social network analysis	United States, Australia	2006	Empirical bipartite graphs are compared to simulated random graph distributions conditional on constraints implicit in the observed datasets. It is concluded that the corporate networks compared have many similarities and some differences. Notably, both tend to be influenced by the clustering of directors on boards, while shared multiple board memberships (multiple interlocks) are an important feature of both infrastructures, and company structural power may be relatively more diffuse in the US structure than in Australia

Article	*Methodology*	*Country*	*Period*	*Main Findings*
Romei et al. (2015) **	Social network analysis & Optimization approach	Italy	2012	The main contribution of this article concerns the emergence of interaction in cases of model-building of ownership networks as graphs (through algorithms who take effective advantage of such structures) and the empirical study of an important case, thus recommending a framework for analyzing issues of corporate governance through applying network analysis and graph theory on ownership networks
Rousseau and Stroup (2015) *	Econometric analysis	United States	1996–2006	Prospective buyers-companies are almost five times more likely to acquire firms in which their board members have served in the past. Buy-outs are also more likely when there is better corporate governance and the interconnected members have a higher share of ownership in the buyer company

(continued)

Table 4.A1 (continued)

Article	*Methodology*	*Country*	*Period*	*Main Findings*
Rungi et al. (2017) **	Social network & Econometric analysis	Multi-national analysis (208 countries)	2015	Among others, a strong concentration of corporate power is ascertained, with less than 1% of the parent companies expanding to more than 100 subsidiaries and being responsible for over 50% of sales internationally. Also, the strategies of indirect control of the subsidiaries by the parent companies correlate with the quality of the institutional environment in every country
Shrader et al. (1991) *	Econometric analysis	United States	-	The study's results indicate that strategic relations of board interlocks constitute significant indicators of the organizational measure of centrality. They are closely related to the central position of companies in the exchange of resources. Thus, board interconnections are used strategically to connect organizations with their environment
Simoni and Caiazza (2012) *	Social network & Econometric analysis	Italy	1998–2006	Board interlocks between companies in the same sector were proven to be mechanisms of cooperation as long as they facilitate deeper connections among competitors, such as their integration through mergers and buy-outs

Article	*Methodology*	*Country*	*Period*	*Main Findings*
Staples (2007) *	Descriptive analysis	Multi-national analysis	2005	In 2005, 75% of the 80 largest international companies had non-nationals on their boards, but only in 10% of those companies, were non-nationals the majority
Stearns and Mizruchi (1986) *	Econometric analysis	United States	1955–1984	Only when a company exerts power over another will the dissolution of board interlocks be reconstituted with the same firm. Otherwise, if the company interconnects with another, this means the absence of relations of corporate control
Stearns and Mizruchi (1993) *	Econometric analysis	United States	1956 – 1983	Through a time-series analysis of 22 large US manufacturing companies from 1956 to 1983, it was found that the types of financial institutions represented on companies' directorial boards correlated with the amounts and types of loans which companies sought

(continued)

Table 4.A1 (continued)

Article	*Methodology*	*Country*	*Period*	*Main Findings*
Takes and Heemskerk (2016) *	Social network analysis	Multi-national analysis	2013	Investigating the concept of centrality in the global corporate board interlock, as well as in different national networks, it is seen that degrees of centrality are correlated and that there are important differences between countries. Also, the importance and centrality of companies don't always go together. Moreover, the article provides additional indications for the peripheral outcomes based on the network's topology
Tuschke et al. (2014) *	Econometric analysis	Germany	1990 –2003	Board interlocks contribute to the companies' learning practices with some types of interconnections having greater importance. In the article, the relevant advantages are seen of the various types such as experience, power and the reliability implicit in the ties among the network's companies, and it is argued that these markers may lead to measurable differences in the companies' learning outcomes

Article	*Methodology*	*Country*	*Period*	*Main Findings*
van Veen and Kratzer (2011) **	Social network analysis	Multi-national analysis (15 European countries)	2006	The results show great quantitative differences in network density in the countries that are closely allied with the capitalist system of each country, while at the level of the European network, the different countries assume completely different positions. This occurs because a country's international position depends significantly on the network's structure and the length of the country's membership in the EU
Vitali and Battiston (2014) **	Social network analysis	Multi-national analysis	2007	The analysis for the detection of community at a global level, showed that a global corporate network is intensely organized and concentrated in communities where geography is the main lever of formation
Vitali et al. (2011) **	Social network analysis	Multi-national analysis	2007	The study shows that the main part of the existing ownership and (flows of) value in international markets is monopolized by a small group of shareholders
Wang et al. (2009) *	Econometric analysis	United States	2000	Overall, findings support the view that it is possible for managers without social and educational credentials to gain access to corporate boards

(continued)

Table 4.A1 (continued)

Article	*Methodology*	*Country*	*Period*	*Main Findings*
Windolf and Beyer (1996) * **	Descriptive analysis & Social network analysis	Germany, United Kingdom	1992–1993	Germany represents a system of "cooperative capitalism" while Britain is an instance of "competitive capitalism"
Yafeh and Yosha (2003) **	Econometric analysis	Japan	1990	The concentrated stock capital correlates with lower expenditure activities, in favor of executive members
Yue (2012) *	Econometric analysis	United States	1996–2002	In the study of the evolution of conventional corporate interactions between internet companies during the period of the dot-com bubble, it was seen that there were asymmetric consequences for the formation and dissolution of corporate networks

References

Aguilera, R. V., & Jackson, G. (2003). The cross-national diversity of corporate governance: Dimensions and determinants. *The Academy of Management Review, 28*(3), 447–465. https://doi.org/10.2307/30040732

Allen, M. P. (1974). The structure of interorganizational elite cooptation: Interlocking corporate directorates. *American Sociological Review, 39*(3), 393–406. https://doi.org/10.2307/2094297

Allen, M. P. (1978). Economic interest groups and the corporate elite structure. *Social Science Quarterly, 58*(4), 597–615.

Allen, M. P. (1981). Power and privilege in the large corporation: Corporate control and managerial compensation. *American Journal of Sociology, 86*(5), 1112–1123. https://doi.org/10.1086/227356

Alley, W. A. (1997). Partial ownership arrangements and collusion in the automobile industry. *The Journal of Industrial Economics, 45*(2), 191–205. https://doi.org/10.1111/1467-6451.00043

Almeida, H. V., & Wolfenzon, D. (2006). A theory of pyramidal ownership and family business groups. *The Journal of Finance, 61*(6), 2637–2680. https://doi.org/10.1111/j.1540-6261.2006.01001.x

Alter, C., & Hage, J. (1993). *Organizations working together*. Sage Publications.

Aminadav, G., Bachrach, Y., Konstantin, K., Rosenschein, J. S., & Wilf, Y. (2011). Rebuilding the great pyramids: A method for identifying control relations in complex ownership structures. SSRN Electronic Journal. https://ssrn.com/abstract=1903941

Andres, C., van den Bongard, I., & Lehmann, M. (2013). Is busy really busy? Board governance revisited. *Journal of Business Finance & Accounting, 40*(9–10), 1221–1246. https://doi.org/10.1111/jbfa.12051

Andrikopoulos, A., Georgakopoulos, A., Merika, A., & Merikas, A. (2019). Corporate governance in the shipping industry: Board interlocks and agency conflicts. *Corporate Governance, 19*(4), 613–630. https://doi.org/10.1108/CG-07-2018-0224

Azar, J., Schmalz, M. C., & Tecu, I. (2018). Anticompetitive effects of common ownership. *Journal of Finance, 73*(4), 1513–1565. https://doi.org/10.1111/jofi.12698

Bardoscia, M., Battiston, S., Caccioli, F., & Caldarelli, G. (2017). Pathways towards instability in financial networks. *Nature Communications, 8*(1), 1–7. https://doi.org/10.1038/ncomms14416

Battiston, S. (2004). Inner structure of capital control networks. *Physica A: Statistical Mechanics and Its Applications, 338*(1–2), 107–112. https://doi.org/10.1016/j.physa.2004.02.031

Battiston, S., & Catanzaro, M. (2004). Statistical properties of corporate board and director networks. *The European Physical Journal B, 38*(2), 345–352. https://doi.org/10.1140/epjb/e2004-00127-8

Battiston, S., Farmer, J. D., Flache, A., Garlaschelli, D., Haldane, A. G., Heesterbeek, H., Hommes, C., Jaeger, C., May, R., & Scheffer, M. (2016). Complexity theory and financial regulation. *Science, 351*(6275), 818–819. https://doi.org/10.1126/science.aad0299

Beckman, C., & Haunschild, P. (2002). Network learning: The effects of partners' heterogeneity of experience on corporate acquisitions. *Administrative Science Quarterly, 47*(1), 92–124. https://doi.org/10.2307/3094892

Ben-Nasr, H., Boubaker, S., & Rouatbi, W. (2015). Ownership structure, control contestability, and corporate debt maturity. *Journal of Corporate Finance, 35*(C), 265–285. https://doi.org/10.1016/j.jcorpfin.2015.10.001

Bizjak, J., Lemmon, M., & Whitby, R. (2009). Option backdating and board interlocks. *The Review of Financial Studies, 22*(11), 4821–4847. https://doi.org/10.1093/rfs/hhn120

Bohman, L. (2012). Bringing the owners back in: An analysis of a 3-mode interlock network. *Social Networks, 34*(2), 275–287. https://doi.org/10.1016/j.socnet.2012.01.005

Bohman, L. (2006). Economic action and interfirm relations: Diffusion of stock repurchases on the Stockholm stock exchange 2000–2003. *European Sociological Review, 22*(4), 383–396. https://doi.org/10.1093/esr/jcl003

Boyd, B. (1990). Corporate linkages and organizational environment: A test of the resource dependence model. *Strategic Management Journal, 11*(6), 419–430. https://doi.org/10.1002/smj.4250110602

Brancaccio, E., Giammetti, R., Lopreite, M., & Puliga, M. (2018). Centralization of capital and financial crisis: a global network analysis. *Structural Change and Economic Dynamics*, *45*(C), 94–104. https://doi.org/10.1016/j.strueco.2018.03.001

Burris, V. (2005). Interlocking directorates and political cohesion among corporate elites. *American Journal of Sociology, 111*(1), 249–283. https://doi.org/10.1086/428817

Burt, R. S. (1978). A structural theory of interlocking corporate directorates. *Social Networks, 1*(4), 415–435. https://doi.org/10.1016/0378-8733(78)90006-0

Burt, R. S. (1983). *Corporate profits and cooptation: Networks of market constraints and directorate ties in the American economy*. Academic Press.

Burt, R. S. (1992). *Structural holes: The social structure of competition*. Harvard University Press.

Cai, Y., & Sevilir, M. (2012). Board connections and M&A transactions. *Journal of Financial Economics*, *103*(2), 327–349. https://doi.org/10.1016/j.jfineco.2011.05.017, Get rights and content.

Cambridge Dictionary. (n.d). Network. In Cambridge Dictionary. Retrieved February 15, 2023, from https://dictionary.cambridge.org/dictionary/english/network

Cardenas, J. (2012). Varieties of corporate networks: Network analysis and FsQCA. *International Journal of Comparative Sociology, 53*(4), 298–322. https://doi.org/10.1177/0020715212460257

Carroll, W. K. (2004). Corporate power in a globalizing world: A study in elite social organization. Oxford University Press.

Castells, M. (1996). The rise of the network society. Blackwell Publishers.

Certo, S. (2003). Influencing initial public offering investors with prestige: Signalling with board structures. *The Academy of Management Review, 28*(3), 432–446. https://doi.org/10.2307/30040731

Chapelle, A., & Szafarz, A. (2005). Controlling firms through the majority voting rule. *Physica a: Statistical Mechanics and Its Applications, 355*(2–4), 509–529. https://doi.org/10.1016/j.physa.2005.03.026

Chisholm, R. F. (1998). Developing network organizations: Learning from practice and theory. Addison Wesley Longman Inc.

Chisholm, R. F. (1996). On the meaning of networks. *Group & Organization Management, 21*(2), 216–235. https://doi.org/10.1177/1059601196212006

Choi, T. Y., & Wu, Z. (2009). Triads in supply networks: Theorizing buyer-supplier-supplier relationships. *Journal of Supply Chain Management, 45*(1), 8–25. https://doi.org/10.1111/j.1745-493X.2009.03151.x

Chu, J. S. G., & Davis, G. F. (2016). Who killed the inner circle? The decline of the American corporate interlock network. *American Journal of Sociology, 122*(3), 714–754. https://doi.org/10.1086/688650

Claessens, S., Djankov, S., & Lang, L. H. P. (2000). The separation of ownership and control in East Asian Corporations. *Journal of Financial Economics, 58*(1–2), 81–112. https://doi.org/10.1016/S0304-405X(00)00067-2

Coleman, J. (1990). *Foundations of Social Theory*. University of Chicago Press.

Compston, H. (2013). The network of global corporate control: Implications for public policy. *Business and Politics, 15*(3), 357–379. https://doi.org/10.1515/bap-2012-0049

Connelly, B. L., Certo, S. T., Ireland, R. D., & Reutzel, C. R. (2011). Signalling theory: A review and assessment. *Journal of Management, 37*(1), 39–67. https://doi.org/10.1177/0149206310388419

Dastkhan, H., & Gharneh, N. S. (2019). Simulation of contagion in the stock markets using cross-shareholding networks: A case from an emerging market. *Computational Economics, 53*(3), 1071–1101. https://doi.org/10.1007/s10614-017-9781-6

Davallou, M., Soltaninejad, M., & Tahmasebi, A. (2015). Analyzing the aspects of cross sharing ownership. Journal of Money and Economy, 10(1), 83–106. http://jme.mbri.ac.ir/article-1-189-en.html

Davis, G. F. (1991). Agents without principles? The Spread of the poison pill through the intercorporate network. *Administrative Science Quarterly, 36*(4), 583–613. https://doi.org/10.2307/2393275

Davis, G. F. (1996). The significance of board interlocks for corporate governance. *Corporate Governance, 4*(3), 154–159. https://doi.org/10.1111/j.1467-8683.1996.tb00144.x

Davis, G. F., & Cobb, J. (2010). Resource dependence theory: Past and future. *Research in the Sociology of Organizations, 28*(1), 21–42. https://doi.org/10.1108/S0733-558X(2010)0000028006

Davis, G. F., & Greve, H. R. (1997). Corporate elite networks and governance changes in the 1980s. *American Journal of Sociology, 103*(1), 1–37. https://doi.org/10.1086/231170

Davis, G. F., Yoo, M., & Baker, W. E. (2003). The small world of the american corporate elite, 1982–2001. *Strategic Organization, 1*(3), 301–326. https://doi.org/10.1177/14761270030013002

David, T., & Westerhuis, G. (Eds.). (2014). *The power of corporate networks: A comparative and historical perspective.* Routledge.

Dietzenbacher, E., Smid, B, & Volkerink, B. (2000). Horizontal integration in the Dutch financial sector. *International Journal of Industrial Organization, 18*(8), 1223–1242. https://doi.org/10.1016/S0167-7187(99)00015-6

Dietzenbacher, E., & Temurshoev, U. (2008). Ownership relations in the presence of cross-shareholding. *Journal of Economics, 95*(3), 189–212. https://doi.org/10.1007/s00712-008-0018-y

Dooley, P. C. (1969). The interlocking directorate. *American Economic Review, 59*(3), 314–332.

Dorofeenko, V., Lang, L. H. P., Ritzberger, K., & Shorish, J. (2007). Who controls Allianz? *Annals of Finance, 4*(1), 75–103. https://doi.org/10.1007/s10436-006-0069-4

Dritsas, M., Eigner, P., & Ottosson, J. (1996). "Big business" networks in three interwar economies: Austria. *Greece and Sweden. Financial History Review, 3*(2), 175–195. https://doi.org/10.1017/S0968565000000652

Edling, C., & Sandell, R. (2001). Social influence and corporate behaviour: A case study of interdependent decision-making Sweden's publicly traded firms. *European Sociological Review, 17*(4), 389–399. https://doi.org/10.1093/esr/17.4.389

Eisenhardt, K. M. (1989). Agency theory: An assessment and review. *Academy of Management Review, 14*(1), 57–74. https://doi.org/10.2307/258191

Elliott, M., Golub, B., & Jackson, M. O. (2014). Financial networks and contagion. *American Economic Review, 104*(10), 3115–3153. https://doi.org/10.1257/aer.104.10.3115

Erdos, P., & Renyi, A. (1959). *On Random Graphs. Publicationes Mathematicae Debrecen, 6*(1959), 290–297.

Fennema, M, & Schijf, H. (1978). Analysing interlocking directorates: Theory and methods. *Social Networks, 1*(4), 297–332. https://doi.org/10.1016/0378-8733(78)90002-3

Flath, D. (1992). Horizontal shareholding interlocks. *Managerial and Decision Economics, 13*(1), 75–77. https://doi.org/10.1002/mde.4090130109

Flath, D. (1993). Shareholding in the keiretsu, Japan's financial groups. *The Review of Economics and Statistics, 75*(2), 249–257. https://doi.org/10.2307/2109430

Fligstein, N. (1990). *The transformation of corporate control*. Harvard University Press.

Fligstein, N., & Brantley, P. (1992). Bank control, owner control, or organizational dynamics: Who controls the large modern corporation? *American Journal of Sociology, 98*(2), 280–307. https://doi.org/10.1086/230009

Franks, J., & Mayer, C. (1997). Corporate ownership and control in the U.K., Germany, and France. Journal of Applied Corporate Finance, 9(4), 30–45. https://doi.org/10.1111/j.1745-6622.1997.tb00622.x

Garcia-Bernardo, J., Fichtner, J., Takes, F. W., & Heemskerk, E. M. (2017). Uncovering offshore financial centers: Conduits and sinks in the global corporate ownership network. *Scientific Reports, 7*(1), 6246–6256. https://doi.org/10.1038/s41598-017-06322-9

Di Giacomo, M., & Cenci, M. (2018). Corporate control and ownership networks. *Corporate Ownership & Control, 15*(4), 86–95. https://doi.org/10.22495/cocv15i4art8

Gilo, D., Moshe, Y., & Spiegel, Y. (2006). Partial cross ownership and tacit collusion. *The RAND Journal of Economics, 37*(1), 81–99. https://doi.org/10.1111/j.1756-2171.2006.tb00005.x

Glattfelder, J. B., & Battiston, S. (2009). Backbone of complex networks of corporations: The flow of control. *Physical Review E, 80*(3), 036104. https://doi.org/10.1103/PhysRevE.80.036104

Green, M. P., & Semple, K. R. (1981). The corporate interlocking directorate as an urban spatial information network. *Urban Geography, 2*(2), 148–160. https://doi.org/10.2747/0272-3638.2.2.148

Gronum, S., Verreynne, M. L., & Kastelle, T. (2012). The role of networks in small and medium-sized enterprise innovation and firm performance. *Journal of Small Business Management, 50*(2), 257–282. https://doi.org/10.1111/j.1540-627X.2012.00353.x

Gulati, R., & Westphal, J. (1999). Cooperative or controlling? The Effects of CEO-board relations and the content of interlocks on the formation of joint ventures. *Administrative Science Quarterly, 44*(3), 473–506. https://doi.org/10.2307/2666959

Hall, P. A., & Soskice, D. W. (2001). *Varieties of capitalism: The institutional foundations of comparative advantage*. Oxford University Press.

Hallock, K. (1997). Reciprocally interlocking boards of directors and executive compensation. *The Journal of Financial and Quantitative Analysis, 32*(3), 331–344. https://doi.org/10.2307/2331203

Haniffa, R., & Hudaib, M. (2006). Corporate governance structure and performance of Malaysian listed companies. *Journal of Business Finance & Accounting, 33*(7–8), 1034–1062. https://doi.org/10.1111/j.1468-5957.2006.00594.x

Harris, I. C., & Shimizu, K. (2004). Too busy to serve? An examination of the influence of over boarded directors. *Journal of Management Studies, 41*(5), 775–798. https://doi.org/10.1111/j.1467-6486.2004.00453.x

Haunschild, P. R. (1993). Interorganizational imitation: The impact of interlocks on corporate acquisition activity. *Administrative Science Quarterly, 38*(4), 564–592. https://doi.org/10.2307/2393337

Haunschild, P. R., & Beckman, C. M. (1998). When do interlocks matter? Alternate sources of information and interlock influence. *Administrative Science Quarterly, 43*(4), 815–844. https://doi.org/10.2307/2393617

Heemskerk, E. M., & Takes, F. W. (2016). The corporate elite community structure of global capitalism. *New Political Economy, 21*(1), 90–118. https://doi.org/10.1080/13563467.2015.1041483

Hilferding, R. (1910). *Das Finanzkapital: Eine Studie über die jüngste Entwicklung des Kapitalismus*. Verlag der Wiener Volksbuchhandlung Ignaz Brand & Co.

Hillman, A. J., Zardkoohi, A., & Bierman, L. (1999). Corporate political strategies and firm performance: Indications of firm-specific benefits from personal service in the U.S. government. *Strategic Management Journal*, *20*(1), 67–81. https://doi.org/10.1002/(SICI)1097-0266(199901)20:1<67::AID-SMJ22>3.0.CO;2-T

Hillman, A. J., Withers, M. C., & Collins, B. J. (2009). Resource dependence theory: A review. *Journal of Management, 35*(6), 1404–1427. https://doi.org/10.1177/0149206309343434

Jarillo, J. C. (1993). *Strategic networks: Creating the borderless organization.* Butterworth-Heinemann.

Jeidels, O. (1905). *Das Verhältnis der deutschen Grossbanken zur Industrie mit besonderer Berücksichtigung der Eisenindustrie*. Duncker & Humblot.

Johnson, S., Schnatterly, K., Bolton, J. F., & Tuggle, C. (2011). Antecedents of new director social capital. *Journal of Management Studies, 48*(8), 1782–1803. https://doi.org/10.1111/j.1467-6486.2011.01020.x

Jurgens, U., Naumann, K., & Rupp, J. (2000). Shareholder value in an adverse environment: The German case. *Economy and Society, 29*(1), 54–79. https://doi.org/10.1080/030851400360569

Kang, E. (2008). Director interlocks and spillover effects of reputational penalties from financial reporting fraud. *Academy of Management Journal, 51*(3), 537–555. https://doi.org/10.5465/AMJ.2008.32626007

Karos, D., & Peters, H. (2015). Indirect control and power in mutual control structures. *Games and Economic Behavior*, *92*(C), 150–165. https://doi.org/10.1016/j.geb.2015.06.003

Koenig, T., & Gogel, R. (1981). Interlocking corporate directorships as a social network. *American Journal of Economics and Sociology, 40*(1), 37–50. https://doi.org/10.1111/j.1536-7150.1981.tb01370.x

Kogut, B. M., & Walker, G. (2001). The small world of Germany and the durability of national networks. *American Sociological Review, 66*(3), 317–335. https://doi.org/10.2307/3088882

Kotz, D. M. (1978). *Bank control of large corporations in the United States.* University of California Press.

Kramarz, F., & Thesmar, D. (2013). Social networks in the boardroom. *Journal of the European Economic Association, 11*(4), 780–807. https://doi.org/10.1111/jeea.12021

Kogut, B. M. (Ed.). (2012). *The small worlds of corporate governance.* The MIT Press.

La Porta, R., Lopez-De-Silanes, F., & Shleifer, A. (1999). Corporate ownership around the world. *The Journal of Finance, 54*(2), 471–517. https://doi.org/10.1111/0022-1082.00115

Laeven, L., & Levine, R. (2008). Complex ownership structures and corporate valuations. *Review of Financial Studies, 21*(2), 579–604. https://doi.org/10.1093/rfs/hhm068

Larcker, D. F., So, E. C., & Wang, C. C. (2013). Boardroom centrality and firm performance. *Journal of Accounting and Economics, 55*(2), 225–250. https://doi.org/10.1016/j.jacceco.2013.01.006

Lemma, T. T., & Nevash, M. (2016). Corporate ownership patterns in developing countries. *Corporate Ownership and Control*, *13*(2), 101–112. https://doi.org/10.22495/COCV13I2P11

Levy, M. (2009). Control in pyramidal structures. *Corporate Governance: An International Review, 17*(1), 77–89. https://doi.org/10.1111/j.1467-8683.2008.00719.x

Levy, M., & Szafarz, A. (2016). Cross-ownership: A device for management entrenchment? *Review of Finance, 21*(4), 1675–1699. https://doi.org/10.1093/rof/rfw009

Lichtenberg, F., & Pushner, G. M. (1994). Ownership structure and corporate performance in Japan. *Japan and the World Economy, 6*(3), 239–261. https://doi.org/10.1016/0922-1425(94)90014-0

Lincoln, J., Gerlach, M., & Takahashi, P. (1992). Keiretsu networks in the Japanese economy: A dyad analysis of intercorporate ties. *American Sociological Review, 57*(5), 561–585. https://doi.org/10.2307/2095913

Lingmin, X. (2016). Ultimate ownership structure and capital structure: Evidence from Chinese listed companies. *Corporate Ownership & Control, 13*(4–2), 297–306. https://doi.org/10.22495/cocv13i4c2p3

Lorsch, J. W., & MacIver, E. (1989). *Pawns or potentates: The reality of America's corporate boards*. Harvard Business School Press.

Mariolis, P., & Jones, M. H. (1982). Centrality in corporate interlock networks: Reliability and stability. *Administrative Science Quarterly, 27*(4), 571–585. https://doi.org/10.2307/2392531

Martin, G., Gozubuyuk, R., & Becerra, M. (2015). Interlocks and firm performance: The role of uncertainty in the directorate interlock-performance relationship. *Strategic Management Journal, 36*(2), 235–253. https://doi.org/10.1002/smj.2216

Martins, P., & Neves, E. (2017). Corporates' control strategies using network optimization. *International Transactions in Operational Research, 24*(5), 1041–1059. https://doi.org/10.1111/itor.12288

Milgram, S. (1967). *The Small World Problem. Psychology Today, 2*(1), 60–67.

Mizruchi, M. S. (1982). *The American corporate network: 1904–1974*. Sage Publications.

Mizruchi, M. S. (1996). What do interlocks do? An analysis, critique, and assessment of research on interlocking directorates. *Annual Review of Sociology, 22*(1), 271–298. https://doi.org/10.1146/annurev.soc.22.1.271

Mizruchi, M. S., & Stearns, L. (1988). A longitudinal study of the formation of interlocking Directorates. *Administrative Science Quarterly, 33*(2), 194–210. https://doi.org/10.2307/2393055

Moore, C. B., Bell, R. G., Filatochev, I., & Rasheed, A. A. (2012). Foreign IPO Capital market choice: Understanding the institutional fit of corporate governance. *Strategic Management Journal, 33*(8), 914–937. https://doi.org/10.1002/smj.1953

Morck, R., Nakamura, M., & Shivdasani, A. (2000). Banks, ownership structure, and firm value in Japan. *The Journal of Business, 73*(4), 539–567. https://doi.org/10.1086/209654

Napoli, F. (2018). Corporate governance and firm networks: An empirical research based on Italy. *Corporate Ownership & Control, 15*(2–1), 231–247. https://doi.org/10.22495/cocv15i2c1p9

Newman, M. E. J., Strogatz, S. H., & Watts, D. J. (2001). Random graphs with arbitrary degree distributions and their applications. *Physical Review E, 64*(2), 1–17. https://doi.org/10.1103/PhysRevE.64.026118

O'Brien, D., & Salop, S. (2000). Competitive effects of partial ownership: Financial interest and corporate control. *Antitrust Law Journal, 67*(3), 559–614.

Ong, C., Wan, D., & Ong, K. (2003). An exploratory study on interlocking directorates in listed firms in Singapore. *Corporate Governance: An International Review, 11*(4), 322–334. https://doi.org/10.1111/1467-8683.00330

Ornstein, M. (1984). Interlocking directorates in Canada: Intercorporate or class alliance? *Administrative Science Quarterly, 29*(2), 210–231. https://doi.org/10.2307/2393174

Paligorova, T., & Xu, Z. (2012). Complex ownership and capital structure. *Journal of Corporate Finance, 18*(4), 701–716. https://doi.org/10.1016/j.jcorpfin.2012.05.001

Palmer, D. (1983). Interpreting corporate interlocks from broken ties. *Social Science History, 7*(2), 217–231. https://doi.org/10.2307/1170841

Palmer, D., Jennings, P. D., & Zhou, X. (1993). Late adoption of the multidivisional form by large US corporations: Institutional, political, and economic accounts. *Administrative Science Quarterly, 38*(1), 100–131. https://doi.org/10.2307/2393256

Pastra, A. S., Koufopoulos, D. N., & Gkliatis, I. P. (2015). Board characteristics and the presence of women on the board of directors: The case of the Greek shipping sector. In M. Kitada, E. Williams, & L. Froholdt (Eds.), *WMU studies in maritime affairs (Vol. 3). Maritime women: Global leadership* (pp. 35–54). Springer.

Pennings, J. M. (1980). *Interlocking directorates*. Jossey-Bass.

Pfeffer, J., & Salancik, G. R. (1978). *The external control of organizations: A resource dependence perspective*. Harper and Row.

Pfeffer, J. (1972). Size and composition of corporate boards of directors: The organization and its environment. *Administrative Science Quarterly, 17*(2), 218–228. https://doi.org/10.2307/2393956

Piccardi, C., Calatroni, L., & Bertoni, F. (2010). Communities in Italian corporate networks. *Physica a: Statistical Mechanics and Its Applications, 389*(22), 5247–5258. https://doi.org/10.1016/j.physa.2010.06.038

Reitman, D. (1994). Partial ownership arrangements and the potential for collusion. *The Journal of Industrial Economics, 42*(3), 313–322. https://doi.org/10.2307/2950573

Richardson, G., Wang, B., & Zhang, X. (2016). Ownership structure and corporate tax avoidance: Evidence from publicly listed private firms in China. *Journal of Contemporary Accounting & Economics, 12*(2), 141–158. https://doi.org/10.1016/j.jcae.2016.06.003

Robins, G., & Alexander, M. (2004). Small worlds among interlocking directors: Network structure and distance in bipartite graphs. *Computational &*

Mathematical Organization Theory, 10(1), 69–94. https://doi.org/10.1023/B:CMOT.0000032580.12184.c0

Romei, A., Ruggieri, S., & Turini, F. (2015, October 19–21). The layered structure of company share networks [Paper presentation]. IEEE International Conference on Data Science and Advanced Analytics (DSAA), Paris, France. https://doi.org/10.1109/DSAA.2015.7344809

Rousseau, P., & Stroup, C. (2015). Director histories and the pattern of acquisitions. *The Journal of Financial and Quantitative Analysis, 50*(4), 671–698. https://doi.org/10.1017/S0022109015000289

Rungi, A., Morrison, G., & Pammolli, F. (2017). *Global ownership and corporate control networks*. IMT Lucca EIC Working Paper Series 07/2017. http://eprints.imtlucca.it/id/eprint/3767

Salinger, L. M. (Ed.). (2005). Encyclopedia of white-collar and corporate crime. Sage Publications.

Scott, J. (1997). *Corporations, Classes and Capitalism* (3rd ed.). Oxford University Press.

Scott, J. (1991). Networks of corporate power: A comparative assessment. *Annual Review of Sociology, 17*(1), 181–203. https://doi.org/10.1146/annurev.so.17.080191.001145

Shrader, C., Hoffman, A., & Stearns, T. (1991). Agency directors and network centrality: An examination of resource dependencies. *Journal of Managerial Issues, 3*(1), 46–61.

Shropshire, C. (2010). The role of the interlocking director and board receptivity in the diffusion of practices. *Academy of Management Review, 35*(2), 246–264. https://doi.org/10.5465/amr.35.2.zok246

Simoni, M., & Caiazza, R. (2012). Interlocks network structure as driving force of competition among Italian firms. *Corporate Governance, 12*(3), 319–336. https://doi.org/10.1108/14720701211234582

Staples, C. L. (2007). Board globalization in the world's largest TNCs 1993–2005. *Corporate Governance: An International Review, 15*(2), 311–321. https://doi.org/10.1111/j.1467-8683.2007.00573.x

Stearns, L. B., & Mizruchi, M. S. (1986). Broken-tie reconstitution and the functions of interorganizational interlocks: A reexamination. *Administrative Science Quarterly, 31*(4), 522–538. https://doi.org/10.2307/2392962

Stearns, L., & Mizruchi, M. (1993). Board composition and corporate financing: The impact of financial institution representation on borrowing. *The Academy of Management Journal, 36*(3), 603–618. https://doi.org/10.5465/256594

Stokman, F. N., Ziegler, R., & Scott, J. (Eds.). (1985). *Networks of corporate power: A comparative analysis of ten countries*. Polity Press.

Takes, F. W., & Heemskerk, E. M. (2016). Centrality in the global network of corporate control. *Social Network Analysis and Mining, 6*(1), 1–18. https://doi.org/10.1007/s13278-016-0402-5

Tuschke, A., Sanders, W., & Hernandez, E. (2014). Whose experience matters in the boardroom? The effects of experiential and vicarious learning on emerging market entry. *Strategic Management Journal, 35*(3), 398–418. https://doi.org/10.1002/smj.2100

Useem, M. (1982). Classwide rationality in the politics of managers and directors of large corporations in the United States and Great Britain. *Administrative Science Quarterly, 27*(2), 199–226. https://doi.org/10.2307/2392300

Useem, M., (1984). *The inner circle: Large corporations and the rise of business political activity in the U.S. and U.K.* Oxford University Press.

Useem, M., (1996). *Investor capitalism: How money managers are changing the face of corporate America*. Basic Books.

van Veen, K., & Kratzer, J. (2011). National and international interlocking directorates within Europe: Corporate networks within and among fifteen European countries. *Economy and Society, 40*(1), 1–25. https://doi.org/10.1080/03085147.2011.529376

Vitali, S., & Battiston, S. (2014). The community structure of the global corporate network. *PLoS ONE, 9*(8), e104655. https://doi.org/10.1371/journal.pone.0104655

Vitali, S., Glattfelder, J. B., & Battiston, S. (2011). The network of global corporate control. *PLoS ONE, 6*(10), e25995. https://doi.org/10.1371/journal.pone.0025995

Wardrip-Fruin, N., & Montfort, N. (Eds.). (2003). *New media reader*. MIT Press.

Wang, P., Sharpe, K., Robins, G. L., & Pattison, P. E. (2009). Exponential random graph (p*) models for affiliation networks. *Social Networks, 31*(1), 12–25. https://doi.org/10.1016/j.socnet.2008.08.002

Watts, D. J., & Strogatz, S. H. (1998). Collective dynamics of "small-world" networks. *Nature, 393*(6684), 440–442. https://doi.org/10.1038/30918

Westphal, J. D., & Stern, I. (2006). The other pathway to the boardroom: Interpersonal influence behavior as a substitute for elite credentials and majority status in obtaining board appointments. *Administrative Science Quarterly, 51*(2), 169–204. https://doi.org/10.2189/asqu.51.2.169

White, H. C. (1970). Search parameters for the small world problem. *Social Forces, 49*(2), 259–264. https://doi.org/10.1093/sf/49.2.259

Wilhite, A. (2001). Bilateral trade and "small-world" networks. *Computational Economics, 18*(1), 49–64. https://doi.org/10.1023/A:1013814511151

Windolf, P., & Beyer, J. (1996). Co-operative capitalism: Corporate networks in Germany and Britain. *The British Journal of Sociology, 47*(2), 205–231. https://doi.org/10.2307/591724

Wolfenzon, D. (1999). A theory of pyramidal ownership. [Unpublished manuscript]. http://citeseerx.ist.psu.edu/viewdoc/download?doi=10.1.1.198.3874&rep=rep1&type=pdf

Yafeh, Y., & Yosha, O. (2003). Large shareholder and banks: Who monitors and how? *The Economic Journal, 113*(484), 128–146. https://doi.org/10.1111/1468-0297.00087

Yue, L. Q. (2012). Asymmetric effects of fashions on the formation and dissolution of networks: Board interlocks with internet companies, 1996–2006. *Organization Science, 23*(4), 1114–1134. https://doi.org/10.1287/orsc.1110.0683

Zajac, E. (1988). Interlocking directorates as an interorganizational strategy: A test of critical assumptions. *The Academy of Management Journal, 31*(2), 428–438. https://doi.org/10.5465/256558

Zeitlin, M. (1974). Corporate ownership and control: The large corporation and the capitalist class. *American Journal of Sociology, 79*(5), 1073–1119. https://doi.org/10.1086/225672

CHAPTER 5

Connected Corporate Networks I: Definitions, Metrics and Empirical Results from the Greek Telecommunications Sector

Michalis Vafopoulos, Charalampos Agiropoulos, Artemis Gourgioti, and Michalis Klonaras

5.1 Introduction

In recent decades, it has been substantiated that enterprises are not independent units of the economy. Each company belongs to a network with which it interacts and which, at the same time, influences its efficiency and

M. Vafopoulos
Institute of Informatics & Telecommunications, National Center for Scientific Research "Demokritos", Athens, Greece

C. Agiropoulos (✉)
Department of International and European Studies, University of Piraeus, Piraeus, Greece
e-mail: hagyropoylos@unipi.gr

A. Gourgioti
Linked Business PLC, Athens, Greece
e-mail: a.gourgioti@lbsuite.eu

P. E. Petrakis (ed.), *Interconnections in the Greek Economy*, The Political Economy of Greek Growth up to 2030,
https://doi.org/10.1007/978-3-031-31335-6_5

strategy. Key elements of these networks are the interconnections between executives and companies. Directors holding positions on the boards of more than one company, become a bridge and a channel of information between the strong players in each market, essentially shaping both the formal and the social ties that exist between companies. Executives define the long-term strategy of each company, which has a significant impact on its financial performance and, collectively, on the economy of a country.

Mathematical metrics and techniques in market analysis are introduced using network theory. The importance of a node (person or company) is measurable, and it is evaluated based on its narrow or wider network. In connected networks, centrality is considered a key indicator of the position of power held by a node in the network. Since strong companies are usually the largest and strongest players in an economy, a comparison of centrality with an economic performance index (e.g. node turnover) could possibly provide evidence in order to identify strong players in an economy as a whole or in a particular business sector.

Over the last few years, the analysis of business interconnections (formed through the identification of common executives between enterprises) has accelerated and has been enriched, as most commercial registers provide open data on information management for the sum total of all enterprises. Interconnection, in addition to facilitating the dissemination of information and best practices between companies, may also accelerate the spread of problems and lead to a widespread crisis throughout an economy or a part of the market. Modelling of the financial system as a connected network helps to separate clusters of companies with continuous cooperation and common practices. In the light of corporate groups, the additional analysis of companies further identifies clusters in the market and strengthens the interpretive power of the interconnections between them. Corporate groups are a solid corporate network with common business policies and resources. Although the individual subsidiaries are independent of each other, their basic principles, such as investment policies and cooperation with companies outside the group,

M. Vafopoulos · M. Klonaras
OTE Group, Athens, Greece
e-mail: mklonaras@ote.gr

appear identical. Therefore, for the interpretation of the connections between nodes (companies of a business network), an individual analysis of the internal processes and collaborations of a corporate group does not offer significant business insights. The association of the individual subsidiaries in one node, on the other hand, allows for the most accurate analysis of the network, as the group's position in the market is investigated and evaluated.

In this study, the research becomes more targeted, aiming to contribute to the literature on how to identify corporate relations (business networks), through the corporate capital and board network analysis for the telecommunications sector in Greece, including a method of evaluation of the corporate relations therein.

The structure of the chapter is the following: Sect. 5.2 presents the most relevant studies in corporate networking and board interlocks. Then (Sect. 5.3) analyses the data and the methodology used to identify business networks through the corporate capital and board network analysis. The next Sect. 5.4 presents the empirical results for the telecommunications sector in Greece. Finally, Sect. 5.5 discusses the policy implications of the present analysis.

5.2 Literature Review

As has been mentioned, the main function of networks is to focus on the process of interaction in the service of exchanging information and developing contacts. A network can be defined as a set of autonomous organizations that come together to achieve goals which none of them can achieve separately. According to the literature, the network offers a competitive advantage due to the organizational power that characterizes it and is a decentralized organization while ensuring interdependent relations between the parties. In most of the research on boards and corporate interlocks, the network consists of a type of node, the companies, which are linked by a type of connection, those directors who sit on two or more boards (Andrikopoulos et al., 2019; Davis, 1991; Galavotti, 2020; Hernández-Lara et al., 2019). Furthermore, the network can be analysed as a graph of the connections between directors and companies, where, each time, the director is a board member of the specific company.

Corporate networks are formed if we define companies as the nodes and, as a link between two companies, the existence of at least one common board member. Respectively, we can capture these relations from the point of view of the member of the board. In this case, we define as nodes the board members and as a link between two persons, the existence of at least one company, where both members have served on its board. The biography of corporate networks focuses on two forms. One concerns board interlocks and the second ownership interlocks.

Board interlocks appear when a board member (director) of a company is also on one or more boards (Mizruchi, 1996; Pennings, 1980). Therefore, two boards share at least one common member, with the board interlocking network being the total of company boards together with all the interconnections that exist between them (Mizruchi, 1996). Board interlocks are considered beneficial as interconnected members transfer their experiences to other companies by providing valuable information. They also help networked businesses overcome resource dependency by developing a set of strategies (Drobnik, 2012; Hillman et al., 2009; Shrader et al., 1991; Simoni & Caiazza, 2012; Van Veen & Kratzer, 2011) and have real consequences in terms of influencing the performance and behaviour of affiliated companies.

With respect to the second form of corporate networks, those are the connection between the enterprises that assume the form of ownership interlocks or ownership networks. Here, in the simplest composition, two companies are connected if one owns a certain percentage of the other. Ownership networks are very interesting to study, for a variety of reasons. Ownership networks have been used to measure the impact of globalization or institutional interventions, and they are related to issues of corporate social responsibility and sustainability (Wheeler et al., 2003). More complex ownership patterns are cross-shareholdings. These occur when corporations own shares in each other. Generally, cross-shareholdings are sub-networks where companies own each other directly or indirectly, through chains of ownership relations.

Wang et al. (2021) indicate that direct connections, indirect connections and the number of connections (total connections) related to interlocking directorates have significant positive influences on the dynamic corporate performance of companies. The results of their study suggest that more interlocks at board level lead to better corporate performance over a long-term period.

Board interlocks consist in interconnections of organizational objectives and choices. Interlocking directorates describe strategic interdependence between companies in all major capitalist economies

(Andrikopoulos et al., 2019). Furthermore, they affect corporate strategic choices such as alliances, the design of executive compensation, mergers and acquisitions and initial public offerings; there has also been a documented effect of interlocking directorates on auditor choice and accounting practices (Andrikopoulos et al., 2019; Sapinski et al., 2018).

Interlocks may be due to the desire of major players to be part of the capital asset allocation process. This motive can be associated with processes which reinforce cohesion in an upper social class populated by, among other individuals, members of a corporate elite who act as directors of major corporations (Andrikopoulos et al., 2019; Sapinski et al., 2018).

Andrikopoulos et al. (2019) found that interlocking corporate leadership can help resolve agency conflicts, thus reducing agency costs. The extent of leadership overlaps is associated with board size, financial leverage and profitability. There is a bidirectional relationship between profits and interlocks, as interlocking directorates bear a positive effect on asset returns.

Interlocking directorates are regarded as an indicator of social embeddedness, which creates the conditions for exercising a social influence on corporate decisions (Galavotti, 2020). Indeed, firms are likely to imitate the decisions of other firms to which they are connected by social network ties.

The directorial boards of large companies often have a certain number of shared directors, which can be motivated by social structures that foster different types of links, including investments and vertical relationships (Hernández-Lara et al., 2019). Hernández-Lara et al. suggested that the typology of interlocks determined their effects on innovation, which were positive when independent and extra-industry directors held multiple directorships, whereas it was negative in the case of intra-industry interlocking directors. Their study provided evidence for the diverse effects of interlocking directorates and supported that an optimal board composition can improve business innovation, given the common feature of shared directorships (Hernández-Lara et al., 2019).

Caiazza et al., 2019, examine the effect that interlocks have on wealth creation and distribution, and those interlocks can tell us how elites network within a society. Their theoretical perspectives about the research on interlocking directorates are based on the premise that the Anglo-American perspective dominates. Most international studies use agency theory to investigate the welfare implications of interlocks, but many countries do not use the Anglo-American legal regime, which is the basis for agency theory (Caiazza et al, 2019). Moreover, they argue that those institutions have an important influence on interlocks, so that the latter can be welfare-depleting in one institutional setting, while welfare-enhancing in another (Caiazza et al., 2019).

An interlocking directorate occurs when a director sits on the boards of multiple corporations (Zhong et al., 2017). Through an interlocking directorate, firms are widely connected, which potentially serves as a conduit for spreading behaviours across firms. Zhong et al. (2017) investigate whether monitoring caused by regulatory sanctions spreads through interlocking corporate boards. By contrast to other literature, their study illuminates the positive spillover of corporate governance via board interlocks.

Debellis et al. (2020) hypothesize and test the assumption that the board of directors has an important effect on the willingness to engage in international Joint Ventures (JV). Specifically, they found that board interlock ties to other firms increase the likelihood of SMEs to engage in international rather than domestic JVs. Moreover, they found that the positive effect of board interlocks on the formation of international JVs is amplified when there is high ownership concentration.

5.3 Methodology and Data

This research is designed to focus on the ability of corporate interconnection analysis to record the complexity and composition of interconnection networks using population data from the Greek ecosystem. With respect to the methodology, one should first consider the following definitions.

5.3.1 Definitions

The board of directors (or simply the board) is a group of people who jointly supervise the activities of the company. In the case of capital companies, the board is elected by the shareholders. Commonly, smaller entities are directed by one or two managing partners who own the company themselves. This core element of control and supervision of a company can be depicted as a network of connected entities. Practically, a subset of companies is interconnected through common members of the board or shareholders. In research, interconnected companies are captured through two types of networks: the board and the ownership or capital network.

In the board network, also referred to as network of interlocking directorates or board interlock networks, a node represents a company and an edge (link) between two companies denotes that these companies share at least one board member.

In a capital or ownership network, a node represents a company or a natural person and an edge (link) between two nodes denotes that there is an ownership relation.

A corporate group is a collection of parent and subsidiary companies that operate as a single entity, through a common source of control. A parent-to-subsidiary relationship exists when a company (parent):

a. has the majority of the capital or voting rights of another (subsidiary) company,
b. controls the majority of the voting rights of another (subsidiary) company by agreement with other partners or shareholders of this company.

The composition of the corporate groups can be found on the annual balance sheets. Corporate groups operate as a single entity, and they should be considered as such in any corporate network analysis.

In order to proceed with the analysis of the corporate network, it should be considered that the importance of a node depends on the relationships formed with the other nodes of the network and does not hang solely on its attributes. Two additional metrics of analysing the network dynamics are the betweenness centrality and the Eigenvector centrality (Eigen Centrality).

In an undirected graph G, two nodes u and v are called connected if G contains a path from u to v. In graph theory, betweenness centrality is a measure of centrality in a graph based on shortest paths. The shortest path is calculated by the number of edges that the path passes through (for unweighted graphs) or the sum of the weights of the edges (for weighted graphs) is when minimized. The betweenness centrality measures the extent to which a node lies on paths between other nodes. Nodes with a high betweenness may have considerable influence within a network by virtue of their control over information passing between others. Upon their removal from the network, most communications between nodes will be disrupted and the network could potentially separate into isolated subgraphs.

Betweenness centrality in board and ownership networks demonstrates the degree to which directors and shareholders stand between each other. As a result, directors and shareholders with higher betweenness centrality would have more control over the network, as more information will be available to them.

Eigenvector measures the magnitude of the connected entities and how much direct influence it might have over other connected entities in the network. In particular, the eigenvector scores are also considered for each connected entity. For example, a person with a high eigenvector score is likely to be at the centre of a cluster of key entities who themselves have high eigenvector scores. This metric uncovers nodes whose influence extends beyond their direct connections within the larger network.

Eigenvector measures how connected an entity is and how much direct influence it might have over other connected entities in the network.

Eigenvector in board and ownership networks demonstrates the importance of a director or a shareholder within the network by evaluating the "quality" of their direct and indirect connections, where quality is related to the number of connections which the other actors of the network have.

Eigenvector vs Betweenness centrality: Betweenness centrality evaluates each node based on their position in the network. Eigenvector evaluates each node based on their connections. A node with a high betweenness centrality has access to a large volume of information while a node with a high eigenvector has access to more important information, due to its connections (Table 5.1).

The diameter indicates the size of the network and sets the context for how close the nodes in the network are on average. The importance of diameter lies in the information of how quickly something will spread through the network, in accordance with how integrated different components in the network are likely to be.

5.3.2 *Data*

For the analysis of the sectors, we focused on corporate groups. The annual consolidated financial statements are the source of information for the subsidiary companies of each corporate group. The companies that compose each corporate group are unified in a single node. The nodes that describe those individuals with management or ownership relationships exclusively within the companies of each group, are also unified in the node which represents the corporate group.

Table 5.1 Definitions of descriptive metrics

Metric	*Definition*
Nodes	Number of entities (companies/persons) that appear on the corporate network
Edges	Number of relations between the entities
Diameter	The diameter of a graph is the maximum eccentricity of any node in it. That is, it is the greatest distance between any pair of nodes. In order to calculate the diameter of a graph, we have to find the shortest path between each pair of nodes. The greatest length of any of these paths is the diameter of the graph
Radius	The maximum distance between a node to all other nodes is considered its eccentricity. The radius of a graph is the minimum graph eccentricity of any graph node in a graph. The minimum eccentricity from all the nodes is considered as the radius of the Graph G. The minimum among all the maximum distances between a node to all other nodes is considered the radius of Graph G
Average path length	The minimum number of steps or smallest possible sum of edge weights from one node to another, indicates the shortest path between those nodes. The average path length is the average of the shortest path length, averaged over all pairs of nodes. If two nodes are disconnected (there is no path between them) then the path length between them is infinite. Consequently, if a network contains disconnected components, then the avg. path length also diverges to infinity, unless it is calculated only from nodes in the largest connected component. The avg. path length is a measure of the efficiency of information or mass transport on a network
Average Degree	Average degree is the average number of edges per node in the graph. This metric indicates how well-connected the nodes in the graph are (in which case the average degree is high), or whether the typical node in the graph only has a small number of neighbors (in which case the average degree is low). In a directed graph, we could compute either the average indegree (when the node is the target) or the average outdegree (when the node is the source) of each node

Source Author's creation

The analysis is carried out in a three-level board and capital/ownership network and focuses on the relations among the corporate groups within the sector and the links with other industries.

The size of each node was depicted using the Eigenvector centrality (Eigen Centrality) metric. The links that represent ownership relationships have a label that indicates the percentage of ownership. The open-source tool Gephi supported filtering, clustering, navigation and manipulation of network data used in various disciplines, e.g. social network analysis, biology, genomics and several more (Bastian et al., 2009).

5.4 Empirical Results

5.4.1 *Descriptive Statistics*

By the end of May 2021, a total of 384,310 companies (excluding sole proprietorship enterprises) have been registered on the General Electronic Commercial Registry[1] (GECR), 70% of which (270,928) is still active in the Greek Tax Registry. The companies registered on the GECR are currently run by 165,349 managers and they belong to 131,751 owners.

There are 1,254 parent companies to 1,557 subsidiaries. (Again, a subsidiary is a business whose parent company holds a majority stake of at least 50% of all shares).

5.4.2 *Telcos in Greece*

The telecommunications sector (Telcos) was selected for the analysis due to its prominent role in the Greek economy and its highly concentrated corporate network. The contribution of the sector to the Gross Domestic Product (GDP) of Greece for 2019, ranged at 2.7%, marking an increase compared to 2018. The turnover of telecommunications companies in 2019 amounted to 5 billion euro, recording an increase of 2.4% compared to the fiscal year of 2018, according to the review of the sector published by the National Post and Telecommunications Commission[2] (EETT).

Based on the NACE classification,[3] the telecommunication sector consists in total of 1,055 companies[4] with their main business activity

[1] http://www.businessportal.gr/home/index_en.

[2] https://www.eett.gr/opencms/opencms/admin/News_new/news_1369.html.

[3] Regulation (EC) No 1893/2006 of the European Parliament and of the Council of 20 December 2006 establishing the statistical classification of economic activities NACE Revision 2 and amending Council Regulation (EEC) No 3037/90 as well as certain EC Regulations on specific statistical domains. OJ L 393, 30.12.2006, p. 1–39. EurLex.

[4] Active enterprises in the Greek Tax Register as of 31.05.2021.

Table 5.2 Telecommunication Sector Revenue for the fiscal year 2019

Group	*Revenue (in mm €)*	*% of industry revenue*
OTE	3,300	59
Vodafone	957	17
Wind	532	10
Forthnet	260	5

Source Linked Business Registry statistical business register of Greece (LBR)

in the section J (Media & Information Technology) and more specifically in division "61", Telecommunications.

The J sector is already highly concentrated in a small number of strong players who also show a tendency to cooperate in sharing the cost of providing the service. In Greece, there are four telecommunications and broadband service providers operating, consisting of four different corporate groups with a number of subsidiaries covering various sectors of the industry. These corporate groups are: OTE Group, WIND Group, VODAFONE Group and FORTHNET Group.

The total industry revenue for the fiscal year 2019 is €8.6 billion and OTE Group has the largest share (43%), i.e. €3.3 bn. The Vodafone Group follows with 12% of the industry revenue (€957 m, the Wind Group with 7% (€532 m) and finally the Forthnet Group holds 3% of the industry revenue (€260 m) (Table 5.2).

5.4.3 *Statistics for Corporate Groups*

The construction of the corporate network focuses on the connections among the telco groups and the connections with companies outside of the industry. The network consists of 34 nodes (companies and individuals) with 53 edges. The edges represent the connections between the nodes, which can be ownership or management relations. The diameter of the network is 5 nodes, meaning that the flow of the information must pass through 5 nodes to connect the two furthest parts of the network. On average, a node is connected with three nodes (3.12). The network metrics are presented on the Table 5.3.

The nodes which represent the corporate groups are a union of the subsidiary companies and board members who are only involved with the companies within the group. In particular, the node for the OTE

Table 5.3 Network metrics for the Telecommunication Sector

Network metrics	*LBR Undirected*
nodes	34
edges	53
diameter	5
avg. Degree	3.12

Source Authors' calculations

Table 5.4 Board members' network for the Telecommunication Sector

	Subsidiary companies	*Board members*
OTE	27	14
Vodafone	14	5
Wind	7	3
Forthnet	25	8

Source Authors' calculations

Group consists of 27 companies and 14 board members, marking its broad business activity (Table 5.4).

The corporate groups are interconnected through common companies or common board members and their relations are depicted in the Fig. 5.1. Vodafone and Wind have set up a joint venture company (Victus Networks) to maintain their antennas. In essence, they are utilizing the economies of scale of a common business unit. Respectively, the three main providers (OTE, WIND, VODAFONE) have established a joint company (TELEGNOUS) to register and avoid common low-paying subscribers. Victus Networks for the fiscal year 2019 had a revenue of approximately €59 m, while TELEGNOUS reaches €0.24 m.

The FORTHNET group is connected to the VODAFONE group (specifically with the company HELLAS ON LINE) through the joint member on their board of directors, K.D.[5] K.D. has extensive business activity, as he participates in the management of numerous companies, such as the INTRACOM group (IT Services), the ELLAKTOR group (Construction) and Proton Bank. The FORTHNET group is directly connected with the banking sector, as the large banking groups hold

[5] The full names of natural persons have been replaced by their initial letters.

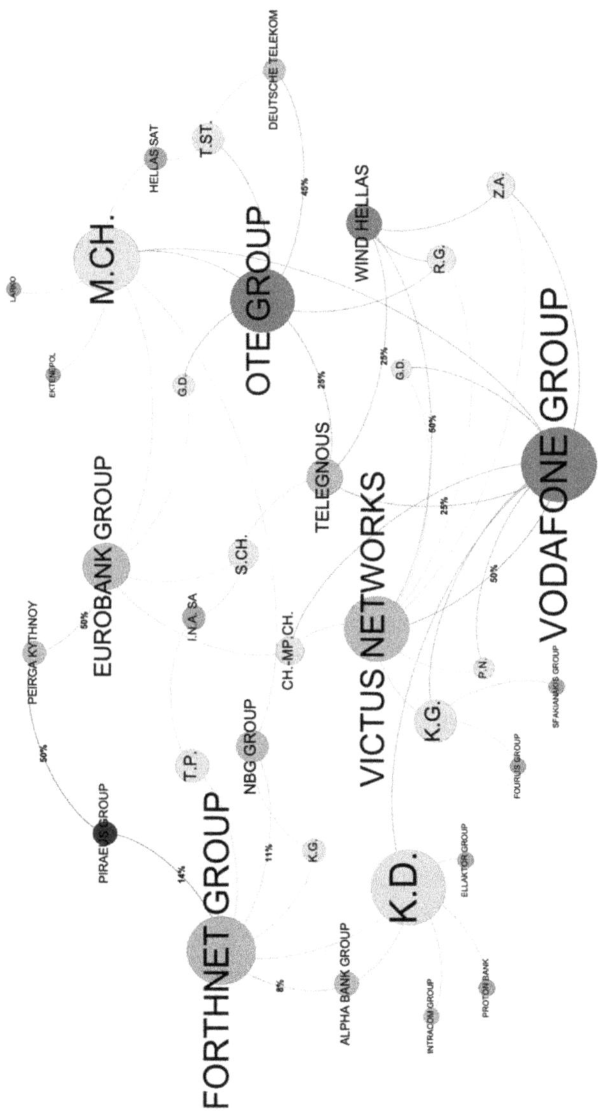

Fig. 5.1 Board members' network for the Telecommunication Sector (*Source* Authors' calculations)

ownership percentages (Alpha Bank-8%, Piraeus Bank-14% and National Bank-11%). The strong presence of banks indicates the existence of financial problems in the group. FORTHNET was left to the banks following the exercise of the option to convert their securities into equities or into equity coupled with stock-options. Almost 33% of their shares passed to the banks which thus assumed control of the group. The forced entry of large banking groups in the network leads to the creation of links between the telecommunications groups and the Greek economy. However, this does not provide useful information on the telecommunications network and its impact on the economy. Therefore, nodes (companies and individuals) that originate from banking groups but are not directly linked to nodes from telecommunications groups, are eliminated from our analysis.

The OTE and VODAFONE groups are also connected through the joint management member named M.CH. M.CH. served as Vice President of the VODAFONE group and General Manager of Financial Affairs for the OTE group, and he has participated in the management of companies of the National Bank, EUROBANK and construction companies (EKTENEPOL, LARCO). Deutsche Telekom owns 45% of the OTE group. The former manager of Deutsche Telekom, T.ST., also participates in the management of companies of the OTE group (COSMOTE—Board Member and OTEPLUS—President & CEO).

The individuals in the telecommunication sector present considerable business activity beyond the sector, thus introducing construction companies and IT companies to the telecommunications corporate network. K.G., for example, has participated in the board of large commercial groups, such as Fourlis and Sfakianakis, and he has served as President of Victus Networks and Board Member for Vodafone.

Further analysis of the network suggests the investigation of the betweenness centrality of the nodes. The ten most important nodes of the telecommunications network are presented on the Table 5.5.

The top nodes of the network act as gatekeepers to the information flow from one part of the network to another. M.CH. and K.D. are the two most highly connected individuals on the network, meaning that they have expanded their business to numerous companies in the industry. Vodafone is the most influential node not only because it is the one with the most links (highest Degree), but it also acts as a bridge between two important clusters, the Forthnet and OTE cluster (Fig. 5.2).

Table 5.5 Order of importance based on the betweenness centrality for the Telecommunication Sector

Order of importance	*Name*
1	VODAFONE GROUP
2	M.CH
3	K.D
4	OTE GROUP
5	FORTHNET GROUP
6	K.G
7	EUROBANK GROUP
8	TELEGNOUS
9	VICTUS NETWORKS
10	S.CH

Source Authors' calculations

Three of the providers rank high, while the Wind Group influences the network to a smaller degree. Vodafone, Forthnet and OTE are interconnected through companies and common individuals, which leads to extending their joint ventures (Victus, Telegnous). Wind, on the other hand, appears to be linked only to nodes related to Victus and Telegnous.

5.5 Discussion

A company's performance is not based solely on its own strategic choices, but is also influenced by its direct or indirect interconnections within its corporate network. Corporate networks represent the environment in which each enterprise applies the mode of interaction within the network. The interpretation of corporate networks based on the existence of corporate groups allows for a more accurate picture of the economy. The individual subsidiaries share management members, know-how, values and strategies. Therefore, the subsidiaries of a group should be considered as business units that jointly and co-ordinately draw up the policy of cooperation both inside and outside the group. The collaboration between the companies of a group is considered a given and the analysis of the relations between them hardly provides additional information for the analysis of a market.

Treating a group of individual subsidiaries as a single entity helps to better identify, visualize and analyse the network. Collaborations with companies outside the group become more visible and the identification of potential problematic areas of the network also become easier to

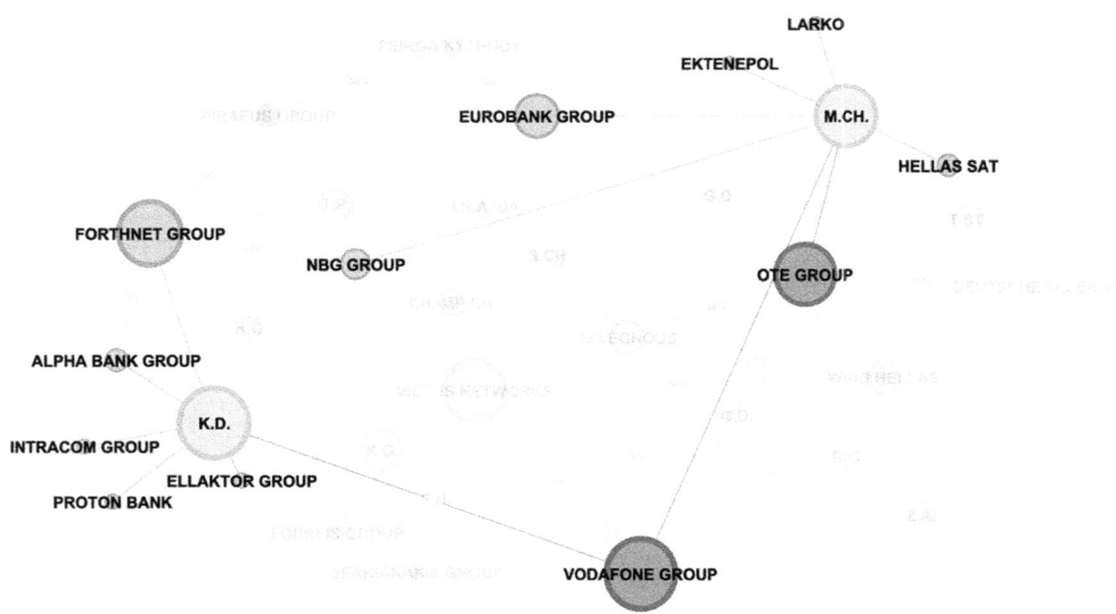

Fig. 5.2 Top ranked nodes of the network for the Telecommunication Sector (*Source* Authors' calculations)

explore. Groups represent the most important players in each market and how they interact with one another. A compact network reveals the existence of extensive connections and partnerships in the market. In addition to the strong flow of information in a network, high connectivity can also indicate problems, especially when banking organizations have entered the network.

Moreover, connections among individuals and companies do not clearly reflect the impact on market formation. A system for evaluating relationships is necessary to measure the influence of each node in the market. This system can be based on the type of relationship, as in the case of management relationships where an executive holds a position of responsibility in the company and what the results are on company performance (positive or negative) during their tenure.

The telecommunications sector is suitable for the analysis of solid networks with extensive cooperation relations between groups, but also for the analysis of infection groups (i.e. in terms of the connection of the Forthnet group and the banking organizations.) However, the analysis needs to be extended to other sectors, with perhaps less connectivity, in order to assess whether the environment affects the performance and policymaking of each company and provides answers to industrial policy problems, such as revenue concentration.

Finally, the present analysis offers the opportunity to further investigate a series of questions relevant to policy such as power concentration, anti-trust investigation, corporate knowledge transfer, macroeconomic implications and business strategy in various industries.

References

Andrikopoulos, A., Georgakopoulos, A., Merika, A., & Merikas, A. (2019). Corporate governance in the shipping industry: Board interlocks and agency conflicts. *Corporate Governance: The International Journal of Business in Society*.

Bastian, M., Heymann, S., & Jacomy, M. (2009, March). Gephi: An open source software for exploring and manipulating networks. In *Third international AAAI conference on weblogs and social media*.

Caiazza, R., Cannella, A. A., Jr., Phan, P. H., & Simoni, M. (2019). An institutional contingency perspective of interlocking directorates. *International Journal of Management Reviews, 21*(3), 277–293.

Davis, G. F. (1991). Agents without principles? The spread of the poison pill through the intercorporate network. *Administrative Science Quarterly, 36*(4), 583–613.

Debellis, F., & Pinelli, M. (2020). Board interlocks in SMEs and the formation of international joint ventures. *PiccolaImpresa/Small Business,* (2).

Drobnik, M. (2012). Corporate networks in Poland: Interlocking directorates and business systems (Doctoral dissertation, NSBE-UNL).

Galavotti, I. (2020). Board interlocks and isomorphism in acquisitions: A review and research agenda. *An Interdisciplinary Outlook in the Wake of Pandemic,* 34.

Hernández-Lara, A. B., & Gonzales-Bustos, J. P. (2019). The impact of interlocking directorates on innovation: The effects of business and social ties. *Management Decision.*

Hillman, A. J., Withers, M. C., & Collins, B. J. (2009). Resource dependence theory: A review. *Journal of Management, 35*(6), 1404–1427.

Mizruchi, M. S. (1996). What do interlocks do? An analysis, critique, and assessment of research on interlocking directorates. *Annual Review of Sociology, 22*(1), 271–298.

Pennings, J. M. (1980). *Interlocking directorates.* Jossey-Bass.

Sapinski, J. P., & Carroll, W. K. (2018). Interlocking directorates and corporate networks. In *Handbook of the international political economy of the corporation.* Edward Elgar Publishing.

Shrader, C., Hoffman, A., & Stearns, T. (1991). Agency directors and network centrality: An examination of resource dependencies. *Journal of Managerial Issues, 3*(1), 46–61.

Simoni, M., & Caiazza, R. (2012). Interlocks network structure as driving force of coopetition among Italian firms. *Corporate Governance, 12*(3), 319–336.

Van Veen, K., & Kratzer, J. (2011). National and international interlocking directorates within Europe: Corporate networks within and among fifteen European countries. *Economy and Society, 40*(1), 1–25.

Wang, W. K., Lu, W. M., Kweh, Q. L., Nourani, M., & Hong, R. S. (2021). Interlocking directorates and dynamic corporate performance: The roles of centrality, structural holes and number of connections in social networks. *Review of Managerial Science, 15*(2), 437–457.

Wheeler, D., Colbert, B., & Freeman, R. E. (2003). Focusing on value: Reconciling corporate social responsibility, sustainability and a stakeholder approach in a network world. *Journal of General Management, 28*(3), 1–28.

Zajac, E. (1988). Interlocking directorates as an interorganizational strategy: A test of critical assumptions. *The Academy of Management Journal, 31*(2), 428–438.

Zhong, Q., Liu, Y., & Yuan, C. (2017). Director interlocks and spillover effects of board monitoring: Evidence from regulatory sanctions. *Accounting & Finance, 57*(5), 1605–1633.

CHAPTER 6

Connected Corporate Networks II: A Novel Approach to the Competition Measure

Charalampos Agiropoulos, Michalis Vafopoulos, Artemis Gourgioti, and George Galanos

6.1 Introduction

In recent decades, competition between companies is considered a major element of a well-functioning economy. Over the past years, it has been well documented in literature that market competition favors investment and innovation (Trėsor-Economics, 2008) and at the same time

C. Agiropoulos (✉) · G. Galanos
Department of International and European Studies, University of Piraeus, Piraeus, Greece
e-mail: hagyropoylos@unipi.gr

G. Galanos
e-mail: galgeorg@unipi.gr

M. Vafopoulos
Institute of Informatics &, Telecommunications of the National Center for Scientific Research "Demokritos", Athens, Greece

P. E. Petrakis (ed.), *Interconnections in the Greek Economy*, The Political Economy of Greek Growth up to 2030,
https://doi.org/10.1007/978-3-031-31335-6_6

ensures consumer well-being. Historical data proves that lack of compe tition entails political implications, from anti-trust to monetary policy and income redistribution. In the previous chapter, the telecommunications industry was analyzed in the light of the business network. The industry analysis is based on the theorem that the existence of connections between executives and companies affects the performance and policymaking of each company that belongs to the business network. Network theory introduces mathematical concepts (e.g., Betweenness—Eigenvector centrality, diameter) in industry analysis, making measurable the influence of companies (nodes) on their network. The existing corporate groups (Vodafone, Wind, Forthnet, OTE) were utilized for the modeling of the network. Corporate groups are created when one company (parent) holds at least 51% of the capital of another company (subsidiary). A group's subsidiaries are considered a business unit, insofar as they operate as a single entity through a common source of control.

Business relationships are based fundamentally on trust. In-market transactions are based on a broad form of voluntary cooperation between business units, which provides mutual benefits. In addition, collaborations are governed by a variety of institutional forms, such as anti-trust and sectoral regulations, which reflect political, historical, and cultural factors. The management of a business unit (company or group) bestows a higher level of confidence in its future, imposing its hierarchical and corporate policies on those who become members of its team. Collaborations with third parties are not necessarily permanent and mutual trust must be established in order not to take advantage of the information obtained during the cooperation.

The business network of the telecommunications market consists of a connected component, i.e., there is at least one path that connects all the nodes of the network. The nodes—companies are connected either through collaborations in third companies (Telegnous, Victus) or through joint executives (Klonis, Mazarakis). This chapter will present a comparative assessment of the our methodology in six additional sectors (Oil Refining, Metallurgy, Air Transport, Publishing, Manufacture of Tobacco

M. Vafopoulos · A. Gourgioti
Linked Business PLC, Athens, Greece
e-mail: a.gourgioti@lbsuite.eu

Products and Short Sea Shipping) that do not have such a cohesive network, nor trends in cooperation between industry groups.

The traditional example of industrial organization argues that market structure is directly related to market behavior and that their interaction also determines market performance (Peterson, 1980, pp. 22–36). These interfaces express competition and monopoly. Competition between companies is a central element of a well-functioning economy.

Measuring the degree of competition in a market is extremely difficult. The most widely used indicators of the degree of competition are the concentration ratios, e.g., the Herfindahl–Hirschman index (HH) and the concentration ratio (CR). These indices are inversely proportional to the market competition, thus the higher the value, the less competitive and monopolistic the market is. Although HH and CR indicators manage to capture a significant portion of the concentration of a market, they are not sufficient to measure market power considering macroeconomic variables over time.

This study proposes a new anti-trust measure based on the CR and HH indices as they are applicable to the corporate network. Companies that are subsidiaries of a group are considered as a business unit, given that they operate as a single entity through a common source of control. The proposed index evaluates the position of each business unit in terms of turnover plus its position in the corporate network. The position of a business unit in the corporate network is evaluated in terms of its ownership and management relations with third-party business units.

In the following Sect. 6.2, this chapter provides a comprehensive overview of the current state of the business concentration and how it is measured through a thorough literature review. The methodology Sect. 6.3 details the new proposed index for measuring corporate network interconnections. The empirical results in Sect. 6.4 present the findings of the study based on the application of the new proposed concentration index and the discussion Sect. 6.5 delves into the implications of the results and how they contribute to the connected corporate networks. Overall, this chapter aims to offer a comprehensive and up-to-date understanding of the competition measures at hand, and the insights gained through this research will be valuable to researchers, practitioners, and policymakers alike.

6.2 Literature Review

The degree of competition, also known as the degree of concentration, is a critical variable for employment, investment, and economic growth. Many studies argue that low concentration (competition) in a market leads to economic growth, creates a favorable environment for investment, drives businesses to innovation, and creates jobs (Trèsor-Economics, 2008). At the same time, ensuring the well-being of consumers depends on the degree of competition.

Many studies in the international literature (Amountzias, 2017; Polemis, 2014a, 2014b; Rezitis & Kalantzi, 2013) investigate the degree of market power of the sectors of the Greek economy, through the price–cost margin (Roeger, 1995). The above-mentioned empirical studies use the method of Hall (1988), which has its roots in the price–cost margin approach (Roeger, 1995). The price–cost margin method assumes that in case of full competition, the marginal cost will be equal to the prices. When equality between prices and marginal costs does not apply, then the market structure is not competitive, in other words the focus is on the range of the mark up.

In addition, indicators are frequently used to measure the degree of competition, such as the concentration ratio $CR(r)$ and the Herfindahl–Hirschman index (HH). The concentration ratio is the sum of the market shares of the largest companies in the market, while the HH index is equal to the sum of the total squares of the market shares. The concentration ratio is calculated as:

$$CR(r) = \sum_{i=1}^{r} \frac{x_i}{X}$$

where x_i is the value of the sales of the enterprise i and r is the total number of enterprises in the market, and X is the total turnover of the total set of enterprises in the market. The higher the market concentration, the less intense is the competition in the market. It should be noted that the concentration ratio provides limited information on the structure of shares between companies in the industry, i.e., the degree of inequality of sales shares.

The Herfindahl–Hirschman (HH) index is often used in empirical research to measure the level of competition in an industry. More specifically, the HH index is a measure of the degree of concentration of sales of companies in each market. This index uses the turnover shares of the companies and is (then?) subtracted from the sum of the squares of the sales shares of all the companies.

The HH index is based on the following formula:

$$HH = \sum_{i=1}^{r} s_1^2 = \sum_{i=1}^{r} \left(\frac{x_i}{X}\right)^2$$

where x_i is the sales value of i company, $i = 1, 2, 3, \ldots,$ r are the businesses in the industry, and X are the total sales of the industry/market in question.

From the two measures, HH seems to be the more generally preferred in terms of its properties. This is because the HH index has a strong advantage over $CR(r)$ indicators, as it could reflect both the average size of the business and the size inequality between companies.

In 1968, the concentration rate was used in the first merger guidelines, and later, in the 2010 horizontal merger guidelines, the HH index was used as a screening tool for potential anti-trust concerns raised by a proposed merger (Kvålseth, 2018).

$CR(r)$ and HH are different so that no functional relationship can exist between them. This notwithstanding, it would be informative to approximate relationships if bounds and inequalities between the measures can be derived (Kvålseth, 2018). Such research was done by Pautler, Kwoka, and Sleuwaegen et al., in which they obtain bounds on HH in terms of $CR(r)$. Their work was a response to the change in the U.S. merger guidelines, replacing the four-firm concentration ratio $CR(4)$ with the HH index. Results showed that the absolute variation in values of HH increased greatly with an increasing CR4. Regarding these early explorations of potential HH-$CR(4)$ relationships, there doesn't seem to be any record of an attempt to verify, correct, or expand on these results (Kvålseth, 2018).

Kvålseth (2018) takes another critical look at those earlier findings using a more rigorous and transparent approach, resulting in some corrections or modifications and alternative formulations. The analytic approach used is that of majorization theory supported by data from computer simulation, generating random market-share distributions.

Kwoka used a statistical model using regression analysis to determine the "best" function to describe the relationship between HH and $CR(r)$

(or vice versa). Such analysis is performed for real or simulated market-share data. Kwoka reported this effort by relating the logarithm $logCR_m$ linearly to $logHH$ for $r = 2$ and $r = 4$ and obtained quite a good fit to real market-share data. More recently, Pavic et al. fitted real data to a model in which CR4 is expressed as a power function of HH. Those authors fitted market-share data at different levels of aggregation and also obtained good model fits.

By contrast, instead of using a function that aims to relate each value of HH to an approximate single value of $CR(r)$ or vice versa, Kvålseth uses majorization theory to develop bounds that can in turn be used to approximately relate one measure to another. This approach also provides tolerance or error limits within which the value of HH must lie given any particular value of $CR(r)$ and vice versa.

In recent bibliography, Bukvic (2019) analyzes the degree of concentration and competition in the Serbian banking sector during the 2010–2017 period and in its current state, by considering the financial statements of banks for the years 2016 and 2017. For this purpose, both traditional concentration indicators (concentration ratio $CR(r)$ and the Herfindahl–Hirschman index), and the rarely used Linda indices have been used. Bukvic has demonstrated that in the current case of a relatively large number of banks operating in Serbia, the existing degree of concentration is relatively low. This provides suitable conditions for the development of healthy competition among them. However, the approximation of the indices to moderate concentration within the period analyzed, warns of the appearance of an oligopoly.

A study by Kostić (2009) provides and promotes many indices that could be used for measuring the market power of companies. Anti-trust policymakers often rely on the calculated values of these indicators to make important decisions regarding the appearance of certain economic entities in the relevant market. They enable the analysis of the current market situation, considering the changes that are happening in it, and they are also used to predict and analyze future market trends (Kostić, 2009).

Concentration indices are subject to changes which those economic entities go through, and they are related to their market share in the relevant market. Therefore, under these changes, the value of the concentration index also changes. For the concentration indices to be comparable between different branches and periods, they are often subject to appropriate mathematical operations to reduce their value in the interval from 0 to 1 (Veselinović & Radukić, 2021).

In general, the restrictions on competition in the market depend on market participants and the distribution of market share, sales, revenue, region, and resources in one market, but also the availability of data (Veselinović & Radukić, 2021). If the level of concentration is methodologically accurate, then, the difference in the size of market share between all companies in the relevant market is accurate and the picture of the level of competition restrictions in the relevant market can be much clearer (Veselinović & Radukić, 2021). Thus, further decisions could be substantiated regarding the strengthening of competitive relations.

6.3 Methodology

The new index revises and recalculates the industry concentration ratio (CR) based on the common entities (nodes) of the network. Each entity—node is evaluated based on its position in the network and its interfaces. The innovation of the new index is the additional multiplier (M) to the algorithm, which evaluates the company's position in the network and increases or decreases the CR value. To calculate the new index, the following steps are followed:

Step 1: Locate the entities from the business network that are related to the company in question.

Step 2: Calculate the concentration ratio (CR) of the common entities according to the formula previously analyzed.

Step 3: To calculate the multiplier, four categories of criteria are considered, and the weights are defined.

$$M = \left(\text{weight}_1 \times \text{score}_1 + \text{weight}_2 \times \text{score}_2 + \text{weight}_3 \times \text{score}_3\right) + \left(\text{weight}_4 \times \text{score}_4\right)/10^5$$

where weight values are presented in Table 6.1.

6.3.1 *Management Positions in Related Entities*

Each management relationship (Table 6.2) between the examined node and the entities/groups of the industry is evaluated and a score is

Table 6.1 Weight values per category

Category	*Description*	*Weight*
Management positions in related entities	The node is connected with affiliated entities/groups	30
Ownership relations in related entities	The node has ownership relationship with affiliated entities/groups	30
Distance in the business network	The level of connection within connected entities	20
Turnover of the connected business entity	Turnover of the node as a percentage of the total turnover of the sector	20

Source Author's calculations

Table 6.2 Scoring values based on their role

Role	*Score*
CEO	100
President	80
Vice president	70
Executive member	50
Non-Executive member	30
Combined (e.g., President & CEO)	Hierarchical selection

Source Author's calculations

obtained which corresponds to the importance of its role in the management of the company. In case there is no management relationship, the score equals zero, while in cases of more than one role, the one with the highest score prevails.

6.3.2 *Ownership Relations in Related Entities*

The ownership relations of the examined node with the industry are evaluated based on the percentage of capital holding. For each unit of capital of the examined node held by an entity, a point is added to the score, e.g., for 70% holding of the capital, the node is evaluated with 70 points.

Table 6.3 Scoring values based on the level of relationship

Level	*Score*
level 1	100
level 2	50
level 3	25

Source Author's calculations

6.3.3 *Distance in the Business Network*

The analysis of the corporate network is performed at three levels (Table 6.3). The first level implies a direct relationship between two entities, i.e., a node actively participates in the administration or ownership of the other. At the second level, there is a node between the examined entities, i.e., there is a direct relationship with the entity of the first level. At the third level, there are two nodes between the examined entities.

6.3.4 *Turnover of the Connected Business Entity*

The turnover of the node is calculated in terms of the percentage that participates in the total turnover of the branch. The higher the participation rate in the total turnover, the greater the influence the node has on the industry (Table 6.4).

Step 4: Following the calculation of the multiplier, the CR of the common entities is re-calculated. The added value which results from the relationship of the examined entity with its business network is fully identified.

$$\text{Addedvalue} = \text{Multiplier} \times \text{CR(commonentities)}$$

Table 6.4 Scoring values based on the percentage of participation

Percentage	*Score*
up to 1%	10
1–10	
...	
> 20%	100

Source Author's calculations

Step 5: The algorithm is completed by calculating the revised CR.

$$\text{AdjustedCR}(\text{commonentities}) = \text{Addedvalue} + \text{CR}(\text{commonentities})$$

Step 6: Each common entity contributes proportionally to CR. Therefore, the percentage of the value added for each entity is estimated and, thus, the revised CR is calculated for each entity, respectively.

$$\text{Addedvalueshare} = (\text{CR}(\text{entity})/\text{CR}(\text{commonentities})) * \text{Addedvalue}$$

$$\text{AdjustedCR}(\text{entity}) = \text{CR}(\text{entity}) + \text{Addedsharedvalue}$$

6.4 Empirical Results

6.4.1 Telecommunications Sector

For the empirical application of the revised CR, this study initially examines the company Telegnous Private Company from the telecommunications sector. According to the traditional methodology, the distribution of CR based on the financial results of 2019 is presented in Table 6.5.

According to the revised CR, the distribution is affected by the relationship of the examined company (Telegnous) within its business network. Table 6.6 presents the input data for Telegnous based on the proposed methodology. Telegnous is associated with three of the four

Table 6.5 CR estimation using the traditional approach

Group (Entity)	*Concentration Rate (as of 2019) (%)*
OTE Group	58.85
WIND Group	9.48
VODAFONE Group	17.06
FORTHNET Group	4.63
Rest	9.99

Source Authors' calculations based on the Linked Business Registry statistical business register of Greece (established by Linked Business PLC, linkedbusiness.eu) defined as the set of legal entities that have been assigned with a valid identification number by the General Electronic Commercial Registry combined with a valid Tax Identification Number by the Greek Tax Register

Table 6.6 Input data for the calculation of the revised CR

Common Entity	*Telegnous (TELECOMMUNICATIONS SOLVENCY ASSESSMENT AGENCY Private Company)*
Involved Entities	*OTE Group, WIND Group, VODAFONE Group*
Management positions in related entities	none
Ownership relations in related entities	100%
Distance in the business network	level 1
Turnover of the connected business entity	up to 1%

Source Author's calculations

groups in the telecommunications sector, namely OTE, WIND, and Vodafone. The groups collectively own 100% of the company; however, there is no management relationship between groups and the company, given that none of the management members are shared. The company is directly connected to the groups and is not mediated by another entity; therefore, the relationship is at the first level of the network. Finally, the turnover of Telegnous for the financial year 2019 was 241.84 K, amount that corresponds to a percentage of 0.004% of the total turnover of the sector for that particular year.

The updated distribution based on the revised CR is presented in Table 6.7.

The CR of the entities associated with Telegnous (OTE, WIND, VODAFONE) is 85.38%. Following the methodology for the calculation of the revised CR applied to Table 6.6, we calculate the multiplier which will define the added value resulting from the relationship of the groups with Telegnous. Table 6.7 presents the added value from this relationship which stands at 4.44%, formulating (bringing?) the revised CR of the three groups to 89.82%. Each entity is affected to a different level and has a distinctive percentage of added value. In other words, the revised CR should be calculated with respect to each entity (separately). Subsequently, the multiplier for OTE group comes to 3.06% while the revised CR amounts to 61.91%. Having said that, it is worth noting that, as the revised CR is calculated for all entities of the industry, in some cases the revised CR decreases respectively (accordingly). Thus, in the examined example the Forthnet group ends up with a revised CR of 3.23%.

Table 6.7 Adjusted CR distribution based on Telegnous effect

TELEGNOUS EFFECT	
CR (3) (initial)	85.38%
REST (initial)	14.62%
MULTIPLIER	0.052
ADDED VALUE	4.44%
ADJUSTED CR(3)	89.82%
ADJUSTED REST CR(3)	10.18%
Added value WIND Group	0.49%
Added value VODAFONE Group	0.89%
Added value OTE Group	3.06%
CR FORTHNET (adjusted)	3.23%
CR WIND Group (adjusted)	9.97%
CR VODAFONE Group (adjusted)	17.94%
CR OTE Group (adjusted)	61.91%
CR REST (adjusted)	6.95%

Source Author's calculations

As can be seen in Fig. 6.1, the affiliated groups (OTE, WIND and VODAFONE) are strengthened in their position while for the other participants, the revised CR is significantly decreased. The largest increase within the telecommunications sector appears in the OTE group, which is the dominant entity of the industry. By contrast, entities without any similar affiliation with Telegnous, e.g., the FORTHNET group, show a significant reduction in their revised CR, and therefore, their influence on the industry is weakened.

6.4.2 *Oil Refining Sector*

The oil refining sector is dominated by the ELPE and Motor Oil Groups. According to the financial data of 2019, Table 6.8 shows the estimations of the traditional CR.

The two groups have entered a partnership with Athens Airport Fuel Pipeline Company. The distribution of CR is clearly affected by this collaboration as Table 6.10 shows, according to the input data (Table 6.9).

Motor Oil and ELPE dominate 80% of the market. In addition, Motor Oil group holds 16% of the Athens Airport Fuel Pipeline, which is a private company while, at the same time, these entities share management members. Moreover, 50% of Athens Airport Fuel Pipeline belongs to the

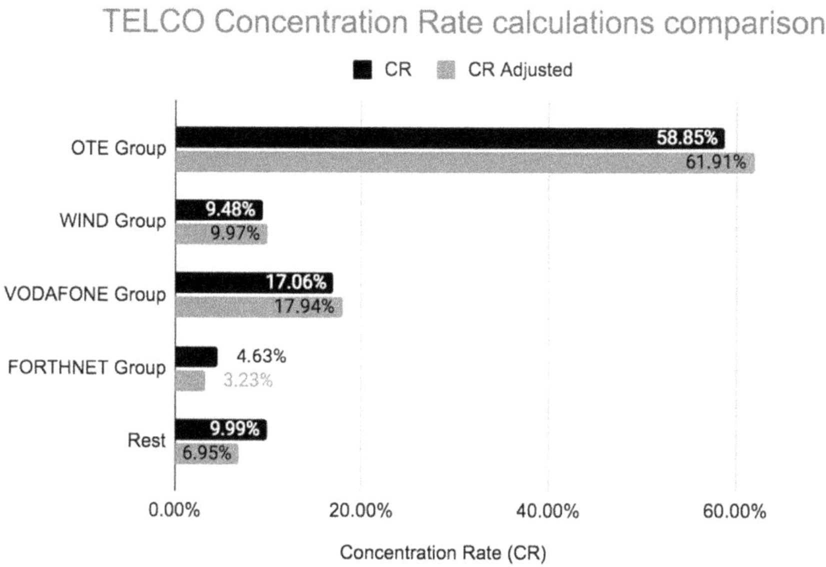

Fig. 6.1 The revised and the initial concentration rate for the Telecommunications sector

Table 6.8 CR estimation using the traditional approach

Group (Entity)	*2019 Revenue (in mm €)*	*CR (%)*
Motor Oil Group	€9,372.00	41.13
ELPE Group	€8,856.00	38.87
Rest	€4,557.00	20.00
Market total	€22,787.00	100

Source Author's calculations

ELPE group. Athens Airport Fuel Pipeline had a turnover of 4.36 m for the fiscal year 2019, corresponding to 0.02% of the total turnover of the industry.

The updated distribution based on the revised CR is presented in Table 6.10.

For the fiscal year 2019, the two groups hold 80% of the total turnover of the sector. Table 6.10 shows that an added value of 4.54% is created by the relationship between the groups and the Athens Airport Fuel Pipeline

Table 6.9 Input data for the calculation of the revised CR

Common Entity	*Athens Airport Fuel Pipeline private company*	
Involved Entities	*Motor Oil Group*	*ELPE Group*
Management positions in related entities	Executive Member	–
Ownership relations in related entities	16%	50%
Distance in the business network	level 1	
Turnover of the connected business entity	up to 1%	

Source Author's calculations

Table 6.10 Adjusted CR distribution based on the effect of the Athens Airport Fuel Pipeline

Athens Airport Fuel Pipeline	
CR (2) (initial)	80.00%
REST (initial)	20.00%
MULTIPLIER	0.0568
ADDED VALUE	4.54%
ADJUSTED CR (2)	84.54%
ADJUSTED CR (REST)	15.46%
Motor Oil Group	2.34%
ELPE Group	2.21%
Motor Oil Group (adjusted)	43.47%
ELPE Group (adjusted)	41.08%

Source Author's calculations

private company. Based on the revised CR, it is estimated that the two groups account for 84.54% of the market, while the influence of the other entities is limited to 15.46%.

Figure 6.2 represents the revised and the conventional CRs. The industry leaders (Motor Oil, ELPE) hold approximately the same market share, with a small lead by the Motor Oil group. Their relationship with the Athens Airport Fuel Pipeline private company strengthens the Motor Oil and ELPE groups by 2.34% and 2.21%, respectively, significantly reducing the market influence of other entities.

6.4.3 *Metallurgical Activities Sector*

Although in the Metallurgical activities sector there are no collaborations between the groups, the existence of a connection is present through

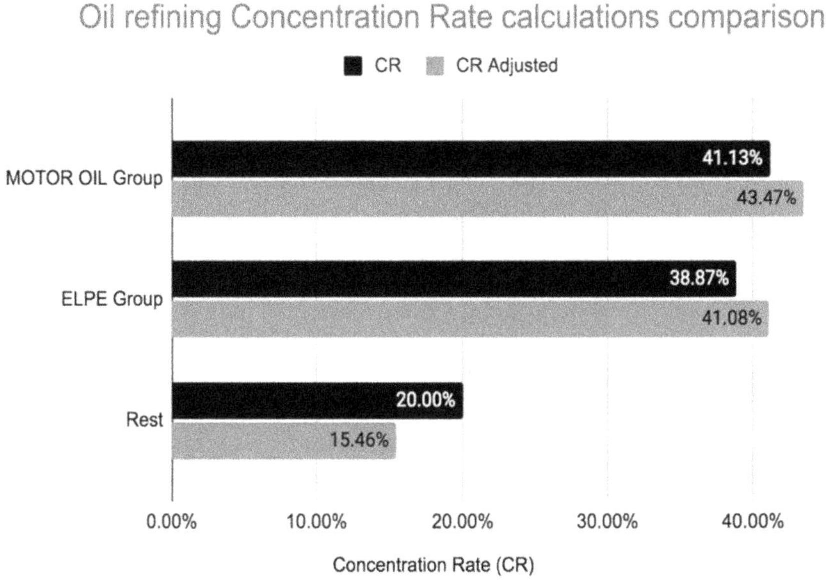

Fig. 6.2 The revised and the initial concentration rate for the Oil refining sector

other companies and members of their management. The president of the Viohalco Group, Stasinopoulos Nikolaos, has been a non-executive member of the management of the Eurobank Group together with Wade Sebastian Burton. Wade Sebastian Burton was also a non-executive member of the Mytilineos Group, creating an indirect connection with the Viohalco Group.

According to the financial data of 2019, Table 6.11 shows the estimations of the traditional CR.

The updated distribution based on the revised CR is presented in Table 6.13.

As mentioned earlier, in the minerals sector there are no collaborations either at company level or in the sharing of management members. However, the indirect relationship of the VIOHALCO and MYTILINEOS groups affects the CR of the companies. Stasinopoulos owns 32% of the shares of the VIOHALCO group performing executive duties, while in a third level of the network, a connection can be found with the

Table 6.11 CR estimation using the traditional approach

Group (Entity)	*2019 Revenue (in mm €)*	*CR (%)*
VIOHALCO Group	€4,198.00	57.72
MYTILINEOS Group	€2,256.00	31.02
HELLENIC HALYVOURGIA	€187.60	2.58
PROMETAL	€118.20	1.63
PIRAIKI METALS	€6.90	0.10
EXALCO	€117.30	1.61
Rest	€388.60	5.34
Market total	€7,273.00	100

Source Author's calculations

MYTILINEOS group; in other words, two other nodes mediate between them (Table 6.12).

The relationship between the groups is of minor importance, as is reflected in the small added value that results from it. The two-related groups (VIOHALCO, MYTILINEOS) had a cumulative CR of 88.74%, while the revised CR is 90.48%. The support rates of the other players are just as small and, in some cases, e.g., PIRAIKI Metals, negligible.

Figure 6.3 shows that the benefit of the affiliated entities is small; however, their influence in the industry was already high and there is no room for significant growth.

Table 6.12 Input data for the calculation of the revised CR

Common Entity	*Stasinopoulos N*	
Involved Entities	*VIOHALCO Group*	*MYTILINEOS Group*
Management positions in related entities	President	none
Ownership relations in related entities	32%	
Distance in the business network	level 1	level 3
Turnover of the connected business entity	–	

Source Author's calculations

Table 6.13 Adjusted CR distribution based on the Stasinopoulos effect

Stasinopoulos EFFECT	
CR (2) (initial)	88.74%
REST (initial)	13.84%
MULTIPLIER	0.0196
ADDED VALUE	1.74%
ADJUSTED CR(2)	90.48%
ADJUSTED CR (Rest)	12.10%
VIOHALCO	1.13%
MYTILINEOS	0.61%
HELLENIC HALYVOURGIA	0.32%
PROMETAL	0.32%
PIRAIKI METALS	0.01%
EXALCO	0.20%
VIOHALCO (Adjusted)	58.85%
MYTILINEOS(Adjusted)	31.63%
HELLENIC HALYVOURGIA (Adjusted)	2.90%
PROMETAL (Adjusted)	1.95%
PIRAIKI METALS (Adjusted)	0.11%
EXALCO (Adjusted)	1.82%

Source Author's calculations

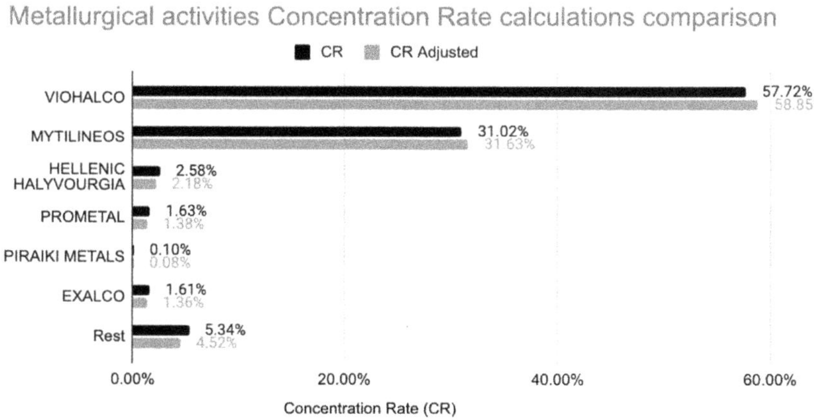

Fig. 6.3 The revised and the initial concentration rate for the Metallurgical sector

6.4.4 *Publishing Sector*

The industry of Newspaper and Magazines Publishing has special characteristics given the nature of information collecting, promotion, publicizing and, in general, the diffusion of news. The Kathimerini Group and Attica Media Group have jointly established a corporation (E-One) which offers online entertainment, information, and communication. Table 6.14 shows the estimations of the traditional CR, according to the 2019 fiscal year financial standings.

Kathimerini and Attica Media own 25% of the E-One company, respectively, while at the same time they share executives. In particular, Diamantopoulos Vassilis has served as CEO of E-One and Vice President of the Kathimerini group (Table 6.15).

Table 6.14 CR estimation using the traditional approach

Group (Entity)	*2019 Revenue (in mm €)*	*CR (%)*
KATHIMERINI GROUP	€39.23	19.44
ATTICA MEDIA GROUP	€28.35	14.05
Market total	€201.80	100

Source Author's calculations

Table 6.15 Input data for the calculation of the revised CR

Common Entity	*E-One*	
Involved Entities	*ATTICA MEDIA GROUP*	*KATHIMERINI GROUP*
Management positions in related entities	President	None
Ownership relations in related entities	25%	25%
Distance in the business network	level 1	level 1
Turnover of the connected business entity	–	

Source Author's calculations

Table 6.16 Adjusted CR distribution based on E-ONE effect

E-ONE EFFECT	
CR (2) (initial)	33.49%
REST (initial)	66.51%
MULTIPLIER	0.065
ADDED VALUE	2.18%
ADJUSTED CR (2)	35.67%
ADJUSTED CR (Rest)	64.33%
Added value ATTICA MEDIA GROUP	0.91%
Added value KATHIMERINI GROUP	1.26%
CR ATTICA MEDIA GROUP (Adjusted)	14.96%
CR KATHIMERINI GROUP (Adjusted)	20.79%

Source Author's calculations

The two-related groups had a cumulative CR of 33.49%, while the revised CR is 35.67%. The Kathimerini group was strengthened by 1.26%, while Attica publications by 0.91%. The recalculation of CR is presented in detail in Table 6.16.

The Figure below shows the output from Table 6.16. The benefit of the affiliated entities is significant, even though they still represent a small share of the industry (Fig. 6.4).

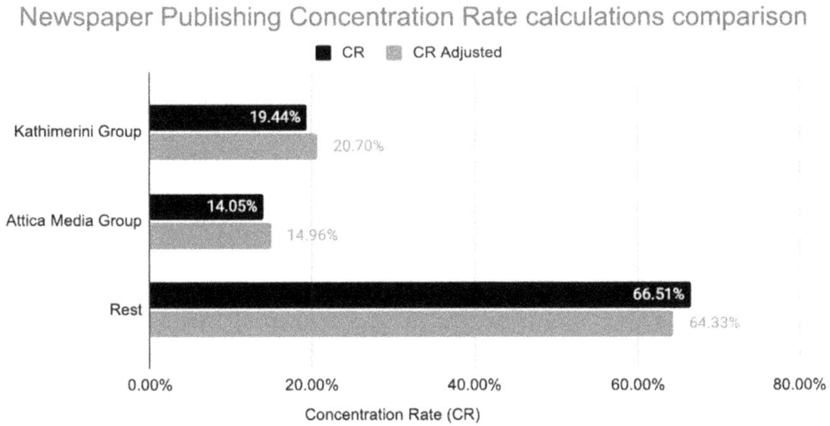

Fig. 6.4 The revised and the initial concentration rate for the Newspaper Publishing sector

6.4.5 *Manufacture of Tobacco Products*

The tobacco industry is particularly concentrated in two strong groups with excessive competition (the Papastratos Group and the Karelia Group). The sector is characterized by limited staff movement while a third smaller player (Greek Cooperative Cigarette Manufacturing Company or in short G.C.C.M./"ΣΕΚΑΠ" in Greek) has inserted itself in the sector. G.C.C.M. is interconnected with several third sectors.

According to the financial data of 2019, Table 6.17 shows the estimations of the traditional CR.

The groups have not cooperated; however, a connection can be found between the Karelia group and the G.C.C.M. (SEKAP), through the Thessaloniki Port Authority and the shared members of the Board of Directors (Table 6.18).

The two-related groups had a cumulative CR of 65.53%, while the revised CR is 66.65%. The Karelia group was strengthened by 1.06%,

Table 6.17 CR estimation using the traditional approach

Group (Entity)	*2019 Revenue (in mm €)*	*CR (%)*
PAPASTRATOS GROUP	€414.69	24.90
KARELIA GROUP	€1,035.70	62.34
G.C.C.M. (ΣΕΚΑΠ)	€52.96	3.19
Market total	€1,661.2	100

Source Author's calculations

Table 6.18 Input data for the calculation of the revised CR

Common Entity	*THESSALONIKI PORT AUTHORITY*	
Involved Entities	*G.C.C.M. (ΣΕΚΑΠ)*	*KARELIA GROUP*
Management positions in related entities	executive member	non-executive member
Ownership relations in related entities	–%	–%
Distance in the business network	level 3	level 3
Turnover of the connected business entity	–	

Source Author's calculations

Table 6.19 Adjusted CR distribution based on the effect of the THESSALONIKI PORT AUTHORITY

THESSALONIKI PORT AUTHORITY	
CR (2) (initial)	65.53%
REST (initial)	34.47%
MULTIPLIER	0.017
ADDED VALUE	1.11%
ADJUSTED CR (2)	66.65%
ADJUSTED CR (Rest)	33.35%
Added value KARELIA GROUP	1.06%
Added value G.C.C.M. (ΣΕΚΑΠ)	0.05%
CR KARELIA GROUP (Adjusted)	63.4%
CR G.C.C.M. (ΣΕΚΑΠ) (Adjusted)	3.24%
CR PAPASTRATOS GROUP (Adjusted)	24.1%

Source Author's calculations

while SEKAP by 0.05%. The recalculation of CR is presented in detail in Table 6.19.

The Figure below shows the output from Table 6.19. The benefit of affiliated entities is of minor importance, as their relationship to the joint entity is not strong, neither does it belong to the same industry (Fig. 6.5).

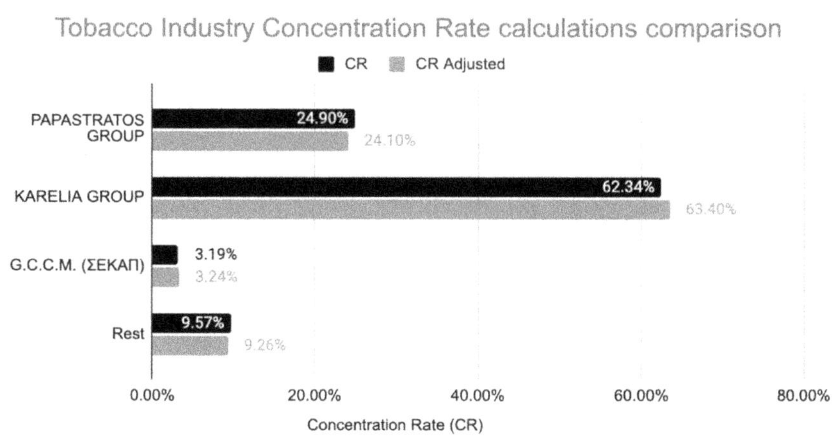

Fig. 6.5 The revised and the initial concentration rate for the Tobacco Industry

6.4.6 *Short Sea Shipping Sector*

The Sea and Coastal passenger water transport sector is highly concentrated. The three main participants (ATTICA Group, ANEK LINES Group, MINOAN LINES Group) are connected to each other, sharing executives in different levels.

According to the financial data of 2019, Table 6.20 shows the estimations of the traditional CR.

The groups have not cooperated, but a connection can be identified between them through the Vardinogiannis and Laskaridis families. The Table 6.21 analyzes the connection of the ANEK Lines and ATTICA groups.

The two-related groups had a cumulative CR of 84.22%, while the revised CR is 85.82%. The ATTICA group was strengthened by 2.77%, while ANEK LINES by 1.19%. The recalculation of CR is presented in detail in Table 6.22.

Table 6.20 CR estimation using the traditional approach

Group (Entity)	*2019 Revenue (in mm €)*	*CR (%)*
ATTICA Group	€405.40	58.94
ANEK LINES Group	€173.90	25.28
MINOAN LINES	€92.10	13.39
Market total	€687.80	100

Source Author's calculations

Table 6.21 Input data for the calculation of the revised CR

Common Entity	*VARDINOGIANNIS IOANNIS IOSIF*	
Involved Entities	*ATTICA GROUP*	*ANEK LINES GROUP*
Management positions in related entities	President	CEO
Ownership relations in related entities	–%	–%
Distance in the business network	level 1	level 1
Turnover of the connected business entity	–	

Source Author's calculations

Table 6.22 Adjusted CR distribution based on VARDINOGIANNIS IOANNIS IOSIF effect

VARDINOGIANNIS IOANNIS IOSIF	
CR (2) (initial)	84.22%
REST (initial)	15.78%
MULTIPLIER	0.047
ADDED VALUE	3.96%
ADJUSTED CR (2)	88.18%
ADJUSTED CR (Rest)	11.82%
Added value ATTICA GROUP	2.77%
Added value ANEK LINES GROUP	1.19%
CR ATTICA GROUP (Adjusted)	61.71%
CR ANEK LINES GROUP (Adjusted)	26.47%
CR MINOAN LINES (Adjusted)	10.03%

Source Author's calculations

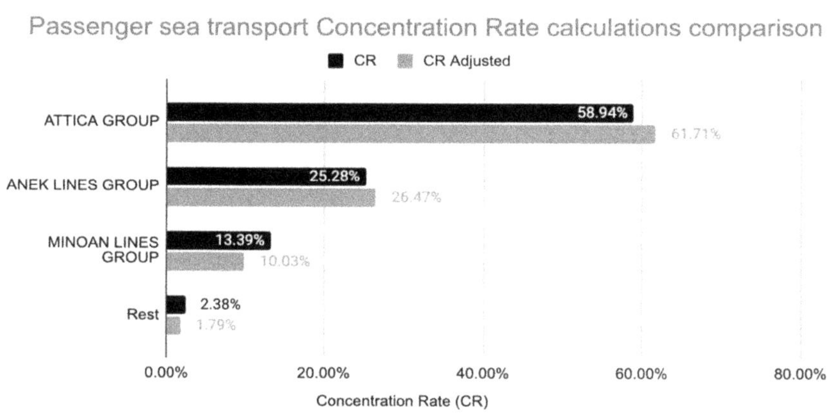

Fig. 6.6 The revised and the initial concentration rate for the Passenger Sea Transport sector

The figure below shows the output of Table 6.21. The joint venture mainly affected the MINOAN LINES group, as its influence in the industry decreased by 3.36% (Fig. 6.6).

6.4.7 *Air Transport Sector*

The Air Transport industry is concentrated in a small number of entities and executives with the dominant groups AEGEAN, AVIAPERS,

MOUZENIDIS (via ELLINAIR), and INTERSALONIKA (via AIR INTERSALONIKA). The executives of the companies are active in several external sector entities (e.g., TITAN, Athens Stock Exchange, MOTOR OIL) thus expanding the business network. Major characteristics of the industry include the partnership in the field of tourism through the association of large shipping and air transport groups, as well as the strong presence of companies with the main objective of promoting tourism (e.g., Marketing Greece S.A.). The presence of the Mouzenidis Group is not strong in the industry, as it has no connections with other entities of the industry. According to the financial data of 2019, Table 6.23 shows the estimations of the traditional CR.

In the sector of passenger air transport, there is an intense cooperation and exchange of executives. A typical example is Mastorantonakis Iosif, who has been Managing Director at Skyserv (a subsidiary of the AVIAPERS group) and a member of the AEGEAN group (Table 6.24).

The two-related groups had a cumulative CR of 81.73%, while the revised CR is 84.59%. The AEGEAN GROUP benefited the most from the relationship (+2.49%) and the AVIAPERS GROUP was strengthened by just 0.37%. The recalculation of CR is presented in detail in Table 6.25.

Table 6.23 CR estimation using the traditional approach[1]

Group (Entity)	*2019 Revenue (in mm €)*	*CR (%)*
AEGEAN Group	€1,308.80	71.12
INTERSALONIKA Group (AIR INTEPΣAΛONIKA)	€2.58	0.14
MOUZENIDIS Group	€112.45	6.11
AVIAPERS Group	€195.19	10.61
Market total	€1,840.30	100

Source Author's calculations

[1] For the INTERSALONIKA and MOUZENIDIS groups, this study accounts only for the turnovers of their active subsidiaries in the sector. The turnover of the MOUZENIDIS group refers to the fiscal year 2018, as no financial standings have been published for 2019.

Table 6.24 Input data for the calculation of the revised CR

Common Entity	*MastorantonakisIosif*	
Involved Entities	*AEGEAN GROUP*	*AVIAPERS GROUP*
Management positions in related entities	executive member	CEO
Ownership relations in related entities	–%	–%
Distance in the business network	level 1	level 1
Turnover of the connected business entity	–	

Source Author's calculations

Table 6.25 Adjusted CR distribution based on VARDINOGIANNIS IOANNIS IOSIF effect

MASTORANTONAKIS IOSIF	
CR (2) (initial)	84.22%
REST (initial)	18.27%
MULTIPLIER	0.035
ADDED VALUE	2.86%
ADJUSTED CR (2)	84.59%
ADJUSTED CR (Rest)	15.41%
Added value AEGEAN GROUP	2.49%
Added value AVIAPERS GROUP	0.37%
CR AEGEAN GROUP (Adjusted)	73.61%
CR AVIAPERS GROUP (Adjusted)	10.98%
CR INTERSALONIKA (Adjusted)	0.12%
CR MOUZENIDIS GROUP (Adjusted)	5.15%

Source Author's calculations

The Figure below shows the output of Table 6.25. The presented interconnection mainly strengthened the AEGEAN group, as AEGEAN is the dominant industry (Fig. 6.7).

6.5 Discussion

A company's business network influences its performance and its strategic choices. The effect of a company on its industry is evaluated based on the holding market share, i.e., the percentage of the total turnover of the sector accrued by the particular entity. However, since the company is also affected by its direct or indirect relationships with other market entities,

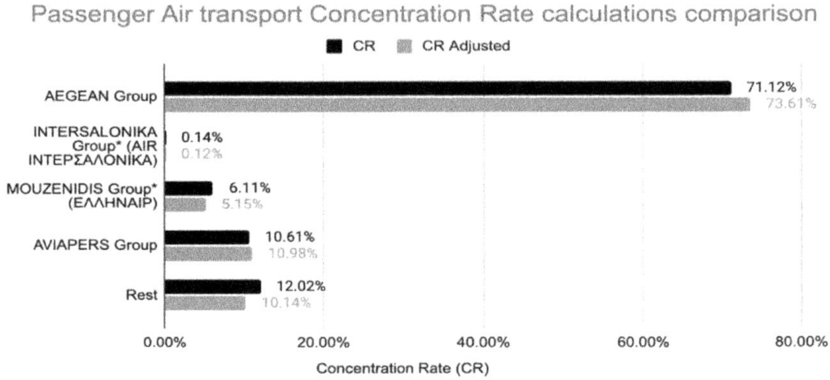

Fig. 6.7 The revised and the initial concentration rate for the Passenger Air Transport sector

its percentage of influence on the industry cannot be based solely on its own turnover.

Current business concentration indicators assume that companies operate independently. In actual fact, this is rarely the case. In most cases, companies in the same sector (usually the strongest) establish joint companies and/or their management members collaborate with third parties. This study attempts to present the existing conventional indicators in a more realistic form using available business data on entities which, under specific circumstances, establish their business relationships.

In this context, our initial effort paves the way for the enrichment of the business concentration indicators. The improvement on traditional indicators is achieved by adding innovative features that record the type of the relationship among entities of the same industry as they aim to improve of their effectiveness.

This study attempts to advance the significance of the existing ratios using objective, unbiased variables, such as joint ventures and the persons that constitute the management of affiliated companies, who provide open data and establish business cooperation. In this context, we utilize data on the cooperation of companies in the same industry through the news and social networks. To more accurately capture the influence of a company on its industry, the recalculation of the concentration index is proposed in light of a corporate network, rather than considering a company as an individual/independent unit. This innovative method of calculating the index is based on a system of evaluating the company's relations to clearly determine the importance of interaction between the nodes. The new index essentially calculates to what extent the examined node has contributed to its own turnover as well as to the turnover of its interfaces.

A company's business network influences its performance and strategic choices. The influence of a company in its branch of activity is evaluated in terms of the market share it holds and more specifically in the percentage of the total turnover of the branch that the specific company produces. However, as the company is affected by both its direct and indirect relationships with other market entities, its percentage of influence in the industry cannot be based solely on its own turnover.

References

Amountzias, C. (2017). An investigation of the degree of market power in the greek manufacturing and service industries. *Journal of Industry, Competition and Trade, 17*(4), 447–464.

Bukvic, R. (2019). Evolution and current status of the competitive environment in the Serbian Banking Sector: Concentration indices analysis. *Serbia: Current political, economic and social issues and challenges*. Nova Science Publishers, Inc., 23–42.

Kostić, M. (2009). Supply concentration analysis in Serbian insurance sector. *Industrija, 37*(2), 59–77.

Kvålseth, T. O. (2018). Relationship between concentration ratio and Herfindahl-Hirschman index: A re-examination based on majorization theory. *Heliyon, 4*(10), e00846.

Kwoka, J. E., Jr. (1985). The Herfindahl index in theory and practice. *Antitrust Bulletin, 30*, 915.

Pautler, P. A. (1983). A guide to the Herfindahl index for antitrust attorneys. *Research in Law & Economics, 5*, 167–190.

Pavic, I., Galetic, F., & Piplica, D. (2016). Similarities and differences between the CR and HHI as an indicator of market concentration and market power. *Journal of Economics, Management and Trade*, 1–8.

Peterson, R. D. (1980, Spring). Product differentiation, implicit theorizing, and the methodology of industrial organization. *Nebraska Journal of Business and Economics*, 22–36.

Polemis, M. (2014a). Empirical estimation of market power in Greece. *Applied Economics Letters, 21*(11), 747–750.

Polemis, ML. (2014b). Measuring market power in the Greek manufacturing and services industries. *International Review of Applied Economics, 28*(6), 742–766. https://doi.org/10.1080/02692171.2014.923386

Rezitis, A. N., & Kalantzi, M. A. (2013). Measuring the degree of market power in the Greek manufacturing industry. *International Review of Applied Economics, 27*(3), 339–359.

Roeger, W. (1995). Can imperfect competition explain the difference between primal and dual productivity measures? Estimates for U.S. *Manufacturing. Journal of Political Economy, 103*, 316–331.

Sleuwaegen, L. E., De Bondt, R. R., & Dehandschutter, W. V. (1989). The Herfindahl index and concentration ratios revisited. *Antitrust Bulletin, 34*, 625.

Sleuwaegen, L., & Dehandschutter, W. (1986).The critical choice between the concentration ratio and the H-index in assessing industry performance. *The Journal of Industrial Economics*, 193–208.

Trėsor-Economics. (2008). Competition within Sectors in France. Treasury and Economic Policy No. 27. General Directorate.

Veselinović, M., & Radukić, S. (2021). Measuring supply concentration on the Serbian oil and oil derivates market by Herfindahl-Hirschman Index. *FactaUniversitatis, Series: Economics and Organization, 1*, 343–356.

PART III

Economic Shocks, Diversification and Economic Interconnections

CHAPTER 7

Economic Shocks in Greece and the Effects on the Gross Value Added Per Economic Sector

Kyriaki I. Kafka

7.1 Introduction

The outbreak of the recent global financial crisis, the COVID-19 pandemic, and the energy crisis fueled by the effects of the Russian-Ukrainian war caused significant economic turbulence in the Greek economy. Those shocks significantly affected the Greek economy's economic development and growth path and the behaviors and decisions made by economic actors. Simultaneously, those shocks highlighted the speed with which shocks are transmitted in the economy and the significant problems of the Greek economy associated with its structure and function.

K. I. Kafka (✉)
Department of Economics, National and Kapodistrian University of Athens, Athens, Greece
e-mail: kkafka@econ.uoa.gr

P. E. Petrakis (ed.), *Interconnections in the Greek Economy*, The Political Economy of Greek Growth up to 2030,
https://doi.org/10.1007/978-3-031-31335-6_7

The effects of Economic Policy Uncertainty (EPU) on various sectors of the economy continue to be a focus of ongoing research in economics, with a growing interest in the impact of EPU on sectoral Gross Value Added (GVA). Although the number of studies on the impact of EPU on sectoral GVA has increased, there is still much to be discovered about this relationship. For instance, there needs to be more research on the effects of EPU on service sectors, and the specific impacts of EPU on different sectors still need to be well comprehended.

EPU refers to the degree of unpredictability regarding government policies that affect economic activity, which encompasses ambiguity concerning taxes, regulations, trade policies, and monetary policy. EPU can significantly impact various sectors of the economy, influencing investment, consumption, and the economy's overall growth.

This chapter investigates how the economic sectors in the Greek economy are affected by the economic shocks that have hit the economy during the period from the first quarter of 1998 up to the third quarter of 2022, leading to the determination of the more vulnerable and the more resilient economic sectors in the Greek economy. Policy recommendations about the transformation of the Greek economy emerge. To the author's knowledge, this is a novel examination of the effects of EPU on various sectors of the economy, specifically in the Greek economy.

The structure of the chapter is as follows. Section 7.2 presents a literature review on how Economic Policy Uncertainty affects sectoral Gross Value Added. Then, Sect. 7.3 describes the data and methodology used in the analysis. Finally, Sect. 7.4 presents the analysis of the empirical analysis results, as well as a discussion of the analysis. Finally, Sect. 7.5 presents the conclusions and some policy recommendations.

7.2 How Economic Policy Uncertainty Affects Sectoral Gross Value Added

Many research studies have used the Economic Policy Uncertainty Index created by Baker et al. (2016) to explore the impact of economic policy uncertainty on corporate investment across various economic sectors. Wang et al. (2014) investigated how economic policy uncertainty affects corporate investment in Chinese listed companies and found that firms tend to reduce their investment when uncertainty rises. Similar findings have been seen by Gulen and Ion (2016), who discovered a significant negative correlation between capital investment at the firm level and economic policy uncertainty, suggesting that uncertainty can discourage corporate investment due to the irreversible nature of the investment. Additionally, Wang et al. (2022) determined that an increase in EPU suppresses corporate investment. On the other hand, when EPU is low, it positively influences corporate investment, and this effect gradually decreases as uncertainty levels rise.

Zhu and Yu (2022) are based on China's industry to examine the effects of EPU on industrial output. Using data for the period 2005–2017, they conclude that EPU has a significant inverted "U"-nonlinear type effect on industrial output.

Kun et al. (2022) highlight that uncertainty in economic policy, particularly regarding monetary policy, in China positively impacts R&D investments made by businesses. This suggests that a rise in EPU may positively affect the professional, scientific, and technical activities and the administrative and support activities sector.

Zhao (2022) finds that when both importing and exporting countries experience increased EPU, it reduces the value-added trade flows in manufacturing. The study also shows that the negative impact of EPU on exporting countries is more significant than that of importing countries. The study concludes that the rise in EPU in exporting countries primarily impacts the value-added trade flows in manufacturing through the cost of exporting. In contrast, the rise in EPU in importing countries primarily affects it through market demand.

Hu and Yan (2021) analyzed the impact of economic policy uncertainty on the structural upgrading of the manufacturing sector in China from 1997 to 2018. The study's findings suggest that economic policy uncertainty significantly affects structural upgrading in manufacturing, particularly in regions with advanced manufacturing structures. The results suggest that economic policy uncertainty drives the manufacturing industry to adopt service transformation strategies and pursue vertical integration, which is the mechanism through which it affects structural upgrading in manufacturing.

Kostis (2021, 2022a, 2022b) analyzed data from 2001 to 2019 for Greece's retail sector and found that uncertainty had a significant impact on the economy. The largest effects were seen in car fuels and lubricants, department stores, and books, stationery and other items. Conversely, uncertainty did not appear to impact the pharmaceutical and cosmetic sector or other stores (excluding fuel). The relationship between uncertainty and retail trade turnover was found to vary between different branches of the retail trade.

Li and Wu (2020) conducted a study to assess economic policy uncertainty's effect on China's real estate development at the macro level. Using the EPU Index developed by Baker et al. (2016), they discovered that economic policy uncertainty has a negative and leading impact on real estate development investment.

Previous research has looked into the relationship between economic policy uncertainty, and housing market returns in various countries such as Germany (Su et al., 2016), Japan (Anoruo et al., 2017), the United States (André et al., 2017), developed economies (Christou et al., 2017), and developing economies (Aye, 2018). Most research has found that the EPU index can be used to predict real housing returns. However, Aye (2018) found no connection between economic policy uncertainty and real housing returns, except for Chile and China.

Aye and Kotur (2022) have determined that there is a long-term association between economic policy uncertainty and agricultural growth, with a negative impact in the long run. They found that economic policy uncertainty negatively and significantly affects agricultural growth and welfare in the short term. Additionally, they note that a stable economic policy environment positively contributes to agricultural growth.

7.3 Data and Methodology

The analysis of this chapter is based on quarterly data on the gross added value of the sectors of economic activity and the economic uncertainty for the Greek economy. The period under analysis starts in the first quarter of 1998 and ends in the third quarter of 2022.

The GVA for each sector of economic activity is derived from the Hellenic Statistical Authority (EL.STAT.). The seasonally adjusted chain volume indicators are used (the base year is 2015) in millions of euros. The sectors under analysis are the following:

- Agriculture, forestry, and fishing
- Mining and Quarrying, Manufacturing, Energy, Water Supply, Wastewater Treatment, Waste Management, and Sanitation
- Construction

- Wholesale and retail trade, repair of vehicles and motorcycles, transport and storage, provision of accommodation, and catering services
- Information and communication
- Financial and insurance activities
- Real estate
- Professional, scientific, and technical activities, administrative, and support activities
- Public administration and defense, compulsory social security, education, activities related to human health and social welfare
- Arts, entertainment and entertainment, household repair, and other services

The economic uncertainty data are derived from the EPU index calculated by Hardouvelis et al. (2018). The methodology they follow is based on the index of Baker et al. (2016).

The data analysis methodology concerns a vector autoregressive model (VAR) to examine the effects (impulse responses) created by a negative disturbance of economic uncertainty for the ten branches of economic activity. The variables included in the VAR are the EPU index and the GVA of the ten sectors of economic activity.

This system is determined by following the standard procedure of the recursive form of the included variables. To determine the appropriate length of VAR (4 lags), stationarity, and non-autocorrelation, the following criteria are used: Akaike criterion, Schwarz criterion, Hannan Quinn criterion, AR Roots, Residual correlogram, Autocorrelation LM test, Granger Causality, ADF test. To ensure the robustness of the results, tests with different VAR lengths and with different orders of the variables were performed. Then an impulse response function (IRF) analysis is carried out to show the effects of economic policy uncertainty on the ten sectors of economic activity for twelve periods after the economic uncertainty shock (3 years).

Table 7.1 presents the descriptive statistics of the variables under analysis.

Table 7.1 Descriptive statistics

	N	*Stdev*	*Mean*	*Min*	*Max*
Economic Policy Uncertainty	99	24,6	95,4	41,3	159,5
Agriculture, forestry, and fishing	99	145,1	1752,2	1362,1	1978,2
Mining and Quarrying, Manufacturing, Energy, Water Supply, Wastewater Treatment, Waste Management, Sanitation	99	615,1	6333,0	5124,7	7460,0
Construction	99	1007,1	1812,7	594,9	4235,9
Wholesale and retail trade, repair of vehicles and motorcycles, transport and storage, provision of accommodation and catering services	99	1769,5	11,067,4	6875,1	15,182,7
Information and Communication	99	391,1	1467,3	1010,9	2245,1
Financial and insurance activities	99	285,1	2016,4	1304,1	2867,1
Real Estate	99	680,1	6430,9	5184,9	7821,7
Professional, scientific and technical activities, administrative and support activities	99	548,5	2502,6	1772,0	3645,7
Public administration and defense, compulsory social security, education, activities related to human health and social welfare	99	1317,0	8981,0	7607,4	11,558,5
Arts, entertainment and entertainment, household repair and other services	99	471,9	1687,5	794,3	2650,7

Source Author's creation

7.4 The Effects of an Economic Policy Uncertainty Shock on the Greek Sectors of Economic Activity

Figure 7.1 presents the effects of a two standard deviations shock of economic policy uncertainty on the Greek economy's ten sectors of economic activity. The period for the impulse response function is 12 quarters after the shock.

There are several economic policy uncertainty shock effects in the Greek economy. There are sectors negatively affected, some others positively affected, and others presenting moderate effects.

The "arts, entertainment and entertainment, household repair, and other services" sector presents an essential variance regarding the effects

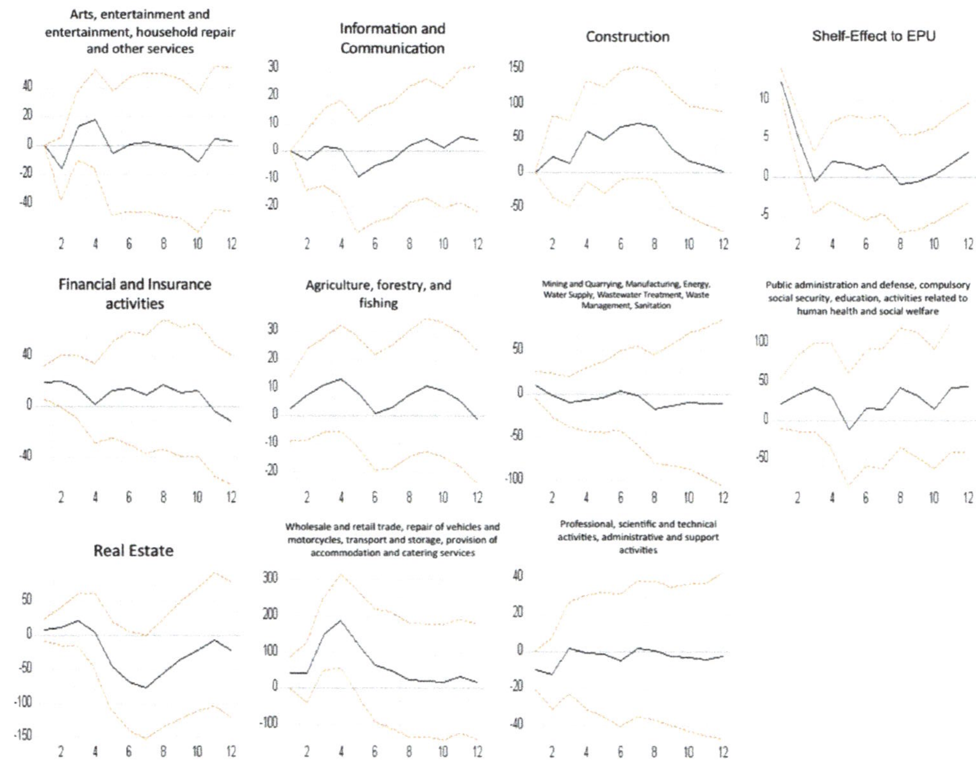

Fig. 7.1 The effects of an uncertainty shock on the Greek sectors of economic activity (*Source* Author's creation)

of an economic policy uncertainty shock. The primary effects of an uncertainty shock exist during the first four quarters after the shock. There is a negative effect two quarters after the shock, which then turns positive effects for the next two quarters. After the first year, the effects of an uncertainty shock turn almost to zero, although there is a return to a negative shock in the 10th quarter.

The sector "Information and Communication" appears to have minor effects. The most damaging effects are realized five quarters after the shock and last until the 8th quarter, and then the sector's GVA is slightly positively affected by the shock.

The "construction" section presents significant positive effects after an uncertainty shock. These positive effects start from the 1st quarter until the 12th quarter after the shock. The positive effects are the highest eight quarters after the shock. This positive effect on the GVA may appear due to increased government spending and infrastructure investments to stimulate the economy and increase employment. In addition, if increased economic policy uncertainty leads to low-interest rates (as a central bank response), this can lead to higher investment in the construction sector. Besides, looking for safer investment decisions, households, and firms may turn to increase their investments in the construction sector instead of other types since they prioritize stability in their living arrangements.

An economic policy uncertainty shock seems to positively affect the GVA of the "financial and insurance activities" as well. However, this effect is much lower than in the construction sector. These positive effects last for the first 11 quarters after the economic policy uncertainty shock. The main reason this happens is that due to increased uncertainty, investors, firms, and households are looking for safer economic actions, and the "financial and insurance activities" sector may satisfy the increased demand for safe assets and the increased demand for insurance products to protect from increased uncertainty.

An economic policy uncertainty shock seems to positively affect the GVA of the "agriculture, forestry, and fishing" sector. The economic policy uncertainty shock is bigger in the 4th and the 9th quarter, while it gets minimized in the 6th and the 12th quarter. This positive effect on the GVA of the agriculture, forestry, and fishing sectors may exist because this sector is often seen as a relatively stable investment. Additionally, agricultural products and fisheries are considered essential goods, meaning their demand is almost constant regardless of economic uncertainty. Finally, the agriculture, forestry, and fishing sectors may benefit from the decrease in competition from other sectors during periods of uncertainty.

The sector "Mining and Quarrying, Manufacturing, Energy, Water Supply, Wastewater Treatment, Waste Management, Sanitation" appears to have a negative due to the shock in economic policy uncertainty from the 2nd to the 5th quarter and from the 8th to the 12th quarter after the economic policy uncertainty shock. Including manufacturing, this is a sector that may is highly affected by increased costs for the economic actors caused by regulatory burdens or other forms of economic policy uncertainty. The increased cost for the firms and the decrease in investments and consumption for the households lead to an uncertain business environment, which delays investment decisions and slows economic activity.

An economic policy uncertainty shock seems to positively affect the GVA of the "public administration and defense, compulsory social security, education, activities related to human health and social welfare" sector for 12 quarters after the shock. However, this positive effect gets negative five quarters after the economic policy uncertainty shock and returns to positive. The main reason for these positive effects is that public administration tries to increase confidence and welfare in the economy in times of high uncertainty. However, increased economic policy uncertainty can lead to decreased investment and consumer confidence, government budget cuts, decreased government revenue, and public sector employment, which can negatively impact the production of goods and services in these sectors. Therefore, there is a negative effect on the 5th quarter.

The most significant adverse effect of economic policy uncertainty, among all sectors of economic activity, is over the GVA of the "real estate" sector. The main negative effects are from the 5th to the 11th quarter, while the highest negative effect comes in the 7th quarter after the economic policy uncertainty shock. The main reasons are reduced investment, decreased consumer confidence, and increased uncertainty, which leads to decreased lending from financial institutions.

An economic policy uncertainty shock seems to positively affect the GVA of the "wholesale and retail trade, repair of vehicles and motorcycles, transport and storage, provision of accommodation and catering services" sector. The main positive effects come in the 4th quarter after the economic policy uncertainty shock, and the positive effects are reduced and almost minimized after the 8th quarter. During periods of high uncertainty, economic actors may try to protect and maintain their standard of living, leading to increased consumption and changed consumption patterns, even toward essential goods. Moreover, new consumer behaviors may emerge under increased economic policy uncertainty, such as an increased shift toward online consumption benefiting the retail trade sector.

Finally, another adverse effect of economic policy uncertainty is over the GVA of the "professional, scientific and technical activities, administrative and support activities" sector. The main negative effects come from the emergence of the shock until the 3rd quarter, the 6th, and the 11th quarter. The main reason for those negative effects is that during high uncertainty, consumers focus on essential goods and services, not nonessential services such as those offered by this sector. Moreover, increased uncertainty may lead to reduced spending on research and development since this does not seem to be a priority for enterprises in times of uncertainty.

7.5 Conclusions and Policy Recommendations

The analysis presented in the present chapter concerns the use of quarterly data for the period 1998–2022 (up to the third quarter), which uses a vector autoregressive model to examine the impulse responses created by a harmful disturbance of economic uncertainty for ten branches of economic activity in the Greek economy.

The duration of the effects varies and can last from a few quarters after the onset of a shock to 12 quarters or more. The effects can be positive and negative for the gross added value of the sectors of economic activity. The most significant adverse effects characterize the real estate management sector. Most uncertainty effects are also adverse for the sector professional, scientific and technical activities, and administrative and support activities. On the other hand, the most positive effects of uncertainty are observed in the construction sector and the wholesale and retail trade, repair of vehicles and motorcycles, transport and storage, provision of accommodation, and catering services sector.

Thus, the direct adverse effects of economic policy uncertainty on the Greek economy are insignificant and concern mainly the real estate sector. However, the interconnections between the sectors of economic activity are high in the Greek economy, resulting in a decrease in demand in some sectors strengthening the Gross Value Added of other sectors and vice versa.

The Greek economy can tackle and better manage EPU and promote sustainable and inclusive growth, ensuring that government policies and regulations are clear and stable, minimizing uncertainty for businesses and investors. Moreover, investment and innovation should be boosted through tax breaks and funding for research and development. In addition, a solid and adaptive financial sector capable of managing changing conditions can be created. Moreover, a crucial point would be the development of more stable and effective government institutions, thus removing obstacles to investment and trade. Another critical issue is expanding trade agreements and foreign investments and strengthening key industries through human capital, innovation, and infrastructure investments. Finally, a critical issue in dealing with increased EPU is maintaining a stable macroeconomic environment.

References

André, C., Bonga-Bonga, L., Gupta, R., & Muteba Mwamba, J. W. (2017). Economic policy uncertainty, US real housing returns and their volatility: A nonparametric approach. *Journal of Real Estate Research, 39*(4), 493–513.

Anoruo, E., Akpom, U., & Nwoye, Y. (2017). Dynamic relationship between economic policy uncertainty and housing market returns in Japan. *Journal of International Business and Economics, 5*(2), 28–37.

Aye, G. C., & Kotur, L. V. (2022). Effect of economic policy uncertainty on agricultural growth in Nigeria. *African Journal of Agricultural Growth in Nigeria, 17*(2), 106–114.

Aye, G. C. (2018). Causality between economic policy uncertainty and real housing returns in emerging economies: A cross-sample validation approach. *Cogent Economics & Finance, 6*(1), 1473708.

Baker, S. R., Bloom, N., & Davis, S. J. (2016). Measuring economic policy uncertainty. *The Quarterly Journal of Economics, 131*(4), 1593–1636.

Christou, C., Gupta, R., & Hassapis, C. (2017). Does economic policy uncertainty forecast real housing returns in a panel of OECD countries? *A Bayesian Approach, the Quarterly Review of Economics and Finance, 65*, 50–60.

Gulen, H., & Ion, M. (2016, March). Policy uncertainty and corporate investment. *The Review of Financial Studies*, *29*(3), 523–564. https://doi.org/10.1093/rfs/hhv050

Hardouvelis, G. A., Karalas, G., Karanastasis, D., & Samartzis, P. (2018). Economic policy uncertainty, political uncertainty and the greek economic crisis. Working Paper.

Hu, R., & Yan, Y. (2021). Effects of economic policy uncertainty on manufacturing structural upgrading: Evidence from China. *Discrete Dynamics in Nature and Society*. https://doi.org/10.1155/2021/7364528

Kostis, P. C. (2021). The effects of economic uncertainty in retail trade in Greek Economy. In B. Aranitou (Ed.), *The history, the economy and the transformation of retail trade and the Greek case*. Kerkyra Publications - Economia Publishing (in Greek).

Kostis, P. C. (2022a). Economic recovery after uncertainty shocks. In *Proceedings of the International Conference on Empirical Economy and Social Sciences (ICEESS)*, 29 Ιουλίου 2022a, Bandirma University, Τουρκία.

Kostis, P. C. (2022b). Winners and losers: The recovery of the Greek retail trade after uncertainty shocks. International Conference on Business & Economics of the Hellenic Open University 2022b (ICBE -HOU), 16–17 June, Athens.

Kun, W., Hu, X., & Liu, F. (2022). *The Impact of Economic Policy Uncertainty on Firms' Investment in Innovation: Evidence from Chinese Listed Firms*. https://doi.org/10.1371/journal.pone.0272983

Li, M., & Wu, G. (2020). The impact of economic policy uncertainty on real estate development in China. *Journal of Applied Finance & Banking, SCIENPRESS Ltd, 10*(4), 1–2.

Su, D., Li, X., Lobont, O. R., & Zhao, Y. (2016). Economic policy uncertainty and housing returns in Germany: Evidence from a bootstrap rolling window. *Zbornik radova Ekonomskog fakulteta u Rijeci/Proceedings of Rijeka Faculty of Economics, 34*(1), 43–61.

Wang, Y., Chen, C. R., & Huang, Y. S. (2014). Economic policy uncertainty and corporate investment: Evidence from China. *Pacific-Basin Finance Journal, 26*, 227–243.

Wang, D., Liu, T., Huang, Y., & Zhou, Y. (2022). Identifying the dynamic influence of economic policy uncertainty on enterprise investment using functional data analysis. *Mathematical Problems in Engineering*. https://doi.org/10.1155/2022/7822710

Zhao, T. (2022). Economic policy uncertainty and manufacturing value-added exports. *Engineering Economics, 33*, 1. https://doi.org/10.5755/j01.ee.33.1.27373

Zhu, S., & Yu, G. (2022). The impact of economic policy uncertainty on industrial output: The regulatory role of technological progress. *Sustainability, 14*, 10428. https://doi.org/10.3390/su141610428

CHAPTER 8

Identifying Smart Growth Policies for Economic Diversification and Sustainable and Inclusive Growth in the Greek Economy

Pantelis C. Kostis

8.1 Introduction

A country's productive structure determines its future path of economic diversification, economic growth, and sustainable and inclusive growth. The Greek economy relies significantly on the production of a few economic sectors and, as a result, is vulnerable to external or internal economic shocks.

This chapter defines Greece's structural constraints and opportunities for economic diversification and sustainable and inclusive growth. For this purpose, the analysis describes the production model of the Greek economy and its vulnerabilities. Those vulnerabilities generate the

P. C. Kostis (✉)
Department of Economics, National and Kapodistrian University of Athens, Athens, Greece
e-mail: pkostis@econ.uoa.gr

P. E. Petrakis (ed.), *Interconnections in the Greek Economy*, The Political Economy of Greek Growth up to 2030,
https://doi.org/10.1007/978-3-031-31335-6_8

need for its change to a more diversified economy based on sustainable and inclusive growth. Then smart growth policies for the future of the Greek economy are presented based on a Quintuple Helix model, which recognizes the importance of collaboration and cooperation between government, industry, civil society, the environment, and the knowledge and innovation system.

The structure of the chapter is as follows: Sect. 8.2 describes that the Greek economy has long been dependent on a small number of sectors, leading to economic vulnerability and a lack of resilience and the need to diversify the economy and promote new sectors and industries. Then, Sect. 8.3 presents smart growth policies that can play a crucial role in achieving this goal under the prism of a Quintuple Helix model for the Greek economy.

8.2 The Need to Change the Production Model of the Greek Economy

The Greek economy heavily relies on a few industries, such as tourism and shipping, which makes it susceptible to external shocks. To mitigate this risk, it is crucial to shift the production model of the economy to increase its diversity.

Diversifying the economy is crucial for overall economic growth, as diversifying investment and production is vital (Petrakis et al., 2016). This viewpoint has been extensively studied in the field of economics. Nobel Prize winner Simon S. Kuznets (1971) believes that a country's economic growth can be described as a sustained rise in the ability to offer more diverse economic goods to its citizens. This idea is further supported by Grossman and Helpman (1992), who suggest that economic growth requires producing an increasing quantity, quality, and range of goods and services.

An economy is considered diverse when its income comes from various unrelated sources (Shayah, 2015). If a country's income relies solely on the production of one product, changes in the price of that product can lead to variations in the standard of living. Imbs and Wacziarg (2003) noted that during the development process, countries tend first to diversify—spreading economic activity evenly across various sectors. Eventually, some countries start to specialize again once they reach a certain level of per capita income. In essence, sectoral diversification initially rises but then begins to concentrate again once a certain level of per capita income is reached.

Additionally, the growth and transformation of an economy depend on the diversity of products being traded (Hausmann & Klinger, 2006; Hwang, 2006). By diversifying exports, an economy can shift toward producing and exporting advanced products that significantly contribute to sustainable growth, meet macroeconomic goals, achieve export revenue stability, and reduce unemployment and income inequality. Therefore, Romer (1990) recognizes diversification as a factor that contributes to and affects the efficiency of other production elements. Furthermore, Acemoglu and Zilibotti (1997) assert that diversification can raise income by expanding the opportunity for spreading investment risk to a more extensive portfolio.

More recently, the current COVID-19 pandemic has significantly impacted Greece's economy, particularly its tourism sector, one of the most dependent on global tourism. According to the OECD annual report published in March 2020, Greece is the 6th most dependent country regarding the industry's contribution to GDP and the 4th in employment among the 35 monitored by the organization. The high dependence on tourism has made the Greek economy particularly vulnerable to adverse circumstances that may affect tourism activity, such as the COVID-19 pandemic. One of the significant economic effects of COVID-19 on Greece is a decrease in international travel receipts due to travelers' fear and the strict policies implemented by various countries to prevent the spread of the virus.

As a result of the COVID-19 pandemic, the hotel and catering industry experienced the most significant decrease in gross value added. The arts, entertainment, and recreation sector also experienced a significant decrease in value added. Significant adverse changes are also expected for the value added in sectors such as trade, other services, transport and communication, manufacturing, and construction, with changes going from positive to negative after the pandemic.

Therefore, the Greek economy's sectoral policy for addressing the COVID-19 pandemic requires closer examination. The decision on which sectors to prioritize for support involves balancing two goals: boosting the sectors that contribute the most to the GDP, to shorten the duration of the recession and extending the recovery after shocks, or supporting the sectors with the highest employment, to minimize losses in human capital. The outcome of this trade-off depends on the cost-effectiveness of supporting each sector.

It is suggested that sectors with high employment levels and a significant impact from support compared to the required budget should be prioritized for support. This means that priority should be given to the hotel and catering industry, manufacturing, and construction. However, consideration should also be given to the real estate management, transport and logistics services, and professional services sectors.

As a result, changes need to be made to the production model to improve its risk diversification and reduce the likelihood of systemic crises causing severe recessions, or if that is not possible, to facilitate a quick recovery. In particular, the manufacturing sector deserves special attention because it, directly and indirectly, accounts for about a third of total employment in the economy and contributes to about 10% of GDP. Efforts should be made to strengthen the industry and increase its participation in the economy's production to at least 15%, even though the EU target is to raise manufacturing's participation to 20% at the European level. Manufacturing has a GDP multiplier of 2.8 and an employment multiplier of 3.5, benefiting services and trade and creating a robust network of small and medium-sized businesses. Manufacturing also accounts for 44% of total exports, pays wages that are, on average, notably higher than the rest of the economy and contributes more to the state's revenues than its share. Boosting manufacturing's participation in GDP has multiplier benefits. Additionally, increasing the manufacturing sector's role in economic production will result in significant job growth, addressing important economic inclusivity issues. Furthermore, the decline of manufacturing and its inability to respond to the challenges posed by the modern globalized environment contributed to the 2008 crisis in the Greek economy (Argeitis & Nikolaidi, 2014).

Furthermore, the Greek economy can enhance the significance of other sectors in its GDP by leveraging its comparative advantages in various sectors, including metals, food, pharmaceuticals, green energy, minerals, and specific high-tech sectors. To alter the production model, specific reforms are necessary to make it easier for businesses to operate in most of their sectors. Strategic planning is also crucial to create a well-structured industrial policy and for the digital transformation of the economy.

8.3 Smart Growth Policies for the Greek Economy

Besides a change in the production model of the economy, there is a need to use modern and holistic approaches to promote smart growth for sustainability and inclusiveness in the Greek economy. Such approaches fall within a Quintuple Helix model (Carayannis & Campbell, 2009, 2010; Carayannis et al., 2012), which recognizes the importance of collaboration and cooperation between five critical stakeholders: government, industry, culture, environment, and academia (Carayannis & Campbell, 2019). In this way, smart growth policies are considered a more comprehensive and integrated approach to economic development and sustainable and inclusive growth for the Greek economy.

8.3.1 Government

The importance and, ultimately, the meaning of seeking more effective and democratic methods of governance (political and economic) lies in the fact that governance can not only influence the performance and form of the economic system at present, but it essentially shapes incentives and institutions for the future distribution of resources and incomes within society. This is a critical issue given the high uncertainty surrounding the Greek economy and society and the recent external shocks caused by the 2008 global financial crisis and the COVID-19 pandemic.

The Greek economy should also become a modern state in line with the requirements of the international environment in which it operates. Four areas break down the priority for activating the strategic development policies of a modern state: (a) Public Infrastructure Investments, (b) Effective management of the public sector, (c) the strategic plan against corruption, and (d) the elaboration of a plan to combat significant tax evasion.

(a) Public Infrastructure Investments

The significance of infrastructure investment in determining overall productivity must be considered. During the 1970–2008 period in Greece, when the potential for product improvement in the economy was strong (averaging 2.7% annually), infrastructure investment played a crucial role in shaping capital and overall productivity. Predictions for the next 37 years (until 2060) indicate a potential increase in the product by 1.3% for Greece. Given the adverse effects of an aging population and climate change, the only way to sustain growth in the Greek economy is through an increase in overall productivity. Thus, infrastructure investment will be of paramount importance.

Additionally, infrastructure investments serve as the foundation for a modern economy and society, providing resilience and contributing to economic growth by reducing social costs, improving efficiency, increasing productivity, and boosting competitiveness (Bell, 2012). Infrastructure encompasses investment systems in capital-intensive sectors such as road networks, utility networks, and public buildings and includes investment in innovation and human capital (tangibles and intangibles). Essential societal structures like housing, water, schools, hospitals, and transportation are all supported by infrastructure, and investing in this area is imperative for economic growth, sustainability, and resilience (Straub, 2008).

Economic infrastructure and social infrastructure are two crucial types of public infrastructure. Economic infrastructure comprises the physical structures that support the production process, providing essential goods and services for economic activity, including transportation, communication, water supply, energy, etc. This makes it a necessary component for the development of supply chains, the exchange of information and knowledge, and the connection between producers and consumers. Social infrastructure, on the other hand, refers to the basic needs of society, such as education and health. Although they are not directly tied to the production process, they play a vital role in maintaining and improving the health and skills of the workforce. As such, they are crucial in developing human capital, which ultimately shapes the productivity and efficiency of the economy in the long term. Furthermore, access to these infrastructures helps reduce inequality and promote social cohesion.

The topic of investing in infrastructure has re-emerged as a pressing concern for the Greek economy for the first time since World War II. This resurgence can be attributed to five main reasons: (a) crises limit the government's fiscal capabilities, with infrastructure financing being a primary victim, especially in hard-hit countries; (b) monetary policy has lost its effectiveness due to the Zero Lower Bound, leading to the need for alternative fiscal tools to boost the economy; (c) the impacts of climate change have intensified; (d) changes in the population require more significant investment at both ends of the age spectrum; and (e) technological advancements are driving new demands for innovation and skills.

It needs to be more accurate to categorize public infrastructure products and services as pure public goods, as only some projects completely fit that definition. Take transport networks, for instance; they benefit society, but their economic performance decreases as usage increases. Moreover, the characteristics of public infrastructure are flexible and can change over time due to technological advancements and new political approaches. For example, technological advancements in telecommunications have helped reduce the costs of developing information and communication technology infrastructure. The importance of infrastructure is emphasized by its inclusion as a crucial aspect of the United Nations' 17 Sustainable Development Goals by 2030. These goals include ensuring access to water and sanitation, providing access to affordable, reliable, sustainable, and modern energy forms, creating flexible infrastructure, and promoting sustainable industrialization and innovation.

Investing in modern trade-related infrastructure can bring competitive benefits to the Greek economy by making its export activities more efficient. It also spurs innovation, generating jobs in cutting-edge technologies like renewable energy and high-speed rail. Large infrastructure projects have long been known to enhance productivity and appeal to research and innovation initiatives significantly. The joint report from the European Investment Bank and the World Economic Forum in 2017 highlights the potential of infrastructure investments to impact competitiveness and inclusiveness. The World Economic Forum recognizes infrastructure as one of the 12 essential drivers of competitiveness, defined as the institutions, policies, and factors that determine a country's productivity level.

Investing in infrastructure has a positive impact on the economy by increasing productivity. The inflow of capital into the infrastructure sector expands the economy's production capacity (OECD, 2015). The benefits of infrastructure investment can be significantly magnified when there is strong complementarity with other factors of production. Investments in network infrastructure, such as electricity or telecommunications, enhance access to these services and reduce costs for businesses, encouraging private investment. As a result, public infrastructure investment can stimulate private investment, leading to a positive spillover effect.

(b) Effective management of Public Sector

The Greek public sector's large size is often seen as a significant factor in accumulating long-term deficits, leading to the current debt crisis. Reducing the size of the public sector is a top priority in countries that need to cut spending through structural reforms. Some governments have expanded the public sector to provide jobs in the past, but this solution needs to be revised. This happened in Greece, where the governments from 1980 onwards aimed to absorb the unemployed workforce by expanding the public sector. However, this increased unemployment due to immigration, population growth, and economic changes.

Modernizing the public sector must follow specific rules and conditions, such as evaluating administrative structures and staff, hiring highly qualified staff in key areas, improving services for businesses and citizens, and simplifying regulations. Developing e-government services is also important, including modernizing services, making essential services available online, providing digital services for enterprises, promoting digital literacy and internet access, and addressing digital security issues.

(c) Strategic Plan on Corruption

Reducing corruption is crucial in improving economies that do not rely on markets. Several vital steps must be taken to achieve this: (a) Reinforcing oversight and control measures to tackle corruption and maintain accountability. (b) Strengthening control and oversight mechanisms and demonstrating a zero-tolerance policy toward corruption, mismanagement, or unclear processes. (c) Effective monitoring and punishment should serve as a deterrent. (d) Evaluating the outcomes of audits to guide further reform initiatives. (e) Improving the flow of information in the justice system. (f) Streamlining administrative procedures and improving services for citizens and businesses. (g) Developing a National Anti-Corruption Action Plan with specific tax administration measures to enhance the political, economic, social, and legislative environment through three key pillars: Deterrence, Training, and Prevention. (h) Promoting and monitoring compliance with transparency rules in allocation processes at all levels of government and in all other state functions to effectively combat corruption.

(d) Tax Fraud Elimination

Tax evasion is typically seen to occur among two groups: low-income earners and high-income earners. Both types of tax evasion pose challenges for a well-run state, but the solutions may differ. For the first group, the following established and proven methods are commonly used: (a) Gradual reduction of the tax burden on individuals and businesses. (b) Promoting the importance of tax compliance. (c) Implementing an effective tax collection system. (d) Widening the tax base through improved collection performance. (e) Simplifying the system and distributing the tax burden fairly by limiting exemptions and special schemes, such as single property tax. (f) Streamlining non-contributory taxes benefiting third parties. (g) Creating an autonomous and centralized structure, eliminating the bureaucracy of multiple small services dealing with taxpayers. (h) Connecting computer systems with other government departments for cross-checking purposes. (i) Hiring additional skilled and specialized personnel. (j) Providing incentives for timely reporting, strict audits, and sanctions for violators, improving liquidity through timely payment of state liabilities, and automatic debt/refund netting.

Particular attention should be given to devising strategies for tackling significant tax evasion for high-income earners. The methods proposed in international practice include: (a) Establishing an international information network. (b) Developing robust domestic control mechanisms. (c) Enhancing the independence of administrative mechanisms responsible for capturing tax-evading assets.

8.3.2 *Industry and Sectoral Policies*

The current wave of the Industrial Revolution brings many changes, and the various industries in the Greek economy must adapt to them. Each sector aims to make the most efficient use of resources, provide innovative solutions that enhance competitiveness, participate in international trade agreements that drive economic activity, and actively participate in the supply chain. The goal is to transform the country's production model, which relies on only a few sectors and makes Greece vulnerable to external shocks, such as the impact of the COVID-19 pandemic on the tourism industry. Sectoral policies impact all areas of the economy. However, the focus is on priority sectors, including tourism, marine and transportation, technology and IT, pharmaceutical, logistics, agro-food, and housing (Petrakis & Kostis, 2020b).

In the tourism sector, digital technology should be used to promote services globally. The quality of services should be improved by utilizing unused tourist assets, simplifying the institutional framework, and developing high-end tourism infrastructure. In marine and transportation, services must be improved, and processes streamlined to increase synergies among industry players. Ports should be upgraded, new technologies integrated, new marinas built, skilled labor employed, and long-term financing for transport infrastructure ensured.

In technology and informatics, businesses need training and information to penetrate the IT and internet sectors and increase productivity. Competition can be encouraged by supporting young scientists with innovative ideas. The Hellenic Telecommunications and Post-commission should be strengthened and independent to promote competition and regulate the market.

The competitiveness and international presence of the Greek pharmaceutical industry can be improved by promoting Greek generics in the market, participating in international networks, providing incentives for developing production lines, and encouraging research and development through incentives and standardization. The institutional framework needs to be changed to allow e-government of the industry and a unified pharmaceutical policy established to improve efficiency.

Major ports should be transformed into integrated logistics platforms in the logistics sector, and the industry should be strengthened with a skilled workforce. The state could incentivize companies to create organized supply zones. In the agro-food sector, competitiveness can be increased by producing high-quality products in larger quantities and marketing them as finished products instead of raw materials. Innovation and the skills of the rural population should be strengthened and focus should be placed on emerging and dynamic markets.

Reforms are needed in the real estate sector to stimulate intersectoral partnerships and increase public confidence in real estate investments. A better tax regime that favors the purchase and sale of real estate, the registration of usable real estate, and special regulations on urban planning, the environment, and expropriations for strategic investments are necessary.

During the COVID-19 pandemic, the sectoral policy of dealing with the pandemic in the Greek economy needs to be carefully evaluated. The trade-off decision on the economic policy should prioritize supporting industries with high employment and a high impact from aid, such as the hotel and catering industry, manufacturing, construction, property management, transport and storage services, and professional services, while considering the financial cost–benefit ratio.

Several actions are needed to boost Greek businesses' competitiveness (Ciampi, 1995). Firstly, there needs to be a modern legislative framework that replaces outdated laws. Secondly, the economy needs to tap into the scientific potential to enhance the quality of products, particularly in high-tech sectors. Thirdly, entrepreneurship needs to be encouraged by creating equal opportunities for all (such as women and vulnerable populations) to start businesses, reducing start-up costs, bureaucracy, and access to finance and promoting skills and understanding of entrepreneurship. Fourthly, the country's natural resources and comparative advantages must be fully utilized, public infrastructure needs to be developed to support competitiveness, and everyone must follow fair competition rules.

Finally, new business entry barriers need to be removed to increase competitiveness in specific sectors. For example, this might involve reducing the licensing requirements for new businesses in the wholesale fuel trade. A national development strategy should also be implemented for key sectors that contribute significantly to the economy, such as tourism, shipping, and agriculture.

8.3.3 Culture

Petrakis and Kostis (2020a) have identified some dominant traits in Greek society, including a lack of trust, strong in-group collectivism, uncertainty avoidance, a significant influence of Orthodox religion, performance orientation, and non-acceptance of inequalities. These traits lead to a focus on the familiar, reluctance to compete or take risks, indecision due to uncertainty and anxiety, and low trust. There is also a prevalent aversion to loss and support for the status quo, protection of the in-group, and a strong role of family and Orthodox Christian beliefs. Despite this, there is a desire for equal opportunities and an emphasis on efficiency in daily life. There is also a trend toward Euroscepticism and the protection of national sovereignty while striving to maintain and improve the standard of living.

Another significant distinction in attitudes in Greek society is the divide between the economic situation (economic have-nots) and cultural backlash behavior. This distinction refers to whether citizens decide, and vote based on their economic struggles or in response to cultural changes. The world, starting with the US, then Europe, and finally Greece, is transitioning into a post-materialistic era where economic concerns take a backseat to other issues, such as social status, refugees, and terrorism, following the impacts of the 2010 financial crisis. In Greece, however, economic issues remain a primary concern for citizens, even though there is a tendency for this to change. This reflects the "economic have-not" hypothesis but also the strong presence of "loss aversion" and the "cultural backlash hypothesis."

The Greek government's political actions should focus on increasing confidence, promoting collaboration, and exposing individuals to new perspectives that broaden their intellectual horizons, such as female leadership. Policymakers should remember that incentives are more complex than commonly thought, with social incentives being more influential than economic ones. This insight can help explain why specific policies do not work and lead to developing policies that can reduce poverty and enhance prosperity. To start, the way options are presented can impact the decision-making process. Simplifying the choices can help individuals make better decisions, as too many options or a complex decision environment can lead to indecision or incorrect choices. This has significant implications for policymaking. Additionally, the government can influence behavior through "nudge policies." These policies aim to modify behavior without limiting or incentivizing choices; instead, they steer individuals toward a particular choice (Thaler & Sunstein, 2008).

Moreover, actions are required to shape savings, and investment behaviors should target both the demand and supply. This can involve structural reforms, improving access to finance, macroprudential policies that ensure an efficient allocation of savings, fiscal policies, and nudge policies that use psychological interventions to encourage savings, and improving financial literacy among the population (Abebe et al., 2016; Lusardi, 2008).

8.3.4 Environment

Greece's unique ecological environment makes it a significant member of the European Union in terms of its ecological richness. The country's constitution includes provisions for environmental, climate, and protection of land and water life. Greece was one of the first countries in the world to adopt a Framework Law on Environmental Protection in 1986. Environmental protection is critical to sustainable economic development, mainly through quality tourism and agriculture, which form the basis of the Greek economy. It also promotes social well-being by safeguarding human health and access to high-quality environmental and ecosystem services. The environmental situation in Greece varies by sector, and monitoring is crucial for improvement. Despite progress in recent years, critical environmental issues such as air quality, water management, and climate change mitigation still need to be addressed. Greece has set climate targets until 2030 as part of its National Energy and Climate Plan, focusing on reducing greenhouse gas emissions, improving waste management and recycling, and tackling plastic pollution.

The European Commission's action plan for a circular economy is a priority for Greece and is part of its National Development Strategy. The plan aims to "close the loop" of the product life cycle, focusing on waste management, circular entrepreneurship, and sustainable consumption patterns. To achieve these goals, regulatory, and legislative measures need to be implemented, such as new waste definitions and reduction strategies, increased public education, and improved governance. "Green" project bonds could also be developed to finance green projects. The development of green funding through appropriate tools is a crucial issue supporting the sustainable development goal (Hellenic Federation of Enterprises, 2018).

For waste management, Greece has implemented a National Plan for Hazardous Waste Management since 2016, aimed at reducing waste production, increasing reuse and recycling, and creating new jobs in waste management. Greece has a good record in water management, with high-quality fresh water and fair water pricing that promotes responsible use. However, water management remains a complex issue with political, administrative, and legal challenges.

8.3.5 Academia, Knowledge and Innovation System

The workforce of a country plays a vital role in driving growth and promoting sustainable development in the long term. Improving the skills and education of the workforce is crucial for dynamic growth. There are two main areas in human resources: research and development

(R&D) and continuing education. In Greece, R&D is mainly funded through the European Structural Funds. The funding for human resource R&D focuses on quality research and excellence. Most funding should be used to improve research institutions and encourage knowledge sharing among Greek institutions and the international research community. The objective is also to attract highly educated Greek scientists who left the country during the debt crisis. For company R&D, funding should be directed toward removing restrictions on business operations. The education and training provided by R&D should encourage entrepreneurship, innovation, productivity, and technological development.

To enhance the quality of the workforce in Greece, there needs to be a focus on improving the quality of education. This requires long-term planning and sufficient funding for education. Lifelong education and vocational training are essential for workers to improve their skills continuously. There should also be a better connection between education and the labor market, focusing on acquiring skills early, providing knowledge relevant to the labor market, and promoting practical training through collaboration between education and businesses.

Moreover, to drive growth and development in the Greek economy, both the private and public sectors must promote the creation of new knowledge and stimulate innovation to improve the competitiveness of Greek businesses. This will also boost export activity. To achieve this, measures need to be taken to support R&D in the Greek economy, such as: (a) Reinforcing basic research by establishing and strengthening research centers, encouraging collaboration between higher education and industry, (b) Developing the skills of entrepreneurs and managers to drive innovation and manage its production, (c) Creating innovations that can easily be commercialized and target specific sectors that have a comparative advantage, (d) Improving the institutional, legal, and fiscal framework to support R&D (e.g., clear long-term tax policy), and (e) Supporting start-ups that focus on innovations.

References

Abebe, G., Tekle, B., & Mano, Y. (2016). Changing saving and investment behavior: The impact of financial literacy training and reminders on micro-businesses. *CSEA Working Paper* No. 2016–08.

Acemoglu, D., & Zilibotti, F. (1997). Setting standards: Information accumulation in development. *CEPR Discussion Paper* No. 1641.

Argeitis G., & Nikolaidi, M. (2014). *Economic crisis and productive restructuring in Greece: The role of the manufacturing industry* (INE GSEE Studies/28). https://ineobservatory.gr/wp-content/uploads/2014/08/meleth-28.pdf (in Greek).

Bell, K. (2012). Investing in infrastructure means investing in innovation. *Harvard Business Review*. https://hbr.org/2012/03/we-know-the-uss-infras tructure.

Carayannis, E. G., & Campbell, D. F. J. (2009). "Mode 3" and "Quadruple Helix": Toward a 21st Century fractal innovation ecosystem. *International Journal of Technology Management, 46*(3/4), 201–234. http://www.inders cience.com/browse/index.php?journalID=27&year=2009&vol=46%40issu e=3/4 and http://www.inderscience.com/search/index.php?action=record& rec_id=23374%40prevQuery=%40ps=10&m=or

Carayannis, E. G. & Campbell, D. F. J. (2010). Triple helix, quadruple helix and quintuple helix and how do knowledge, innovation and the environment relate to each other? A proposed framework for a trans-disciplinary analysis of sustainable development and social ecology. *International Journal of Social Ecology and Sustainable Development, 1*(1), 41–69. (https://www.igi-global. com/article/triple-helix-quadruple-helix-quintuple/41959.

Carayannis, E. G., & Campbell, D. F. J. (2019, March). *Smart quintuple helix innovation systems*. SpringerBriefs in Business, Springer. 978-3-030-01517-6.

Carayannis, E. G. Barth, T. D., & Campbell, D. F. J. (2012). The quintuple helix innovation model: Global warming as a challenge and driver for innovation. *Journal of Innovation and Entrepreneur- ship, 1*(1), 1–12. http://www.inn ovation-entrepreneurship.com/content/pdf/2192-5372-1-2.pdf.

Ciampi, C. (1995). *Enhancing European competitiveness (2nd Report to the President of the Commission, the Prime Ministers and the Heads of States)*. Office for Official Publications of the European Communities.

Grossman, G. M., & Helpman, E. (1992). *Innovation and growth in the global economy*. MIT Press.

Hausmann, R., & Klinger, B. (2006). *Structural transformation and patterns of comparative advantage in the product space* (Harvard University Center for International Development Working Paper No. 128).

Hellenic Federation of Enterprises. (2018). *Toolbox for the acceleration of productive investments*.

Hwang, J. (2006). *Introduction of new goods, convergence and growth*. Harvard University, Mimeo.

Imbs, J., & Wacziarg, R. (2003). Stages of diversification. *American Economic Review, 93*(1), 63–86.

Kuznets, S. S. (1971). Modern economic growth: Findings and reflections (Prize Lecture). *The NobelPrize.org*. https://www.nobelprize.org/prizes/economic-sciences/1971/kuznets/lecture/.

Lusardi, A. (2008). Household saving behavior: The role of financial literacy, information, and financial education programs. *NBER Working Paper* No. 13824

OECD. (2015). *Lifting investment for higher sustainable growth*. OECD Publishing. https://doi.org/10.1787/eco_outlook-v2015-1-46-en

Petrakis P. E., Kostis P.C. (2020a). *The evolution of the Greek economy: Past challenges and future approaches*, Palgrave Macmillan, ISBN 978–3–030–47209–2.

Petrakis P. E., Kostis P.C. (2020b). *Policies for a stronger Greek economy: Actions for the next decade*, Palgrave Macmillan, ISBN 978–3–030–47078–4.

Petrakis, P. E., Valsamis, D. G., & Kafka, K. I. (2016). From an optimal to a stagnated growth prototype: The role of institutions and culture. *Journal of Innovation & Knowledge*. https://doi.org/10.1016/j.jik.2016.01.011

Romer, P. M. (1990). Capital, labor, and productivity. *Brookings Papers on Economic Activity, 21*(1990 Microeconomics), 337–367.

Shayah, M. H. (2015). Economic diversification by boosting non-oil exports (case of UAE). *Journal of Business Economics and Management, 3*(7), 735–738. https://doi.org/10.7763/JOEBM.2015.V3.276

Straub, S. (2008). Infrastructure and growth in developing countries: Recent advances and research challenges. *World Bank Policy Research Working Paper* No. 4460. http://documents.worldbank.org/curated/en/349701468138569134/pdf/wps4460.pdf.

Thaler, R. H., & Sunstein, C. R. (2008). *Nudge: Improving decisions about health, wealth, and happiness*. Yale University Press.

CHAPTER 9

Networks and Interconnections in an Era of Trending Divergence

Anna-Maria Kanzola

9.1 Introduction

Economic growth depends on the combination of three elements: financial and natural capital; human capital; and social capital. Focusing on the latter element, Burt (1992) claims that social capital is the final determinant of economic growth because it generates networking activities. Networks are an important aspect of social and economic interactions since they are a source of interdisciplinary concentration due to the fact that social bonds are correlated with individual, social, and institutional goal-setting (Barnes, 1972). Consequently, networks impact social and economic structures through mutually beneficial relationships and concentration effects. By definition, networks promote cooperation and support within their framework. Their significance is established from an

A.-M. Kanzola (✉)
Department of Economics, National and Kapodistrian University of Athens, Athens, Greece
e-mail: annmkanz@econ.uoa.gr

P. E. Petrakis (ed.), *Interconnections in the Greek Economy*, The Political Economy of Greek Growth up to 2030,
https://doi.org/10.1007/978-3-031-31335-6_9

economic and anthropological perspective. However, regardless of the positive externalities within the networks, there are also adverse situations and results.

Nowadays, economies and societies are experiencing greater connectivity caused by technological advancement, globalization, and a reduction in the cost of communication and travel (Watson, 2010). Such advancements have positive and negative implications for economic constructs but, they also, lead to higher complexity in terms of network formation. For instance, connectivity increases transparency and promotes social interactions and identification. On the other hand, global connectivity relates to higher levels of systematic risk and over-information anxiety, resulting in poor decision-making, bounded rationality, and adverse selection. In a world where everything is connected, economic and social shocks spread faster than ever and have severe consequences that are more challenging to mitigate.

The present chapter examines the aforementioned topics through the lens of three pillars. First, there is a critical discussion of the emerging positive effects and challenges of an interconnected world at individual, social, and economic levels (Sect. 9.2). Second, the analysis focuses on the role of networks in the prediction of the future and provides insights for the future of world cooperation under specific circumstances (Sect. 9.3). Lastly, the reasoning is concentrated on the role of human and creative capital in mitigating divergence tendencies, concluding this chapter (Sect. 9.4).

9.2 Interconnection Effects and Challenges: Insights for Global Interactions

Cooperative dynamics comprise a dilemma in economic science due to the contradictory assumption that individuals are selfish and act upon their own interests (Axelrod, 1984). More specifically, Axelrod (1984) develops a theory of cooperation under which individuals are self-centered but cooperate due to their long-term motivations toward mutual benefits. Thus, in such a case, cooperation between selfish agents is possible without the formation of a central authority to force it. Anthropologically, societies balance among three behavioral characteristics, namely: (i) competitiveness, (ii) cooperativeness, and (iii) individualism, depending on the living circumstances (Mead, 1937).

At social, anthropological, and economic levels, cooperative behaviors are established as fundamental to social and economic contacts. In turn, cooperation encourages and frequently "forces" networking activities. Networks are special structures of social and economic significance. Socially, networks satisfy the human need to belong and to affiliate with a wider group of individuals with common traits and social values (Moser & Ashforth, 2022). Economically, networks are mostly generated from hierarchies and refer to the concentration of different interactive behaviors. Broadly, networking generates direct and indirect externalities, which could be either positive or negative, depending on the nature of the network[1] (Economides, 1996). Consequently, interconnectivity refers to the shared relationships among several parties that produce powerful forces and causal relationships affecting the outcomes of a process.

The existence of networks automatically implies the following: First, the emergence of networks is not random but structured around the potential benefits for all the members of the network. Second, conflict could possibly arise between different networks or the members of a network, leading to a failure of cooperation. As a result, to secure the critical mass required as well as cooperation, it is common for network operators to opt for lock-in conditions.

Traditionally, networks are analyzed through firm behavior (Economides, 1996); however, the application of network analysis can be extended to depict the relationships among significant economic agents and the established structures because it addresses social phenomena and power dynamics (Chiesi, 2015). The interplay between networks and various agents in the economy and society is a critical tool for gaining a comprehensive understanding of the evaluation and significance of complex cooperative dynamics in social and economic systems. At this point in the analysis, it is established that (i) networking activities require stimuli and (ii) we can apply network analysis to acquire insights regarding international politics (Axelrod, 1984). To that end, the remainder of this section discusses the power interconnections and challenges for alliances at a country level, considering how they affect global governance.

Global alliances and networks are driven by the need to safeguard national interests, welfare, and global megatrends. To better elaborate on

[1] For instance, networks are classified as one-way or two-way depending on the service they provide and the way they allow for interaction (Economides & White, 1998).

network dynamics, let it be assumed that a set of countries form a simple network where the following assumptions hold true:

Assumption 1 states that utility is a function of a stable direct benefit and of expected participation in the network. The utility is not the same for all the agents because networking effects are assessed differently by different agents. $U_i = a + h_{exp}(n)$.

Assumption 2 states that each agent has a different comparative advantage in terms of production, and after networking, it focuses on this.[2]

Assumption 3 states that the participating agents are of different capacities, but there is no direct way for the other countries to observe due to hidden agendas, indifference, or bounded rationality.

Assumption 4 states that in this network there is no formal authority to force cooperation since all agents are ostensibly the same (Axelrod, 1984).

The following Fig. 9.1 depicts a network with countries as agents that participate in the network in order to reduce the associated cost of individually producing all goods and services and increase their social welfare.

In this simplified network, the most powerful agent is country F because it operates as a "provider" and main link to the other countries. The blue nodes are the most important for this network because they are vital to its existence and all the other agents depend on them. For instance, even though there are reciprocal relationships between countries A, B, E, and D, they depend on country F, meaning that this cooperation could collapse if the most powerful agent decides to stop the supply line towards countries A or D. In that respect, the most powerful agent has the ability to exercise control over the other members. This repercussion emerges based on the position of the most powerful agent, which is at the center of the interactions.

[2] This assumption is relevant for the remainder of the analysis, where the discussion regards the recent turn of countries towards autarky and self-sufficiency.

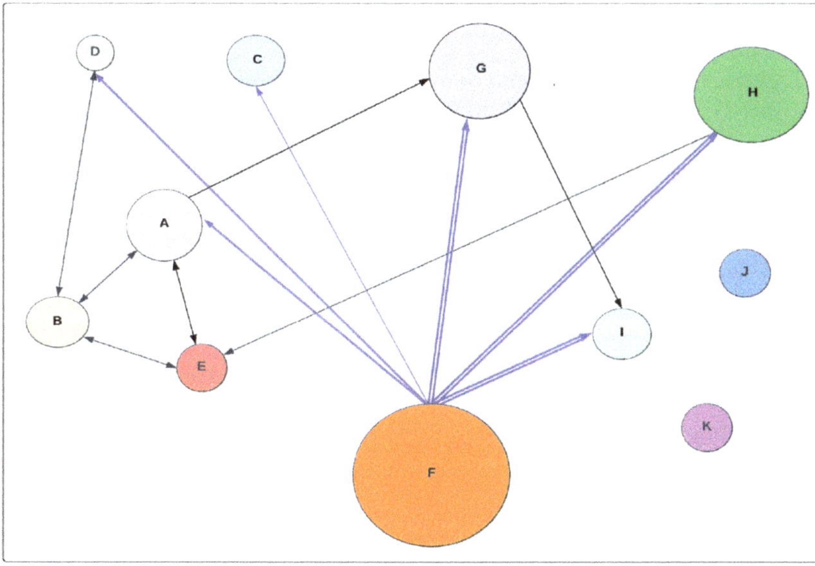

Fig. 9.1 High interdependence and power dynamics (*Source* Author's creation)

Power relationships in network society are fairly complex (Castells, 2011), and there is no single form of power. For instance, all the members of the given network have networking power over countries that are not members of the network; in Fig. 9.1, these are countries J and K (Castells, 2011). On the other hand, the agents in the presented network differentiate in terms of networked power, which refers to the ability to exercise power over the other agents (Castells, 2011). The latter is attributed to some degree to the relative power positions of agents within the network and the fact that some agents may amplify disparities of power that existed prior to the establishment of the network (Faul, 2016). Thus, establishing a formal network does not necessarily moderate existing asymmetries of power (Faul, 2016).

The presented network can be evaluated in the short-term and in the long-term. In the short-term, the benefits refer to the reduction of transactional costs. In the long-term, positive externalities concern the ability of each agent to build local learning by means of the direct and indirect links of the network (Balla & Goyal, 1998), which eventually leads to innovation. Essentially, local learning means that all agents, ceteris paribus, obtain the same benefits in the long run due to spatial diffusion (Balla & Goyal, 1998).

Despite the positive effects, there are some downsides due to structural reasons. To begin, because all of the agents do not have the same capacity, the most powerful agent can (i) impose direct political, economic, social, and cultural violence on the other parties (Bulk, 2015) and (ii) bind local learning (Balla & Goyal, 2000) to maintain position. Furthermore, in this network, which at some point resembles a "star" structure, shocks spread faster (Economides, 1996). Due to its overreliance on one actor, this network is susceptible to endogenous shocks and is characterized by an unstable equilibrium. Consequently, real and expected systematic risks spread faster, challenging the network's resiliency (Acemoglu et al., 2015). As a result, if all agents—except for country F—have the same level of knowledge and are perfectly rational, they will have a strong incentive to avoid participating in this network, and cooperation will not occur.

It is, thus, established that network analysis offers the ability to understand network activities from an intertemporal perspective in order to make assumptions for social welfare and relations among several agents. Broadly, discussing future possible scenarios in terms of networks is related to their evaluation in terms of economic and political power. The following section emphasizes this matter.

9.3 Networks as "Nodes" to the Future

Networks shape and drive action, and therefore, the future. That is, network analysis is an instrument of action to construct or deconstruct relational structures so that they can lead us towards one future or another since we address social phenomena and circumstances that are future-directed (Rodríguez Díaz, 2009). A list of predictions can be structured as a network, especially if we trace those powerful forces that emerge again and again and shape the future (Johnson, 2004). According to van der Duin et al. (2014), a network approach to foresight strengthens the various roles of foresight. The question that arises is: How is future research related to network analysis of global dynamics? To provide an answer to this question, we shall compare global network dynamics with the simple dynamics discussed above.

When investigating foreign affairs and networks, two issues are of paramount importance: (i) whether the agents have the ability to increase their power by enhancing and exploiting their network positions, and (ii) the complex dynamics produced by the different kinds of power (Hafner-Burton et al., 2009). The complexity of global network dynamics is due to the fact that there are several powerful agents (the United States of America, China, Russia, and India), depending on their size, development level, characteristics, and location. Even though the simple network of Fig. 9.1 is of a small scale, at some point it accurately debates the implications of a cooperation where a network is formed as a result of transformative powers such as the megatrends (Naisbitt, 1988). In this case, power asymmetries may or may not be addressed due to the erroneous assumption of a globalized economy and culture. While it is understandable why and how countries wish to protect their interests, it is essential to elaborate on how megatrends promote global cooperation or divergence.

The most distinctive example of the promotion of world cooperation is the "globalization phenomenon," which refers to the interdependence of the world's economies, cultures, and inhabitants as a result of technological improvements and international trade. Globalization is linked with the emergence of world interconnectivity and global networking because it proposed a unified way of life and economic activity (Godet et al., 1994; Holm & Sorensen, 1995). In that respect, one could argue that globalization induced cooperation at individual, social, and country levels based on the similarity of the experiences regarding cultural integration. However, not all countries share similar structural characteristics and agendas, meaning that power asymmetries challenge social welfare and the network's resiliency when major disturbances occur.

Major disturbances could take the form of endogenous shocks of economic, social, and political nature—such as technological shocks, financial crises, and geopolitical conflicts—or exogenous shocks, such as health crises and natural disasters. Subsequently, globalized, interconnected economies and societies are vulnerable because of contagion effects. Historically, global economic convergence was inevitable after the Cold War (Axelrod, 1984); however, recent events such as the Great Depression of 2008, the Coronavirus Pandemic of 2020, and the geopolitical conflicts that resulted in the Energy Crisis of 2022 brought back the past missions for self-sufficiency and autarky (Helleiner, 2021; Malcomson, 2021) based on a general turn to de-globalization (Bello, 2004).

The key concern is how the new age of de-globalization and multipolarity affects the networked economy and the welfare of the participating agents, given that the global economic network is established on the principles of the globalization agenda. To reduce the associated complexity, we suppose that the same four assumptions described above are not far from reality. In this case, many global agents face a lock-in situation where their welfare is bound to the effective operation of the global network. However, there is the possibility of exogenous and endogenous forces that oppose global cooperation. Hence, in an era of established network economies and trending divergence, discussing the future is unavoidable in order to envision and analyze futures and social change (Rodríguez Díaz, 2009) and determine whether societies will deal with a "market of lemons" (Akerlof, 1970) in international politics.

Megatrends that oppose global cooperation trigger divergence, meaning that protectionism is back on the political agenda (Wolf, 2018). More specifically, self-sufficiency is a tactic to distance oneself from the system and is associated with long-term preparedness to guarantee long-term welfare. Along with autarky, which concerns self-reliance, these are the two pivotal notions in an era of great multipolarity and de-globalization tendencies (Malcomson, 2021). The shift toward self-sufficiency and autarky is connected to the rise of global insecurity because of the negative effects of high interdependence, interconnectedness, and contagion (Helleiner, 2021; Malcomson, 2021). Additionally, there is historical path dependence, with some major agents having a tradition of protectionist and self-sufficiency policies (Malcomson, 2021). Major-power autarky is defensive, and it is not necessarily associated with a more dangerous world scenery (Malcomson, 2021). However, because of the inevitable locked-in situations and high interdependence with powerful providers, this is a difficult issue to address in an interconnected, networked global economy. There are two possibilities as mentioned below.

First, an unorganized return of great powers to autarky might result in a "security dilemma" situation (Axelrod, 1984) where agents seek their own security by challenging the security and welfare of others, denoting that the greatest risk is that major nations may attempt to prevent their rivals' access to resources (Malcomson, 2021). Furthermore, a possible collapse of global cooperation and the network economy will radically diminish intertemporal social welfare due to a setback in global sustainable integration.

Second, there is the possibility that despite the trending divergence of the system, the powerful nodes of the network will hold on, providing support and emphasizing multilateral relationships (Ruggie, 1993; Tago, 2017) to protect the established welfare. However, such a development requires (i) a strict legislative framework, (ii) a relative degree of each agent's self-sufficiency, and (iii) distributed, decentralized, and democratized benefits. Hence, the future of global cooperation and welfare depends on mutually beneficial activities and a strict legislative framework that prohibits one party from overruling the other (Axelrod, 1984).

9.4 Conclusions: Randomness and Order Shape Networks and the Future

In the history of human cooperation, there have been forces and changes that bind us together and others that drive us apart. The fates of globalization and cooperation under changing interconnected dynamics depend on elements of order and randomness (McKinsey Global Institute, 2023; Watts, 2003). Regardless of optimism, globalization—as a dynamic term—will continue to play an important role in the determination of global activities because, contrary to the aforementioned Fig. 9.1, every agent depends strongly on other agents, mostly regarding resources (McKinsey Global Institute, 2023). However, such a proposition does not cancel trending divergence, but it does establish a framework in which we recognize that we need each other to maintain and achieve high levels of social welfare. In this case, there are two options: (i) agents cooperate relatively peacefully or (ii) geopolitical revisionism ideologically prevails, altering the geopolitical map as we know it today and leading to a welfare gap for some agents. Given that the first possibility constitutes a desirable future, it is interesting to refer to the evolution of global chains (McKinsey Global Institute, 2023), through social and cultural capital, because in a highly social and technologically interconnected world, the positive externalities from networking go beyond regional growth and classic economic geography (Glückler & Doreian, 2016) because of the spatial patterns that emerge (Malecki, 2002).

Knowledge and creative economies are intellectually based and grow beyond strict geographic terms. Thus, they yield several opportunities for sustainable value creation based on the idea that social beliefs, institutions, power relations, traditions, procedures, and so forth produce social capital and shared norms that reinforce cooperation. Additionally, institutions and legislative frameworks operating at a global level are in a position to define, apply, monitor, and enforce the technical and economic conditions and rules for a set of operators (Agrell, 2015). Nonetheless, when dealing with agents and networks at a country level, these are challenging objectives, yet worth mentioning since they theorize on a set of circumstances where global interconnectedness is beneficial for all and desirable.

Consequently, the role of institutions and certain economic structures, such as knowledge and creative economies, in the promotion of sufficient, sustainable, and inclusive growth by capitalizing on the interconnection effect is of great vitality if societies and countries are oriented toward promoting social welfare. Nonetheless, we should never exclude the possibility of forces which are transformative in an unpredictable manner.

Concluding this chapter, it should be highlighted that when megatrends related to foreign affairs, de-globalization, and multipolarity appear, they produce extreme economic uncertainty, which impacts global constants (Aftab & Phylaktis, 2022). Yet, as societies and economies go through the adjustment phase, induced economic uncertainty is being mitigated thanks to institutional and networking practices. That is, networks can generate equilibria when economies and societies approach several tipping points, provided that these networks promote welfare.

References

Acemoglu, D., Ozdaglar, A., & Tanbaz-Salehi, A. (2015). *Networks, shocks, and systematic risk*. Working Paper No. 20931. http://www.nber.org/papers/w20931

Aftab, M., & Phylaktis, K. (2022). Economic integration and exchange market pressure in a policy uncertain world. *Journal of International Money and Finance, 128*(102701).

Agrell, P. (2015). *Incentive regulation of networks: Concepts, definitions and models*. Reflets et perspectives de la vie économique, LIV, 103–132. https://www.cairn-int.info/journal--2015-1-page-103.htm.

Akerlof, G. A. (1970). The market for "lemons": Quality uncertainty and the market Mechanism. *The Quartelrly Journal of Economics, 84*(3), 488–500. https://doi.org/10.2307/1879431

Axelrod, R. (1984). *The Evolution of Cooperation*. Basic Books Inc.

Balla, V., & Goyal, S. (1998). Learning from neighbours. *The Review of Economic Studies, 65*(3), 595–621. https://doi.org/10.1111/1467-937X.00059

Balla, V., & Goyal, S. (2000). A noncooperative model of network formation. *Econometrica, 68*(5).

Barnes, J. A. (1972). *Social networks*. Addison-Wesley Publishing Company.

Bello, W. (2004). *Deglobalization: Ideas for a new world economy*. Fernwood Publishers.

Bulk, E. W. (2015). Social identity-based threats to human security: Gender practice in sustainable development and conflict transformation. *Capstone Collection* 2757. https://digitalcollections.sit.edu/capstones/2757

Burt, R. S. (1992). *Structural holes: The social structure of competition*. Harvard University Press. http://www.jstor.org/stable/j.ctv1kz4h78

Castells, M. (2011). A network theory of power. *International Journal of Communication, 5*, 773–787.

Chiesi, A. M. (2015). Network analysis in wright, J.D. (Ed.) International encyclopedia of the social & behavioral sciences (Second Edition), *Elsevier*, 518–523. https://doi.org/10.1016/B978-0-08-097086-8.73055-8

Economides, N. (1996). The economics of networks. *International Journal of Industrial Organization, 14*(2).

Economides, N., & White, L. J. (1998). One-way networks, two-way networks, compatibility, and public policy. In Gabel, D., Weiman, D.F. (Eds.), Opening networks to competition. *Topics in Regulatory Economics and Policy Series, 27*. Springer. https://doi.org/10.1007/978-1-4615-5483-7_2

Faul, M. V. (2016). Networks and power: Why Networks are hierarchical not flat and what can be done about it. *Global Policy, 7*(2), 185–197.

Glückler, J., & Doreian, P. (2016). Editorial: Social network analysis and economic geography—positional, evolutionary and multi-level approaches. *Journal of Economic Geography, 16*(6), 1123–1134.

Godet, M., Chapuy, P., & Comyn, G. (1994). Global scenarios: Geopolitical and economic context to the year 2000. *Futures, 26*(3), 275–288. https://doi.org/10.1016/0016-3287(94)90015-9

Hafner-Burton, E., Kahler, M., & Montgomery, A. H. (2009). Network analysis for international relations. *International Organization, 63*(3), 559–592.

Helleiner, E. (2021). The return of national self-sufficiency? Excavating autarkic thought in a de-globalizing era. *International Studies Review, 23*(3), 933–957. https://doi.org/10.1093/isr/viaa092

Holm, H. H., & Sorensen, G. (1995). Introduction: What has changed? In Hans-Henrik Holm and Georg Sorensen (Eds.), *Whose world order?* Uneven globalization and the end of the cold war (Boulder, CO: Westview), 1–17.

Johnson, R. L. (2004). Networks of predictions. *Futures, 36*(10), 1095–1102. https://doi.org/10.1016/j.futures.2004.03.007

Malcomson, S. (2021, April 26). The new age of autarky. Why globalization's biggest winners are now on a mission for self-sufficiency. *Foreign Affairs*.

Malecki, E. J. (2002). The economic geography of the internet's infrastructure. *Economic Geography, 78*(4), 399–424. https://doi.org/10.2307/4140796

McKinsey Global Institute, (2023). How our interconnected world is changing. McKinsey & Company.

Mead, M. (1937a). Interpretative statement. In M. Mead (Ed.), *Cooperation and competition among primitive peoples*. McGraw-Hill.

Moser, J. R., & Ashforth, B. E. (2022). My network, myself: A social network approach to work-based identity. *Research in Organizational Behavior, 41*, 100155. https://doi.org/10.1016/j.riob.2022.100155

Naisbitt, N. (1988). *Megatrends*. Warner Books.

Rodríguez Díaz, J. A. (2009). Networks and the future: A new methodological approach to envision and create the network society of tomorrow. *Futures, 41*(7), 490–501. https://doi.org/10.1016/j.futures.2009.01.004

Ruggie, J. G. (Ed.). (1993). *Multilateralism matters: The theory and praxis on an international form*. Columbia University Press.

Tago, A. (2017). Multilateralism, bilateralism, and unilateralism in foreign policy. *Politics*. https://doi.org/10.1093/acrefore/9780190228637.013.449

van der Duin, P., Heger, T., & Schlesinger, M. D. (2014). Toward networked foresight? Exploring the use of futures research in innovation networks. *Futures, 59*, 62–78. https://doi.org/10.1016/j.futures.2014.01.008

Watson, R. (2010). *Future files. A brief history of the next 50 Years*. Nicholas Brealey Publishing, London-Boston, printed in the UK by Clays Ltd. ISBN: 978-1-85788-534-7

Watts, D. J. (2003). *Small worlds*. Princeton University Press.

Wolf, N. (2018, June 11). *Protectionism: Historical perspectives*. VOX EU, CEPR.

Index

P. E. Petrakis (ed.), *Interconnections in the Greek Economy*, The Political Economy of Greek Growth up to 2030, https://doi.org/10.1007/978-3-031-31335-6

GPSR Compliance
The European Union's (EU) General Product Safety Regulation (GPSR) is a set of rules that requires consumer products to be safe and our obligations to ensure this.

If you have any concerns about our products, you can contact us on

ProductSafety@springernature.com

In case Publisher is established outside the EU, the EU authorized representative is:

Springer Nature Customer Service Center GmbH
Europaplatz 3
69115 Heidelberg, Germany

www.ingramcontent.com/pod-product-compliance
Ingram Content Group UK Ltd.
Pitfield, Milton Keynes, MK11 3LW, UK
UKHW022221051026
15624UKWH00002B/291
* 9 7 8 3 0 3 1 3 1 3 3 4 9 *